JOHN COSIN

JOHN COSIN

Papers presented to a Conference to celebrate the 400th anniversary of his birth

Edited by

Margot Johnson

Durham
Turnstone Ventures
1997

Acknowledgements

The editor acknowledges with gratitude the kind permission of the Bishop of Durham for permitting the reproduction of Cosin's portrait in the Throne Room at Auckland Castle which appears on the front cover; and to H. John Smith and Roy Biggs for the photograph; to Margaret Till for the imaginative illustration of Durham Cathedral choir as it might have looked before the Commonwealth; to the Master and Fellows of Peterhouse, Cambridge, for the photograph of their portrait of a young man in the twentieth year of his age, 1615; to the Bishop of Durham and the Warden, Alastair Yule, for permission to reproduce the pen and wash drawings of Auckland Castle; to Fleur Coppock for photographs of the Durham choir stalls in the chapel on Inner Farne; and to Durham University Library for the reproduction of an opening of Cosin's annotated copy of *The Book of Common Prayer* in Bishop Cosin's Library.

The exhibition at Auckland Castle, telling Cosin's story which is reproduced here, could not have been erected without the hard work of John Franklin and Malcolm and Margaret Forrester, and the support of Alastair Yule. It was on display for two weeks.

Thanks are due to the authors of the Conference papers for allowing their publication and for their patience during the period of preparation for the press. Not least, the editor owes a debt of gratitude to Roger Norris for checking difficult references, to Pauline Walden and Beryl Parker for their expertise in typing scripts in their final form, and to Christine Crisp for editorial assistance.

Turnstone Ventures

37 Hallgarth Street

Durham

DH1 3AT

ISBN 0 946105 11 1

Text in Times New Roman

Printed in Great Britain by Robert Attey & Sons, Sunderland

British Library Cataloguing in Publication Data.
A catalogue record for this book is available from the British Library.

CONTENTS

ILLUSTRATIONS

Preface

A Conference entitled *John Cosin: from priest to Prince Bishop* was held in Durham on 2 - 4 July 1993 as part of the programme celebrating the 900th anniversary of the completion of the great Romanesque monastic cathedral of Durham. The Conference was sponsored by the Friends of the Prayer Book, St Oswald's church, and Durham University's Department of Adult and Continuing Education. The Bishop of Durham, the Rt Revd David Edward Jenkins, opened the proceedings with a lively address in Bishop Cosin's Library, Palace Green, where Roger Norris had arranged an exhibition of Cosin's manuscript material including the famous *Durham Book*, the copy of the 1619 *Book of Common Prayer* annotated in Cosin's hand. Papers were delivered by Dr J.T.D. Hall, University Librarian, on Cosin's Library, and Canon R.J.W. Bevan on Cosin as liturgist. On Saturday, the Conference continued in St Oswald's Institute with seven sessions, followed by Evensong with 17th-century music sung by St Oswald's choir. The sanctuary was set out as it would have been in Cosin's time. After the Conference dinner, St Oswald's choir gave an excellent concert, in church, of choral and instrumental music, both sacred and secular.

On Sunday afternoon, Conference members visited Auckland Castle, where Cosin lies buried in St Peter's chapel, said to be the largest private chapel in Europe, which he created and furnished with great magnificence. An exhibition on Cosin's life and work was mounted on a series of screens in the Throne Room, where it remained for general public viewing for two weeks after the Conference.

John Cosin was not only one of Durham's greatest bishops. He became known as chaplain to two bishops, parish priest, prebendary of Durham, Archdeacon of the East Riding of Yorkshire, royal chaplain to Charles I, Master of St Peter's

College (Peterhouse), Cambridge, vice-chancellor of Cambridge University, Dean of Peterborough, chaplain to the exiled royal court in Paris, and after the restoration of the monarchy, Bishop of Durham. A scholarly and gifted liturgist, he played a leading part in the Savoy Conference and prayer book revision which resulted in *The Book of Common Prayer* of 1662.

In Durham he commissioned much notable rebuilding after the depredations of the Civil War and Commonwealth, and built his Public Library in Durham, to which he gave the fruits of his life-long activities as bibliophile and book collector. Cosin designed the woodwork and interiors of his castles of Durham and Auckland, and the parish churches under his influence displayed a distinctive style admired and valued by connoisseurs today.

The Conference papers, offering some new insights into Cosin's life and work, are presented in this volume to celebrate the 500th anniversary of his birth in 1595.

Note: The spelling of proper names was not standardised in Cosin's time. The forms of names preferred by the authors has been followed.

John Cosin

Contributors' CVs

RICHARD JUSTIN WILLIAM BEVAN is a Canon Emeritus of Carlisle. He was formerly Vicar of St Oswald's, Durham, and Chaplain to Durham University. Subsequently he was Rector of Grasmere, and later Canon Residentiary, Canon Treasurer and Vice-Dean of Carlisle Cathedral. He was a Chaplain to the Queen from 1986-1992. He edited *Steps to Christian Understanding* (1959) and *The Churches and Christian Unity* (1964). He is the author of *A Twig of Evidence - Does Belief in God make Sense?* (1986).

PETER CLACK studied at Newcastle University, graduating BA (1971) and M.Litt (1977). He was Field Archaeologist for County Durham (1974-85), trained as a teacher (1985-6), and taught history in secondary schools in Newcastle (1986-94). He has written numerous papers on the archaeology and history of NE England; revised the Prehistoric and Roman sections for the second edition of Pevsner's *County Durham* (1983), is joint author/editor of seven books on northern England including *Archaeology in the North* (1976), *Weardale Chapels* (1978), *Rural Settlement in the Roman North* (1982) and *Making Sense of Buildings* (1984); he wrote *The Book of Durham City* (1985) and is preparing an edition of Bishop Cosin's Survey for the Surtees Society. He is also a novelist: *Emrys the Singer* (Woodhay Press, 1996), and is currently writing *The Bishop's Gift*, a novel about Bishop Cosin's Durham.

BRIAN CROSBY was born at West Hartlepool, and was educated at the Grammar School there, St John's College, Durham University (1952-57), BA (Theology, 1956), Dip.Ed. (1957), MA (History, 1966), Ph.D. (Music 1993), Palatinate for Cross-Country (1957). Career: The Chorister School,

Durham - Assistant Master Mathematics (1957-90), Deputy Headmaster (1990-66); Alto lay-clerk, Durham Cathedral (1959-88). He says: For over 35 years it has been my delight to explore the Cathedral archives, seeking information about the choir and its music. This has led to articles in *The Durham University Journal, Music & Letters, The Musical Times,* and the publication of *Durham Cathedral: Choristers and their Masters* (1980); and *A Catalogue of Durham Cathedral Music Manuscripts* (OUP, 1986). He has been a member of the Executive Council of *The Friends of Durham Cathedral* since 1991, and Hon. Treasurer from 1992.

JOHN T.D. HALL has been Librarian, University of Durham, since 1989. His first and higher degrees at the University of Manchester were in French Studies and he has written on sixteenth-century French poetry and on Pierre de Ronsard. He was Assistant Librarian in Manchester University Library (1971-78), latterly in the John Rylands Library in the Rare Books collection, and was sub-Librarian in Edinburgh University Library in charge of Special Collections (1978-86). He was a Deputy Librarian of Cambridge University Library (1986-89). He has published articles in scholarly journals, several Exhibition catalogues of books and manuscripts in special collections, and an Anthology of Edinburgh University Student Magazines.

NICK HEPPEL was educated at Reading School and The Queen's College, Oxford, where he read music. He then took the Durham MA course in Seventeenth Century Studies, researching English verse anthems and performance practice. After completing teacher training in Manchester, he taught for a year at Canon Slade School in Bolton, and since 1994 he has been head of music at Holbrook High School in Suffolk.

MARGOT JOHNSON, theologian and historian, has been part-time Tutor in History, Department of Adult and Continuing Education, Durham University (1966-96).

Formerly of Hull University Library (1938-39); East and West Riding County Libraries (1941-43); Durham University Library (1950-52, 1956-57); Deputy Librarian, Durham Cathedral Library (1961-63); Library Association Senior Examiner in Religion and Fellowship Thesis Examiner (1963-76); Lecturer (in Bibliography), Newcastle Polytechnic (1964-65). She has published numerous articles and short books, has others in preparation and has broadcast on radio and television. She is Chairman of the *Friends of the Prayer Book*.

PATRICK MUSSETT was at Corpus Christi College, Cambridge (1957-60) and graduated MA in classics. He was Administrative Assistant in the Extra-Mural Department, University of Manchester (1960-3); Assistant in Palaeography and Diplomatic, University of Durham (1963) and is now Senior Assistant Keeper of Archives and Special Collections, Durham University Library. He is interested in post-Reformation cathedral history and in collaboration with P.G. Woodward gave the Durham Cathedral Lecture, *Estates and Money at Durham, 1660-1985* (1988). He has published *Norwich Cathedral under Dean Prideaux, 1702-24* (in David Marcombe and C.S. Knighton, *Close Encounters: English Cathedrals and Society Since 1540* (1991); and *The reconstituted Chapter, 1660-1820* (in Nigel Yates and Paul A. Welsby, *Faith and Fabric. A history of Rochester Cathedral, 604-1994*, 1996).

DANIEL O'CONNOR is in Anglican orders. His ministry has been in England, Scotland and India, and he is presently located at Wakefield Cathedral, with a diocesan inter-faith brief and an honorary research Fellowship in the University of Edinburgh. In addition to a part in the editing of the 1967 edition of Cosin's *Devotions*, he has written a number of books on literary and missiological themes.

KENNETH WILLIAM STEVENSON became Bishop of Portsmouth in 1995. He was born on 9 November 1949 and was educated at Edinburgh Academy (1957-66); Edinburgh University (1966-70) graduating MA; Salisbury/Wells Theological College (1970-73); Southampton University (1975), Ph.D., Manchester University (1987), DD. He was Curate at Grantham (1973-76), Lecturer (senior curate) Boston (1976-80); part-time tutor Lincoln Theological College (1975-80); Chaplain and Lecturer Manchester University (1980-86); Visiting Professor, University of Notre Dame, Indiana (1983); Rector of Guildford, Holy Trinity & St. Mary (1986-95); Bishop of Portsmouth from 1995. Member of Inter-Anglican Liturgical Consultation (1983-); Secretary, Anglo-Nordic-Baltic Theological Conference (1985-); part of Planning Group for Worship at Lambeth (Worship Book, 1988); Member of Liturgical Commission (1986-); Member of Faith and Order Advisory Group (1991-). Publications: *Nuptial Blessing: a Study of Christian Marriage Rites* (1982); *Eucharist and Offering* (1986); *Jerusalem Revisited* (1988); *The First Rites* (1989); *Covenant of Grace Renewed: a vision of the Eucharist in the 17th Century* (1994); *Handing On: Borderlands of Worship and Tradition* (1996). His other interests are: music (horn and piano) and historical biographies.

MARGARET TILL, before marriage and moving to the north-east, lived and worked in London, doing illustrations for books and periodicals (including *The Radio Times*) and teaching drawing, lithography and wood-engraving at the Sir John Cass College in the City of London. Her paintings and prints have been exhibited in London, Durham and Newcastle. She taught art at Bow School, Durham, Durham Johnston School and Durham Cathedral Chorister School. She has illustrated leaflets written by Canon Stephen Pedley on Bede and St Oswald for Durham Cathedral.

I

Introduction

The Right Reverend David E. Jenkins, Bishop of Durham

When this invitation came, I said I would be delighted to come as long as I was not expected to do more than make a few welcoming remarks. So what follows is nothing like an opening paper; all the papers come tomorrow. However, I am very glad to come and welcome you all to this conference on *John Cosin, Priest to Prince Bishop*. I was particularly pleased to note that *The Friends of the Prayer Book* had got together with St Oswald's Church and Durham University's Department of Adult and Continuing Education to offer this Conference. And to offer it not only for its own intrinsic merit but also as a very proper contribution to the celebrations to mark nine hundred years of Durham Cathedral.

Bishop Cosin is certainly a notable contributor to the nine hundred years of life in the Cathedral. He was what you might call the Restoration Bishop; in many ways, he was a restoring and beautifying bishop. Those of you who come to Auckland Castle on Sunday afternoon will have the chance to see the way in which he picked up the ancient medieval banqueting hall and turned it into a splendid chapel. I am told that this chapel goes well with the other thing associated with the Bishops of Durham, namely, the throne in the Cathedral. I am told that not only is the throne in the Cathedral probably the highest in Christendom (so that I am at least two inches above contradiction even from the Pope, which comes in useful, as you can imagine, for a person like myself!), but also that the chapel at Auckland Castle is alleged to be one of the largest private chapels in Europe, with dimensions to compare with - if they don't surpass - those of the Sistine Chapel. Whatever the truth of the matter, it is a very remarkable chapel, with absolutely splendid woodwork for which Cosin was responsible. He contributed similar woodwork to the Cathedral and also to the church in Brancepeth.

Cosin was certainly a beautifying bishop as well as a restoring bishop. This was part of his expression, as far as I can gather, of his concern with what I think we may dare to call the beauty of holiness, and therefore the glory of devotion. This concern of his is reflected in, and marked by, his notable collection of private devotions in the practice of the ancient Church and the Fathers, called *THE HOURES OF PRAYER. As they were after this manner published by Authoritie of Q. Eliz. 1560. Taken out of the Holy Scriptures, the Ancient Fathers, and the divine Service of our own Church.* This seems to me an absolutely splendid Anglican mix. 'Out of the Holy Scriptures, the Ancient Fathers *and* the divine Service of our own Church'. That is, we have our own contribution to make to the Church's pursuit of holiness and to the Church's expression of catholicity.

So Cosin made a notable contribution to Anglican divinity and, of course, to the Prayer Book of 1662, but this will be discussed tomorrow. I think it appropriate that *The Friends of the Prayer Book* should be the principal sponsors of this Conference. When you get to Auckland Castle you will see an exhibition of Cosin's life and reflection. We hope that in due course, we may be able to find room, close to the chapel and the public rooms, to keep this as a more permanent exhibition. It is a good thing that all this interest in Cosin is being developed at the moment and you are taking such a practical part in it. I believe it may make its permanent mark on the way in which, both here in the Cathedral and in Auckland Castle, we maintain our witness to this very rich past.

I am afraid that I cannot myself be at Auckland Castle when you visit. I shall not be concerned with the seventeenth century that day but with persons under the age of twelve in the twentieth century because I have to preach at two o'clock at the Church Lads' and Church Girls' Brigade service in the Cathedral. I dare say that, while drawing on the Scriptures, I shall not be unduly drawing on the Fathers for that occasion. I would have liked to have heard the papers tomorrow but unfortunately I have an urgent pastoral engagement elsewhere. So I would just like to welcome you and wish you well.

Before I sit down I would like to comment on two matters, ranging more broadly to matters relevant today which still fit into the pattern of Cosin's memory, Cosin's contribution, and especially Cosin's concern with the 1662 Prayer Book.

As a member of the House of Bishops, I have been interested to notice the exchange of views that have taken place between *The Prayer Book Society* (I am not confusing that with *The Friends of the Prayer Book*) and the Liturgical Commission on various matters. I am particularly interested to see contained in the papers for this coming General Synod, a set of essays published by the Liturgical Commission on 'the renewal of common prayer, unity and diversity in Church of England worship'. The essays look to me as though they will be of considerable interest. You have at least one author of one of these essays speaking to you tomorrow.

In carrying on the tradition, in recalling Cosin's great contribution and in looking at the folio edition of the Prayer Book annotated in his hand, we are picking up an approach and concern which this Library embodies, and of which Cosin's contributions to the Castle and the Cathedral speak. This is a continuing concern about what is the place of common prayer? How is *The Book of Common Prayer* related to that place? How do you keep common prayer going? Without being faithless to *The Book of Common Prayer*, what else is needed? And so on.

In this connection, I think I can count myself - without a capital F - a friend of the prayer book, *The Book of Common Prayer*. From a boy onwards the use of *The Book of Common Prayer* certainly sustained my worshipping life and faith. The one service I used to try to make sure I got to, wherever I was from my early teens onwards (and I kept it up through the army too, even in India), was to a *Book of Common Prayer* service at eight o'clock in the morning or as early as I could for Holy Communion. It meant a tremendous lot to me. And the fact remains that if I want to go to a service I can really enjoy and relax in, I still choose a *Book of Common Prayer* Evensong. People may not believe this, but as I get older and older it becomes quite obvious that I am really a traditionalist! However, I believe that the ability to be free to open the Tradition out to the changing circumstances around and about arises from being rooted in the Tradition.

The Friends of the Prayer Book, and people concerned with Cosin, have a contribution to make to how we deal with the various matters of liturgy and its variation nowadays. But I hope that in so doing they will not fall into the error of some people who still write to me on the occasion of a parish falling vacant; the kind who write in all sobriety, honesty and decency: 'Dear Bishop, we want our new vicar to be middle-aged with a very loyal wife and two splendid children and we hope he will change nothing and bring the young people in'. People still do write to me in those terms and I am afraid I continue to be baffled by it. For to keep the Tradition alive you have to move on and develop all sorts of things. I am afraid that the tendency to think that what happened in the seventeenth century must be more definitive than what happened in the fourth century, or at the Reformation, or whatever, is false. Nothing that happens in any century can be totally definitive. Those friends of the Prayer Book who simply look backwards, I think, are doing it no proper befriending. These matters need urgent and detailed consideration - a controversy, indeed - and consultation. I hope that the experience of studying Cosin and all that was around him will help you to make contributions to interpreting for today the deposits and insights of Tradition, including that part added in 1662.

I have already expressed to you my devotion to early morning services in *The Book of Common Prayer*, but I must also pass on to you an experience I had as a college chaplain. When I was chaplain of Queen's College, Oxford, I used to celebrate the 1662 service of Holy Communion in the chapel regularly, especially on Sunday mornings at the college service, to which all sorts of people came in those days. It was only as I got more and more into discussion with lively undergraduates that I made a discovery. As I celebrated that service I had my own internal commentary going on in my head about what the service meant, a commentary which made connections of a three-D nature with things outside the service. My experience of the service was rich, but it was not a richness the young undergraduates were tapping into. I therefore got permission from the Archbishop of York, who was the Visitor of Queen's College, Oxford, to work with my students to build up a slightly modified 1662 service combined with a commentary on it. This experience of mine with young people made it clear to me that you cannot make the 1662 service the sole centre of Anglican worship in this country now.

I relate this to *The Friends of the Prayer Book* in all friendship, openness and honesty and I contribute it to your continuing discussions. (I would add, however, that I am getting more and more tired of what I might call the fidgetiness of fancying that you have to have a new rite every year.) So the whole issue with which the Liturgical Commission is wrestling so hard is one of fundamental importance. Hence also the importance of taking time to consider these matters in this splendid place, with all its associations of Durham and Cosin.

So I renew my welcome to you. I am, after all, in one sense, John Cosin's successor, though I fully acknowledge the temporary nature of that. I welcome you greatly. I hope you will have a splendid time tomorrow and on Sunday. And I do urge you to contribute from your devotion to the Prayer Book, to the liturgical search and richness of the Church of England, and above all to the assertion of Anglicanism for which Cosin so clearly stood: an Anglicanism based on this combination of the Catholic Tradition, the Fathers, the Scriptures and contemporary understanding. It is on this note that I would like to hope you have the very best possible next twenty-four hours, now that you have got over me.

II

John Cosin: An Introduction to his Life and Work

Margot Johnson

There are many facts about Cosin's life which are either at present irrecoverable, or which have been asserted without foundation. Among them are the origins of his father and mother; and the absence of any extant record of his baptism. The date and place of his ordination also remain a mystery. This paper attempts to explore some of these problems, as well as to outline the better known facts about his life and work which may not be available to the general reader. A bibliography is appended to direct those who wish to know more.

In his brief autobiography, Cosin says he was born in Norwich on 30 November 1595; and in a letter to Myles Stapylton, dated 2 January 1671/2, he says he was '76 years at St Andrew's Day last past'.[1] (The article by J.H. Overton in *The Dictionary of National Biography*, Volume 4, 1887, repr.1917, gives his date of birth as 1594, which is an error.) His father, a tradesman of Norwich, was Giles Cosin, whom Peter Smart, among other abuse flung at John Cosin, called a 'prick louse', an old contemptuous term for a tailor; but this may not be specific and is the only hint at his trade.

The *Certificate from the College of Arms of the Death and Funeral Ceremonies of John Lord Bishop of Durham* lists among his benefactions:

> To the poor people within the precincts of the Cathedral at Norwich and within the parish of St Andrew's there, in which he was borne and educated in his minority. xx [£20].

The baptisms of five of his sisters are recorded in St Andrew's register: Anne, 12 December 1591; Elizabeth, 28 December 1593; Alice, 19 March 1597/8; Lidia, 17 February 1599/1600; Mary, 27 April 1606; and there is Pet, baptized at St Giles in 1601, of whom no more is known; but there is no record of either John's baptism, or that of his brother Nathaniel. They do not appear in any other surviving Norwich parish register.

If the boys were regarded as more important than the girls, they may have been baptized at a more prominent church, perhaps Norwich Cathedral, which incorporated the parish church of St Mary; but the registers are defective for the relevant period. The *International Genealogical Index* has the misleading entry: Nov. 1594 & 5 John, son of Giles and Elizabeth Cosin, baptized at St Andrew, Norwich, clearly patron-supplied information from printed books, without reference to the original registers.

The date 1595 is likely to be correct, as presumably John knew his own date of birth, and it fits in with the family pattern of childbearing in alternate years. Both Percy H. Osmond's *A Life of John Cosin* (1913), and the unpublished Ph.D. thesis by the late J.G. Hoffman, *'John Cosin, 1595-1672: Bishop of Durham and Champion of the Caroline Church'* (1977), give the same information but without reference to original sources.

John Cosin's ordination papers, if extant, would be expected to include a record of his baptism, but there are difficulties here also. George Ornsby, writing in 1869, is worth quoting at length:

> The name is certainly one of considerable antiquity in that county [Norfolk]. Roger Cosyn is mentioned in the *Quo warranto* Rolls in the time of Edward I., and in 1314 the same individual, or one of the same names, occurs as lord of the manor of Elyngham Magna. See Bloomfield's Norfolk, ii, p.267; see also i. p.485, and ii. p.491. In 1322 King Edward II. granted to John Cosyn, of Norwich, licence to found a chantry in the parish of St. Peter Mancroft, for two priests daily to celebrate Divine Service,

> endowing it with messuages in Norwich, and lands and tenements in Erlham. See Inq. *ad quod damn.* 12 Edw.II. n.106; 17 Edw.II. n.150. The history of this chantry may be found in Bloomfield's Hist. Norf. iv.p. 201. See also the *Valor Ecclesiasticus* iii. p.294, for the value at the suppression.[2]

According to Surtees (who gives no references), and is quoted by Osmond, Giles Cosin is said to have had connections with Seven Burnhams, a group of villages in Norfolk: Burnham Market, Burnham Deepdale, Burnham Westgate, Burnham Ulph and Sutton, Burnham Norton, Burnham Thorpe and Burnham Overy; and until 1777 there were also Burnham St Edmunds and Burnham St Andrews, both of which have disappeared. No families named Cosin are recorded in any of these places at the right dates; but Burnham Deepdale had Curzons, a name probably a variant of Cosin. Osmond also quotes a tradition that Giles Cosin came from Foxearth, in the south of Suffolk (later north Essex), but although the name Cosin occurs in neighbouring parishes, neither Giles himself nor any likely connection with him has been traced. At this period, the wool trade was the reason for the migration of ambitious or already prosperous merchants and sons of gentry who saw the possibility of increasing their fortunes; and a more northern origin at a remoter period is not unlikely. From Ornsby's evidence it appears likely that the Cosin family had long connections with Norwich itself; and it would be interesting to know the source of the other alleged places of origin of John Cosin's father.

Both Osmond and Hoffman state that Giles Cosin married Elizabeth Remington of Remington Castle, Norfolk, but no place of that name has been found in the county. The burial register of St Andrew's Norwich records: 'Elizabeth Coosin, widoow, buryed December 8 1644', probably John Cosin's mother. A memorial to Rebecca Remyngton, who died in 1604, is in the nave of St Andrew's; and Mr Nicholas Remington, Alderman of Norwich, presented a handsome standing cup to

St Andrew's. At the west end of the nave a memorial was placed to his son Nathaniel, who died in 1617 aged fourteen.[3] The use of 'Mr' was long confined to the gentry; and these references suggest that the Remington family prospered in Norwich at the time. A gentry family of this name flourished at Lund, near Beverley, in the East Riding, in the sixteenth century, and several clergy of that name are found in the sixteenth and early seventeenth centuries elsewhere in Yorkshire. The name is derived from Rimington, a place in West Yorkshire.[4]

Although John was the third child, he was the eldest son, and it is just possible that if John's mother's origins could be traced, they might reveal also his place of baptism, as it was a common practice for a first child to be baptized at the mother's former home church where the marriage took place and this could have happened in the case of the first son. John himself was unable to supply his grandparents' names at the heraldic visitation of 1672; so, if he did not know them personally, they may not have been a Norwich family. Norwich was a leading city and very prosperous through the cloth trade. Often sons of the gentry were entered into apprenticeships there. Puritan influence was strong. In many of its churches the ministers had no surplices and Holy Communion was received sitting.

Education

From 1610 until 1614, John attended Norwich Grammar School, near the cathedral, which would be natural for a bright boy with the advantage of a free place as the son of a burgess. His master was Richard Briggs. The school had a very good reputation and Archbishop Parker had been a pupil there. Unfortunately the school registers are incomplete for the crucial years.[5]

When he was thirteen or fourteen years old, about 1608, his father died, leaving him some property in Norwich. John says he gave most of his inheritance to his mother, retaining only twenty pounds yearly to meet his maintenance at Cambridge University. He was admitted a pensioner at Gonville and Caius College in 1610 at the age of fifteen, no younger than many other boys who went up to the University at the time. He matriculated and entered as a scholar in the same year. In addition to the income retained from his father's bequest, he had been awarded one of the Norwich Scholarships to Gonville and Caius College. The College admission registers, which are probably the best of all the Cambridge College registers, contain unusually full information, but they throw no light on John's baptism.

The College had a strong Norfolk connection. Dr John Kaye (1510-73), a Norwich born physician known as Caius, from the Latin form of his name, refounded in 1557 Gonville Hall, which was founded originally in 1348 by Edmund Gonville, Rector of Torrington, Norfolk. After the benefaction of Kaye, the College became known as Gonville and Caius. Caius built the Gate of Honour, the Gate of Virtue and the Gate of Humility, which were intended to symbolize the passage of the student.

Life was hard for a student in seventeenth-century Cambridge. Chapel was at 5.00a.m., and after breakfast he studied privately with his tutor, attended lectures, or, if actually preparing to take a degree, was engaged in public disputation. Dinner was in hall at noon, followed by further declamations or disputations. The student was then free until evening chapel, which preceded supper in hall at 7.00 p.m. and early bed.

Subjects of study were mostly rhetoric, logic and classics; theology was often part of the student's private study with his tutor. Venn's History of the College is quoted by Osmond (p.7), where he says that the rooms were large

> with three or four 'cupboards' in the corners, each with a window . . . in size between a sentry-box and a bathing-machine. . . . Three or four undergraduates lived and slept in the centre-room,

> sometimes with a tutor. . . . The 'studies' were quiet corners for them to work in. . . . The students had small truckle-beds, which by daytime could be run out of sight under the tutor's bed. . . . Most of the rooms evidently had fireplaces, but some of them certainly had not.

The same writer quotes Dr Leaver of St John's College, who says that after the students had finished their day's work,

> they were fain to go into the court, and walk or run up and down half an hour to get an heat in their feet when they go to bed.

Cosin occurs in the *Biographical History of Gonville and Caius College, 1349*-1897,[6] which records that he graduated B.A. in 1613/14 (nine-tenths of B.A. degrees were given in January); M.A. in 1617; proceeded to the degree of Bachelor of Divinity in 1623; was a Fellow of his college from 1620 to 1624; and was awarded the degree of Doctor of Divinity in 1630.

Cosin retained affection for his old school and college. In 1669, as Bishop of Durham, he gave a twenty-eight pounds annual rent charge from his lands and tenements in Great Chilton, County Durham, for three scholarships of twenty nobles each, such recipients to be Norwich born, and educated at its public Grammar School. These were to be chosen 'by ye master *in concilio sociorum aut Saltem Decanorum Collegii*'. Vacancies were to be reported to the master of Norwich School. If there were no suitable Norwich boys, candidates from elsewhere in Norfolk were eligible under the rules for scholarships laid down by Dr Caius.

At Gonville and Caius, Cosin had two very able contemporaries: Oliver Naylor, who was already a Fellow when Cosin matriculated in 1610; and Eleazor Duncon,[7] who was admitted scholar in 1613. Cosin thought highly of Eleazor who later followed him to Durham.

Cosin's First Post

His obvious promise and good appearance attracted the notice of both Bishop Overall and Bishop Andrewes, both of whom offered to take him as a young graduate into their households as secretary, without interfering with his studies. The introduction to Bishop Overall came from his nephew John Hayward, Rector of Coton, near Cambridge, and a prebendary of Lichfield, who first introduced Cosin to the study of liturgy. Cosin expressed his gratitude by leaving a legacy to Hayward's children, and he paid for his son Peter's education. Bishop Overall had been Regius Professor of Divinity at Cambridge, and both were leading theologians in the new movement against Puritanism, promoting what they termed 'the beauty of holiness', expressed in dignified worship, ritual and music.

On the advice of his tutor, Cosin chose to enter the service of Bishop Overall as his secretary and librarian. He developed a deep affection for him and referred to him as 'dear Lord and master' for the rest of his life. Overall was Bishop of Lichfield and Coventry from 1614 to 1618, and Bishop of Norwich from 30 September 1618 until his death on 12 May 1619. In 1616 Cosin became a junior Fellow of his college and graduated M.A. in 1617. In 1619 he was admitted a Fellow Commoner, and on Bishop Overall's death became a domestic chaplain to Bishop Neile of Durham.

Ordination

At some time during these years, Cosin must have been made deacon, at least, and for this would need a title (an appointment to a post), but the date is unknown; nor, so far, has any record of his ordination to the priesthood come to light. He preached his first sermon in 1621 at Coton for John Hayward. The Coton parish records (now in Cambridgeshire County Record Office) do not mention the occasion. It is not safe to assume that by now he was ordained, as cases are known when unordained graduates and even undergraduates preached.

It is likely that he was in priest's orders in 1622, when he was appointed University Preacher. Who ordained him and when? If ordination papers could be found, they would include a copy of the baptismal entry. It would be reasonable to suppose that Cosin was ordained by Bishop Overall. Unfortunately there is a gap in the series of Bishops' Registers for Lichfield (now in the Staffordshire Record Office) from 1579 to 1619; and no ordinations are included until 1623. Separate ordination papers begin in 1660.

Ordination papers for Ely diocese (now in Cambridge University Library) begin only in 1749. Previous ordinations were recorded in the bishops' registers, but unfortunately the seventeenth-century Ely Registers, covering Bishop Overall's time at Norwich, have been lost. There is a transcript of Lancelot Andrewes' register up to February 1619 when he was translated to Winchester, but if this is complete, Cosin was not ordained by him at that period. There are no later transcripts.

Cosin was a Fellow of Gonville and Caius from 1620 to 1624, and Cambridge University Archives list subscriptions of Fellows when they were ordained. Cosin subscribed on 11 June 1624.[8] Unless he had been in deacon's orders for some time, this seems remarkably late for his ordination as priest and perhaps inconsistent with his appointment as University preacher in 1623. It is too late for his subscription for the degree of B.D. which he obtained in 1623, and too early for his D.D. in 1630.

It is unlikely that Cosin would have been ordained by a bishop other than Overall while he was under his patronage up to his death in 1619; but it is just possible that Bishop Richard Neile ordained him after he entered his service when he was Bishop of Durham (1617-28).

The Lincoln episcopal registers (in Lincoln Record Office) have a gap; the last date in Register XXX is 1609; and Register XXXI begins in 1640. Cosin had no connection with Durham Diocese until 1624, although there may have been some earlier personal association with Bishop Neile. There are no surviving Durham ordination papers as early as this date: and the extant sections of Neile's Register contain no reference to Cosin. Therefore, the dates when Cosin was made deacon and ordained priest remain an open question; but it is possible that he was priested in 1624 and had been a deacon already for some time.

Durham House

As a domestic chaplain to Bishop Richard Neile, Cosin spent much time at Durham House, the Durham bishops' London residence off the Strand. It was not far from the Savoy, and had passed through various hands: Sir Walter Raleigh once lived there; and later it was alienated to the Earl of Pembroke. Neile was a courtier, and although he had no pretensions to scholarship himself, he sought out and encouraged younger men of talent. Durham House therefore became known as 'Durham College'.[9] The Puritans said that the men of Durham House preached Arminianism and practised popery.

Bishop Neile was the early patron of William Laud, and later supported him, so that at Durham House Cosin associated with men of high Anglican views. Here he met Richard Mountague, and became a friend of the older man whose views afterwards aroused so much opposition. A skit entitled *Appeal of the Orthodox Ministers of the Church of England against Richard Mountague* pokes fun at the Durham House party, with exaggerated and distorted descriptions of their dress (a long cloak and cassock), beliefs and meticulous observance of ceremonial.

Mountague saw matters differently and in 1624 wrote to Cosin that the champions of Anglicanism had 'to stand in the gapp against Puritanism and Popery, the Scilla and Charybdis of antient piety'.

At Francis White's consecration as Bishop of Carlisle in Durham House chapel in 1626, Cosin preached at length in praise of the episcopal office, and his sermon aroused great anger among those of Puritan persuasion.

Neile himself rose through rapid promotion, being succesively Bishop of Rochester (1608), Lichfield (1610), Lincoln (1613), Durham (1617), Winchester (1627), and Archbishop of York (1631).

Master of Greatham Hospital

In 1624, Bishop Neile appointed Cosin Master of Greatham Hospital in County Durham, after the death of William Neile, at a salary of one hundred pounds a year. The Hospital had been founded in 1272 by Bishop Robert Stichill, but was refounded in 1610 by James I for thirteen poor unmarried men. Cosin was collated on 22 June, but resigned on 24 July of the same year, when he exchanged the post with Gabriel Clarke, Durham Prebendary and Archdeacon, for the benefice of St Peter's, Elwick.

Cosin as Rector of Elwick

Cosin remained officially Rector here until 1660; but he appears never to have lived in the Rectory House, Elwick Hall. He appointed a curate to look after the parish under his supervision, except during the Commonwealth, when he was expelled and John Bowey, an intruder, officiated.

After his return from exile, between 1660 and 1672, Cosin, as Bishop of Durham, directed the restoration of the church of which he had been rector. A fourteenth-century chantry chapel on the north side was demolished in 1660, and the chancel was rebuilt using the old materials. Two sets of carved bench-ends were placed in the chancel. A silver cup with a cover paten is inscribed: 'The blood of Jesus Christ cleanseth us from all sin'; and round the bottom are the words: 'for elwicke 1667'. The two bells in the tower are one of 1664 by Samuel Smith of York, and the other is inscribed 'Christopher Hodgson' and the date 1694. The church is not quite as Cosin left it: the tower was rebuilt in 1813 and heightened in 1860; and the chancel arch has been reconstructed.

Prebendary of Durham Cathedral

Cosin was installed prebendary of the tenth stall of Durham Cathedral on 4 December 1624. As financial records for the period do not survive, it is unknown whether or not this appointment provided Cosin with a substantial income, and no living appears to have been associated with it. The house allocated to this stall was built on the site of the former monastic infirmary.[10]

Accession of Charles I

On 27 March 1625 Charles I ascended the throne and was warmly received. Two months after his accession, however, in May 1625, Charles I married by proxy Henrietta Maria, the fifteen-year-old daughter of Henry IV of France. His marriage to a Roman Catholic was much disliked by his Protestant subjects. Although young, she had been taught carefully in France to encourage Roman Catholic agencies for obtaining conversions from protestantism. The coronation was delayed because of the marriage and the outbreak of plague.

Cosin as Archdeacon of the East Riding of Yorkshire

In September 1625 Cosin became Archdeacon of the East Riding of Yorkshire, a post previously held by his future father-in-law, Marmaduke Blakiston, another Durham prebendary. He acted through a respected lawyer in York, Robert Claphamson who had long managed the affairs of the archdeaconry; but Cosin's Visitation questions and the replies received show that he was much concerned to remedy a great deal that was amiss. The Rectory of Mappleton had been annexed to the Archdeaconry since 1230, and brought him an annual rent of twenty-two pounds.

Charles I's Coronation

The coronation took place on 2 February 1625/6. The Dean of Westminster, Bishop Williams of Lincoln, was in disgrace, and Laud, then Bishop of St David's, was chosen to act as Dean in his place. As chief ecclesiastical adviser, he aimed at scrupulous correctness in the coronation ceremonial. Cosin was appointed *Magister Ceremoniarum* and placed where he could signal to the choir during the service. Years later Prynne, relating Cosin's supposed offences said:

> Popish Master J.C., when the prayers appointed for the Coronation were then read, kneeled behind the Bishops, giving directions to the Quire when to answer.

Cosin's translation of the *Veni Creator* was printed as an appendix to the copy of the service used by the King, perhaps for his private devotions. The hymn was incorporated later into *The Book of Common Prayer* of 1662. In the service for the ordering of priests it is to be said or sung 'answering by verses as followeth':

> COME, Holy Ghost, our souls inspire,
> *And lighten with celestial fire.*
> Thou the anointing Spirit art,
> *Who dost thy seven-fold gifts impart.*
>
> Thy blessed Unction from above,
> *Is comfort, life, and fire of love.*
> Enable with perpetual light
> *The dulness of our blinded sight.*
>
> Anoint and cheer our soiled face
> *With the abundance of thy grace.*
> Keep far our foes, give peace at home:
> *Where thou art guide, no ill can come.*

Teach us to know the Father, Son,
And thee, of both, to be but one.
That, through the ages all along,
This may be our endless song;
Praise to thy eternal merit,
Father, Son and Holy Spirit.

Puritan suspicions of Cosin aroused by his appointment as Master of Ceremonies at the Coronation seemed to be confirmed by his support of Richard Mountague who faced an onslaught of opposition.

The Duke of Buckingham arranged a Conference at his own residence, York House, in the hope of silencing the accusations. Two Puritan divines, Dr Preston, Master of Emmanuel College, Cambridge, and Bishop Morton were to question Mountague closely. On the chosen day Mountague was unable to attend but Cosin, who claimed to know his mind intimately, faced the charges on his behalf and refuted them ably. After two days Buckingham declared that nothing contrary to the formularies of the English Church had been proved against Mountague. At the time Cosin was twenty-nine and Mountague was forty-seven years old.

Cosin as Rector of Brancepeth

On 20 July 1626, without giving up the living of Elwick, Cosin was collated to the Rectory of Brancepeth (St Brandon's), six miles from Durham, just over three weeks before his marriage (*see below*). He owed the preferment to Laud's acquaintance with the Duke of Buckingham, for whom he had used his influence, a few weeks earlier, to secure the Chancellorship of Cambridge University. When not in residence at Durham Cathedral, or not required at Auckland Castle to attend to the Bishop's affairs, Cosin lived at Brancepeth.

Here, he set in motion the complete re-ordering of the church. The general arrangements and fine woodwork remain much as he left them, and are a remarkable record of his views on how a church should look to express the firm foundation of the Church of England in history.[11] Perhaps he intended to remain at Brancepeth, as on the north wall of the chancel a large blank tablet, with classic pilasters and fruit swags, was intended for his memorial, but never completed as he gave up the living on becoming Bishop of Durham.

Cosin's Marriage, Health, and Children

On 15 August 1626, at St Margaret's Church, Crossgate, Durham, Cosin married Frances Blakiston, daughter of Marmaduke Blakiston, of Newton Hall, which lay in St Margaret's chapelry within the large parish of St Oswald. The original parish register records:

> 1626 Johannes Cosyn, Pastor de Elwick, et Domina Francisca Blakiston, filia Marmaduci Blakiston de Newton, nupt, August 15.[12]

Before his own children were born he won the devotion of Richard Mountague's small daughter, who was often called 'his little wif'. As early as 1627 Cosin's health was not good for Mountague wrote to him 'to condole that which I can never forget, that fit of stone . . .' from which Mountague had suffered also for a long time.

It will be helpful to say something about Cosin's children at this point. There were three sons (two died in infancy) and four daughters of the marriage: John; Mary (who married Sir Gilbert Gerard); Elizabeth (who was married four times: first to Henry Hutton, secondly to Sir Thomas Burton, thirdly to Samuel Davison, and fourthly to Isaac Basire);[13] Frances (who first married Charles Gerard, and second Thomas Blakiston); and Anne (who married Denis Granville).[14] Anne seems to have been a little feeble-minded and too fond of wine, to the embarrassment of her husband, Denis Granville, who was himself no favourite of Cosin as he was always in debt. John was unstable and became a trouble to his father. In exile during the Commonwealth, he attended a Jesuit school in Paris, became a Roman Catholic, recanted and returned to the Church of England, but returned to the Roman Church to Cosin's great sorrow. John was always uncertain in his beliefs. He entered the English College at Rome on 26 October 1652 as Charles Cosins, and was ordained a Roman Catholic priest on 24 February 1657/8. His father was heartbroken and never got over his son's defection. Mary, however, was the comfort of Cosin's old age.

A Book of Private Devotions

At the King's request, Cosin compiled and published on 19 February 1626/7, *A Book of Private Devotions* for the Anglican ladies of Queen Henrietta Maria's court, who had been criticized by her Roman Catholic ladies who used their Books of Hours throughout the day. They were horrified to find no similar provision made for Church of England ladies who had so much spare time on their hands daily. The *Devotions* was based on an Elizabethan *Book of Hours*, but it aroused much opposition from the Puritans. Opponents objected to the sacred monogram IHS at the head of the engraved title-page, as they thought it was popish. Cosin pointed out that the letters are simply an abbreviation representing the first three letters of the name '*Jesus*'. When written in Greek capitals, the second letter of the word is like H.[15]

Durham Cathedral under Change

Cosin was determined to see that due reverence was observed in the Cathedral services, and that worshippers stood, knelt or bowed at the times he thought proper. By now women's stalls had been built at the north side of the choir beside Bishop Skirlaw's tomb, where its railings had been removed to accommodate them. On a famous occasion Cosin seized the sleeve of Margaret Heath (wife of John Heath of Old Durham), tearing it, and calling her a 'lazy sow' because she did not stand up for the Creed. Presumably he went down the choir from his stall to speak to her.

Eleazor Duncon, who had been admitted a scholar of Caius College three years later than Cosin, followed him to Durham where he was installed prebendary in 1628 and became his strong ally, later succeeding him as Bishop Neile's domestic chaplain.

Before the influence of Laud, the Holy Table, made of wood, was placed at the east end of the chancel when not in use, but was moved to stand lengthways in the centre of the choir for Holy Communion so that the celebrant stood on the long north side facing south.

Peter Smart

Peter Smart was a Prebendary of Durham from 1609 to 1641 and therefore was long-established when Cosin arrived. Although the altar installed by Richard Hunt (Dean 1620-1638) had been built before Cosin's time, he was to be accused by his enemies of responsibility for its use. Peter Smart described the altar and the new arrangements:

> You, Dean Hunt, with your associates, holding a conventicle in the Castle of Durham . . . ordered that the old Communion Table of wood . . . should be cast out of the Church; which was done, and in place therof you have set up a double table, very sumptuous of stone, which you always call the altar. This altar stands upon six stone pillars, curiously polished, and fastened to the ground, having upon every black pillar those cherubim-faces as white as snow . . . You beautified the same altar with paintings and gildings, and hangings and coverings of silke and velvet, of silver and gold, so brave and glorious that all the altars in England . . . may set their caps at our Durham altar, which has cost, with the furniture belonging thereunto, above £3000.

This figure is a gross exaggeration. Elsewhere the altar was said to cost two hundred pounds. Even so, this was a considerable sum in those days. Dean Hunt's altar remains in place; but it bears marks where the angel heads have been removed. Except at special seasons such as Passion Week, it is covered by a larger altar.

It is possible that vestments were introduced in 1627 at Cosin's suggestion. In that year a Chapter Order runs:

> The three vestments, and one white cope, now belonging to the vestry of this church, shall be taken and carried to London, to be altered and changed into fair and large copes according to the Canons and Constitutions of the Church of England.

On July 27 1628 Peter Smart preached his famous sermon at Durham attacking the new ideas and especially the activities of John Cosin. Smart said:

> This Cosens hath set up 50 glittering angels round about the quire of Durham Church, in long scarlet gownes, with golden wings and guilded heads.[16]

Smart objected also to lights on the altar and in the choir:

> On Candlemas Day last past: Mr COSENS . . . busied himselfe from two of the clocke in the afternoone till foure, in climbing long ladders to sticke up wax candles in the Cathedrall Church: The number of all the Candles burnt that evening was 220, beside 16 Torches.

Smart hated also the music and the restoration of the copes for all of which he blamed Cosin:

> He chaunts with Organs, Shackbuts, and Cornets, which yield an hydeous noise . . .

In *A Sermon Preached in the Cathedrall Church of Dvrham Jvly 7. 1628*, which Smart had printed, he said:

> I haue heard of a Divell that preacht, I haue heard of a Friar that preacht in a rope; but I neuer heard of, either Divell or Frier, that preached in a Cope.

There is an Appendix to the *Sermon*, entitled *A briefe, but true historicall narration of some notorious acts and speeches of*

Mr. Iohn Cosens, and some other of his companions contracted into Articles. The 10th Article states:

> He hath brought diuers old Copes which have been used in May-games heretofore, one of them hauing the picture of the Trinitie embroydered upon it, and these Copes hee would enjoyne the Praebends constantly to weare.

Smart also complained of bowing to the altar. There was no doubt much bad feeling and name calling on both sides at the time. Smart feared that the new practices tended towards popery, although Cosin and his friends and associates were staunchly protestant and were trying to re-establish the tradition of an English church with ancient foundations. As a result of his sermon, Smart was eventually deprived of his preferments.

On the afternoon of the day Smart preached his sermon, Dean Hunt called the High Commission Court, and Smart was suspended from his prebendal stall. Cosin had no more to do with the case after this. It was later heard in London and then referred to York where Smart was imprisoned from 1629 to 1640. Cosin stated later that during the imprisonment, he had earnestly entreated for him 'that, upon any due sense of his fault, he might be quietly sent back to us again, in the hope that he would hereafter live in better peace and concord with us'.[17] Nick Heppel has written extensively about Smart's accusations against Cosin elsewhere in this volume.[18]

Charles I's Visit to Durham in 1633

Charles I stayed in Durham during his progress to Scotland to be crowned there. The King arrived from Auckland Castle at five o'clock on Saturday evening, 1 June, and after saying the Lord's Prayer quietly, entered the Cathedral under a canopy borne by eight prebendaries in surplices. He sat in a chair by the font to receive a short address of welcome from the Dean, before proceeding to the choir during the singing of the *Te Deum*. After a short service, he visited the tombs of St Cuthbert and of the Venerable Bede. He was presented with a rich cope which the Dean and Chapter had bought, and which, it is said, he gave to Laud for use in the royal chapel; but this seems to be the cope which is now in Durham. It is of crimson satin, powdered all over with stars; David and Goliath's head are worked on the hood; and the border is covered with cherubs in stump work. The bill survives. Charles stayed in the Castle, attended Matins in the Cathedral next morning, and was at Evensong in the Castle on Sunday, leaving on Monday. Cosin had charge of all the arrangements for the reception of the King and for the service in the Cathedral. Charles I wrote a letter to the Dean and Chapter from the Castle, dated 2 June, drawing attention to certain things he wished to see carried out: the removal of certain tenements in the churchyard, and the finding of seats elsewhere than in the choir for the Mayor and Corporation and for the wives of the prebendaries. The letter is preserved in the Dean and Chapter Library.[18a] Cosin's arrangements, however, were a complete success and on Bishop Neile's recommendation he was sworn one of the King's Chaplains-in-ordinary. The appointment had the support of Laud. On Sunday after Evensong, in the Castle, the King touched for the King's Evil. Charles I visited Durham again in 1637.

The royal visits left a great impression on Durham. Panel portraits of Charles I and Queen Henrietta Maria over the fireplace of the Mayor's Chamber in the Town Hall were rumoured to be the gift of Charles I after his lavish entertainment by Bishop Morton.[19] The portraits are probably copies of one of Charles I now in the USA and of a portrait of Henrietta Maria in the Royal Collection at Windsor.

Cosin as Archbishop's Chaplain: Leeds Visit

When Bishop Neile became Archbishop of York (1632-42) Cosin remained his chaplain and at the same time continued as Archdeacon of the East Riding of Yorkshire. On 21 September

1634, when Archbishop Neile consecrated St John's Church, Briggate, Leeds, Cosin, as his chaplain, accompanied him and preached the morning sermon. The occasion is commemorated in a two-light window of nineteenth-century painted glass in the south-east wall of the nave. Cosin is shown on the left and Neile on the right. The church has seventeenth-century furnishings in the style favoured by Cosin.[20]

Cambridge: Master of Peterhouse and Vice-Chancellor

A few months later, in 1634/5, Cosin became Master of Peterhouse (St Peter's College), Cambridge and took with him a Durham Cathedral man, Thomas Wilson, as organist. Copies of part music made for the choir are well known to musicologists and have been used in conjunction with the Durham Cathedral seventeenth-century part-books to establish and complete otherwise unknown scores.

At Peterhouse Cosin took great interest in both the library and the chapel. The library, built in 1590 in accordance with the wishes of Dr Andrew Perne (Master 1554-89), is on the first floor with originally a Long Gallery for the Master above. It was lengthened to the east by some thirty-six feet in 1633 and the date is in the brickwork outside the oriel window. The interior was fitted out with woodwork (1641-48) by William Ashley after he had completed work on the chapel. The bench-ends are thought to be inspired by those in the Laurentinian Library at Florence in the 1620s.

The chapel was built between 1628 and 1632 under the influence of Matthew Wren, who was Master from 1625 to 1634 and so Cosin's immediate predecessor. Its Laudian Gothic style represented the high Anglican ideals of the period. The flanking cloisters are of the same date, but were classicized between 1709 and 1711, and an ornamental porch was removed in 1755. The chapel interior retains many of the furnishings of Cosin's time, including the open balustraded stalls and the cambered timber ceiling. The reredos, flanking panelling and rails are of the 1720s. A contemporary account by William Prynne, on the authority of a Mr Wallis, describes

> . . . the glorious new Altar . . . to which the Master, Fellowes and Schollers bowed and were enjoyned to bow by Doctor Cosens . . .

and the

> Basons, Candlesticks, Tapers standing on it and a great Crucifix hanging over it . . .

There were carved crosses 'at the end of every seat', and a pot on the altar 'which they usually call the incense pot'. Much of this so-called 'Wren's nest' was despoiled in 1643 when Cosin was ejected. When Laud was on trial he was accused of responsibility for these innovations at Peterhouse. In defence he said they were made by Wren and Cosin, and asked why, as both were alive, they could not be required to answer for what they had done. Wren was imprisioned in the Tower for seventeen years. Both Laud and Wren defended their rites and ceremonies as being based on their experience in the Royal Chapels, where Charles I encouraged Armenianism under Wren as Dean of Windsor and Laud as Dean of the Chapel Royal.

The east front of both the chapel and library facing Trumpington Street are of the 1630s; but in 1665, when Cosin was Bishop of Durham, he paid for the erection of an ornamental eastern façade which bears, over the east window, his coat of arms impaled with those of the See of Durham. The façade is not keyed into the structure. His bequest to Peterhouse paid for the octagonal buttresses and the stone facing of the north and south sides.

In 1639 Cosin was made Vice-Chancellor of Cambridge University. For a year he remained solely in Cambridge and was unable to fulfil his duties in Durham, as he wrote to the Dean. As University Vice-Chancellor he became responsible for administering Archbishop Laud's 'Etcetera Oath' (similar to the Scottish League and Covenant). It was considered 'Popish' by its opponents and Cosin advised Laud against it.

He became concerned also with building a University Library and Senate House. The model he had made was approved, and progress was made in raising funds. Cosin promised to contribute one hundred pounds as soon as the ground was cleared ready for building. When the Rebellion broke out, the scheme came to nothing.

At an earlier time, Cosin had complained to Laud about the condition of the University Church of Great St Mary's which dates mainly from the fifteenth and sixteenth centuries although there was a church on the site in 1205. As Vice-Chancellor, Cosin undertook changes there. The puritan, Prynne, says: 'Altars, Crucifixes, Candlesticks, Tapers, and bowing to altars were brought in'. Cosin caused the side-chapels to be separated from the nave by parclose screens, and ordered the erection of a screen to divide the chancel from the nave. The great Cambridge antiquarian, William Cole (1718-42), describes it as 'a beautiful and lofty screen with a canopy and spire-work'. It was to be defaced in 1641 and removed in the mid-eighteenth century.

Peter Smart's Case against Cosin

On 13 April 1640 Parliament met for the first time for eleven years. Within a fortnight, Peter Smart presented a petition for an enquiry into his wrongs. A committee was appointed to consider the matter. Cosin realized his personal danger if this Parliament was in control.

Smart's principal charges against Cosin were:

1. he took the eastward position when celebrating Holy Communion;
2. he had covered cushions and benches with crosses;
3. he had spoken scandalously against the Reformers;
4. he had denied the Royal Supremacy.

Cosin refuted these charges easily, saying that he always took the north side of the Holy Table except for the consecration; that he denied the second charge; that he had always blessed God for the Reformation; and showed that he upheld the Royal Supremacy.

One charge brought against him by his enemies related to a Cambridge don named Nicholas, a Fellow of Peterhouse, claiming that he had enticed him to popery. Cosin proved that the opposite was true: he had argued with Nicholas, made him read a public recantation, as was within his powers as Vice-Chancellor, and expelled him from the University.

In spite of these denials, Smart's charges were upheld and Cosin was imprisoned. He asked for bail and was released on 3 December. On 19 January 1640/1 he was bound in two thousand pounds and his securities in a thousand pounds each for his appearances upon summons. Three days later the committee presented its report, drawn up by Francis Rous the elder (who became Speaker to Cromwell's first Parliament of 1653) and the House of Commons vindicated Smart and condemned Cosin. Resolutions were passed declaring Cosin unfit and unworthy to hold office in the universities or to hold any ecclesiastical preferment. The committee was ordered to prepare the case against Cosin and in mid-March his impeachment was carried to the House of Lords. The twenty-one Articles of impeachment were designed by Rous to draw a picture of 'an army of priests with a great design of bringing Popery'.

Cosin's replies to these charges are worth reading, and show him to have acted always within the law and with moderation.[20a] Cosin was released, but allowed no reparation for his wrongful accusation and imprisonment, while Smart was restored to his Durham prebend and the vicarage of Aycliffe.

Dean of Peterborough

After the second 'Bishops' War' broke out in August 1640, Cosin's Durham income suffered badly. The Dean and Chapter revenues were diverted to the Scots, who demanded eight hundred and fifty pounds a day for maintenance. Because of his poverty, Charles I chose Cosin from four candidates for the post of Dean of Peterborough, which had become vacant by the death of Dr Thomas Jackson, who was also President of Corpus Christi College, Oxford. On 7 November 1640, Cosin took up this appointment whilst retaining the Mastership of Peterhouse.

The Death of his Wife Frances

Amid all these troubles, his wife Frances died on 25 March 1642, after the birth of Anne. A strange story is told about her death. Frances had appeared to make a good recovery after the birth and all was prepared for the baptism. On the Eve of the Feast of the Annunciation, the Chanter at Peterborough took the anthem he had chosen to Cosin, as Dean. It was *I am the Resurrection,* appointed to be sung as part of the Burial Service, to a composition by Wilkinson (whose Christian name is unknown). When Cosin asked the reason for the choice, the Chanter replied, 'It is a good anthem and you have not yet heard it'. Frances died the next morning, and Cosin afterwards regarded the anthem as an omen. Thus it happened that while the child was at the font for baptism, the body of the mother lay on her bier nearby to be carried away for burial. The same anthem was sung again at the funeral. Frances is buried in the north choir aisle of Peterborough Cathedral, opposite the tomb of Katharine of Aragon.

The marble slab bears her Latin epitaph composed by her husband. Instructions for the placing of the inscription, together with the wording, were laid down in the codicil to

Cosin's Will, and forty pounds was entrusted to his daughter Lady Mary Gerard and his executors for carrying out the work.

In 1642 the Master and Fellows of Peterhouse agreed to send the college plate to supply the York mint for the King's cause. They resolved to replenish it at their own cost at the end of the present troubles. There is preserved at Peterhouse a note of the agreement in Cosin's handwriting. Not only Peterhouse, but other colleges in Oxford and Cambridge offered their plate to be melted down in the King's cause. On 13 March 1643/4 Cosin was ejected from the mastership by warrant of the Earl of Manchester, who was commissioned by Parliament 'to purge' Cambridge and the eastern counties. Among the charges made against Cosin was that he had agreed to send the college plate to York, an attempt foiled by Oliver Cromwell and Valentine Walton, the regicide. After the Restoration of the monarchy, Cosin gave to Peterhouse a very fine two-handled cup which bears his episcopal coat of arms. It is used at an annual dinner held to commemorate Cosin.

Suspicions against Cosin: Ejection and Exile

Cosin's position had become increasingly insecure because of his support of Laud. In 1633 Laud had been offered secretly a Cardinal's hat when it was hoped that, as Archbishop of Canterbury, he might become Patriarch of a Uniate Church of England following the pattern of the Greek Orthodox Church in Lithuania and Ruthenia in 1598. Laud, however, remained a faithful Anglican to the last.

A popular belief that Laudianism led to Roman Catholicism found support in the defection of some Cambridge men. An ejected Fellow of Peterhouse who visited Rome in the 1640s met there three others whom he had known at Peterhouse when Cosin was Master; Francis Blakiston (Cosin's nephew), Christopher Barker, and Richard Nichols. William and Thomas Keightley, Fellow Commoners under Cosin, also became ardent Roman Catholics. Another was the poet Richard

Crashaw, whose pupil at Peterhouse was Ferrar Collet (of Little Gidding). When Crashaw left in 1643, Ferrar was passed to Joseph Beaumont, Crashaw's closest friend, a man of extreme views of whom Cosin thought little. Other defaulters to Rome came from Pembroke and St John's Colleges. With such associations, although Cosin was faithful to his Church, it was easy to cast suspicion on him. He was the victim of expediency in the process of the destruction of the establishment.

Now that Cosin was held unfit to hold the Deanery of Peterborough, and was ejected from the mastership of Peterhouse, it became evident that he would have to leave England for his own safety. He sent his four daughters to the Blakistons, their mother's family.

In April 1643 Peterborough Cathedral was ravaged daily for a fortnight by Parliamentarians led by Cromwell's son Richard. They broke the stained glass, destroyed the choir stalls and altar screen, riddling with shot a painting of Christ in glory. They broke up the organs 'with such a strange, furious, and frantic zeal as cannot be well conceived but by them that saw it'. The Prayer Books and the lectern Bible with the Apocrypha were torn up. William Dowsing left a journal of his similar exploits at Cambridge in December 1643:

> We went to Peterhouse with officers and soldiers; and . . . we pulled down two mighty great Angels with wings, and divers other Angels, and the four Evangelists, and Peter with the keys over the Chapel-door, and about a hundred cherubims and Angels, and divers superstitious letters in gold . . . Above the walls was written, in Latin, *We praise thee ever*; and on some of the images was written, *Sanctus, Sanctus, Sanctus*; on other *Gloria Dei et Gloria Patri*, etc., and all *Non nobis Domine*, etc., and six Angels in the windows.

Dowsing makes no mention of Cosin who had probably left Cambridge earlier in the year and gone into hiding in order to avoid Parliamentary arrest.

In the north, Bishop Morton, who had been Bishop of Durham from 1632, fled before the Scots to Stockton-on-Tees, to his castle which was later stripped and demolished. All ecclesiastical property was confiscated and sold.

The Civil War

In February 1642 Charles I, knowing that civil war was inevitable, hastened with Queen Henrietta Maria to Dover, sending her to Holland with the crown jewels which she was to pawn or sell to raise money for the royalist cause. She herself believed that her presence in England was endangering the King's person. From Holland she hoped to return to England when danger had passed. She was well received on her journey to Amsterdam, and a print in The Hague shows her reception outside the Castle of Heemstede.

London and the eastern counties were on the side of Parliament, while support for the Royalists was mainly in the north, the west and the counties bordering on Wales. Hull was the arsenal of the North and in April its Governor had refused to open its gates to the King. Civil War began on 22 August 1642 when Charles I raised his standard at Nottingham.

Cosin with the Court in Paris

When the Queen arrived in Paris she was received by the Queen Regent of France, Anne of Austria, who assigned quarters to her in the Louvre and a pension of one thousand two hundred francs a day. It is not known how and when Cosin reached France; there is no reference to him in Paris before 1645. However, he had been appointed by the King as royal chaplain responsible for the Anglicans in the Queen's court, where the Protestant servants were much more numerous than those who were Catholics. As long as Charles was alive, the Queen was scrupulous in observing his wishes. Cosin was given quarters in the Louvre, a room which was furnished as a chapel for the daily offices, an income, and freedom to minister to his flock. Later, Henrietta Maria was asked by the Queen Regent to dismiss Cosin from her service, a demand she felt bound to comply with since she was dependent on her for charity. She arranged for services to be held in the residence of the English Ambassador, Sir Richard Browne (1605-83), who was to play an important part in keeping alive the services and liturgy of the Church of England among the Paris exiles.

In his large house in Paris Browne created a chapel where regular Sunday Prayer Book services were held by Cosin. The chapel subsequently became the headquarters of the exiled English church and here Cosin is said to have 'supported the honour of the Church of England in the popish country to admiration in an open chapel at Paris with the solemnity of a cathedral service'.[21] The services, which were said to be held there for nineteen years, were well attended by the exiles and notably by well-known English clergy and scholars.

Many bishops and other English theologians, who took refuge in the Embassy chapel, were having to face disputes with Roman Catholics and Continental Protestants at a time when the Church of England, its orders, doctrines and liturgy seemed a lost cause. However, in his *Diary*, John Evelyn says they were able 'to argue for the visibility of the Church from this chapel and congregation'. He also describes various services held in the chapel, including that of his own marriage to Browne's only daughter Mary on 27 June 1647, and the ordination of two young Huguenots on Trinity Sunday, 12 June 1650. Both ordinands were admitted to the diaconate and ordained priests by Dr Sydserf, Bishop of Galloway, at a time when there were few remaining Church of England bishops. The sermon at the ordination was preached by Cosin.

One of the two ordinands was John Durel (chaplain to the Duc de la Force), who became prebendary of the fourth stall at Durham Cathedral in 1668, and Dean of Windsor in 1677. It was he who translated the Prayer Book into French for the use of Anglicans in the Channel Isles and saw through the press Cosin's *History of Transubstantiation*. The other was Daniel Brevint (chaplain to Monsieur de Turenne) whom Cosin presented for ordination. Later, when Cosin became Bishop, he persuaded the King to appoint Brevint to the same prebendal stall at Durham which he had held, as well as to his former Rectory of Brancepeth. Brevint eventually became Dean of Lincoln; his eucharistic manual, *The Christian Sacrifice and Sacrament* was adopted by John and Charles Wesley and had a great influence on the early Methodists.

While Cosin was living in Paris, he was presented with a chalice, bearing a Paris mark of 1651, by the Earl of Clarendon, a member of the Anglican community in Paris. A matching cover was made for Cosin probably after his return to England. A paten made in Paris is also dated 1651, and must have been given at the same time as the chalice. Cosin brought these to Auckland Castle when he became Bishop of Durham, and today they are on display in Durham Cathedral Treasury.

Charles was tried on 20 January 1649 and executed on 30 January. The Queen was informed in Paris. Following his death, she was pressed to withdraw Cosin's pension. Cosin himself was placed under pressure to become a Roman Catholic, but remained faithful to the Protestant cause, and made friends with the Huguenots. It is clear that he accepted the validity of their ministry and Holy Orders.

Cosin himself became impoverished and was reduced to taking gifts from visitors to Paris in order to live. According to Evelyn, one of Cosin's benefactors was Sir Ralph Verney, who was sufficiently well off to be able to offer financial assistance to those less fortunate. Later, when Verney's wife died, Cosin sent him a copy of his *Devotions*. Cosin was also helped by Evelyn himself and William Sancroft (prebendary of the ninth stall at Durham 1662-74 and Archbishop of Canterbury from 1677). Cosin was a book collector, and as conditions became harder, he contemplated selling his valuable library in order to live; but the Restoration came just in time.

His daughters in England must have been improverished for among the Letters of Privy Seal granted by Oliver, Lord Protector is preserved the entry:

> Mary Cosins [afterwards Lady Gerard], daughter of Docto^{r}. Cosins, a pencon of xx^{s}. per weeke from y^{e}. 20th. of Octob^{r}. 1657, for y^{e}. support of her sis^{rs}..., &c.

The Prayer Book and the Commonwealth

Under the Protectorate of Oliver Cromwell use of *The Book of Common Prayer* was forbidden. However, his immediate family continued to use it; and his daughter was married according to the Prayer Book service, when the current law demanded a secular ceremony before a magistrate. It is also known that when James Ussher, Archbishop of Armagh, died in the house of a royalist countess at Reigate in 1656, Cromwell ordered that he should have a state funeral in Westminister Abbey, using the otherwise forbidden Prayer Book liturgy.

Anglicans were persecuted. Many loyal clergy were ejected and replaced by men of Presbyterian or Independent persuasion, known later as 'intruders'; but other parish clergy carried on and defied the law when possible. John Evelyn's *Diary* records an incident in December 1657 when soldiers broke into a Communion Service which they had been sent to prevent; but the service was completed in spite of their threatening attitude.

Restoration of the Monarchy: Cosin as Bishop of Durham

At the Restoration in 1660 Cosin returned to England to Peterborough, where he restored worship according to *The Book of Common Prayer.* He opened negotiations for the restoration of his livings and other ecclesiastical preferments in Durham: his parishes of Elwick and Brancepeth, his prebend at Durham Cathedral, and his archdeaconry. It was suggested that he should become Dean of Durham, but this idea was superseded by his appointment as Bishop of Durham in 1660. He was consecrated in Westminster Abbey on 2 December, and his friend Dr Sancroft preached. As Bishop of Durham he was at Charles II's right hand at his Coronation, a traditional privilege of Durham bishops.

Cosin entered his diocese by crossing the River Tees at Croft, and receiving the Conyers falchion in the traditional manner. The falchion is a tenure sword, now rare, but common in the thirteenth century. The tenure is first mentioned in 1396. The manor of Sockburn was held by many generations by the presentation of a falchion to the bishop on his first entering the County Palatine. The tenant met the Bishop in the middle of Neasham ford or on Croft Bridge with the words:

> My lord Bishop, I here present you with the falchion wherewith the champion Conyers slew the worm, dragon, or fiery flying serpent, which destroyed man, woman, and child; in memory of which the king then reigning gave him the manor of Sockburn to hold by this tenure, that, upon the first entrance of every bishop into the county, this falchion should be presented.

Cosin entered now upon the inheritance and traditions of the medieval prince-bishops of Durham.

The Savoy Conference of 1661

Charles II had received a deputation of Puritan divines in 1660 when he was still in Holland. In November 1661 Convocation attempted reconciliation with the Presbyterians, and a commission was appointed to review *The Book of Common Prayer*. A conference was called to meet at the Savoy House.[22]

Those invited were twelve bishops and twelve Puritan divines, with nine assistants on each side. The bishops heard the views expressed and set about trying to produce a revision of the Prayer Book which it was hoped would satisfy dissenters. Eight distinguished scholars were appointed to plan the work. Because of Cosin's growing reputation as a liturgist, Charles I had asked Cosin to prepare a revision; and from that time and throughout his exile, Cosin had continued to note his ideas in his own folio copy of the Prayer Book, printed by Norton and Bill in 1619. This book, with annotations showing his proposals in his own hand, and some in the hand of William Sancroft, from 1662 a canon of Durham and Cosin's chaplain, is known as *The Durham Book*, because it is preserved in Bishop Cosin's Library in Durham. Cosin became the first secretary of the Conference, and in this position he had much influence. Others who played a prominent part were Robert Sanderson, who had taken part in discussion for revision in 1641; William Sancroft, who followed Cosin as secretary to the Conference; and Matthew Wren, Bishop of Ely, who had vetted the ill-fated Scottish Prayer Book.

The sources for the first English Prayer Book of 1549 were now influenced by new liturgies. Rubrics had to take account of past practices, which included the use of a moveable Holy Table which had been placed lengthways in the chancel or nave to be close to the people, with the celebrant standing on the north (long) side, and any other minister assisting standing on the south side. The people gathered round the Table for the Communion.

Laud had encouraged the practice of leaving the Holy Table against the east wall of the chancel where it stood when there was no Communion, and protecting it with rails to prevent abuse, while retaining the place of the celebrant on the north, which was now one of the short ends of the Holy Table. Cosin himself always stood at the north end during a Communion Service, moving to the west side only for the consecration and thus following ancient practice.

Cosin favoured Genevan principles. The Sentences and Responses used generally at the Gospel reading are of Cosin's recommendation. He wanted to print the words 'Glory be to Thee O Lord' to be said by the congregation before the Gospel reading, and 'Thanks be to Thee O Lord, for thy holy Gospel' said at its conclusion, which are of ancient usage. They appear in the Scottish Liturgy of 1637. In December 1661 Cosin wrote the words with the variant 'Thanks be given to the Lord'. They were omitted from the 1662 Prayer Book but have passed into general use in their earlier form. Cosin also wished to restore the Bidding Prayer before sermons but this proposal was also rejected. He composed five new collects, which are universally loved and familiar today. In the Ordinal was inserted Cosin's own hymn, the translation of the *Veni Creator*, 'Come Holy Ghost our souls inspire . . .', which he had composed for the coronation of Charles I. The amendments finally agreed were written out by Sancroft in a Prayer Book bound with a Psalter and Ordinal, all printed by Barker in 1634, known as *Sancroft's Fair Copy* and now in the Bodleian Library. The completed work of revision was written by Sancroft in a Prayer Book printed by Barker in 1636 and bound with a Psalter and Ordinal of 1639, now in the Library of the House of Lords and known as *The Convocation Book*. This was the official copy from which a fair copy was made to send to the King, and, with the Black Rubric (enjoining the receiving of Holy Communion kneeling) added, was attached to the Act of Uniformity. Convocation deputed to Cosin the task of producing a form of service for the consecration of churches and chapels.

The Act of Uniformity enjoined the use of the new Prayer Book by St Bartholomew's Day, 24 August 1662. Durham Dean and Chapter Library has a copy of the 1662 Prayer Book with a portrait of Charles II as frontispiece.

Cosin: Durham Cathedral and Diocese

Although he was far from well, suffering from stone in the kidneys, swollen legs, shortness of breath and poor eyesight, Cosin was energetic in putting to rights his vast diocese, which stretched from the River Tees to the Scottish Border, including both Northumberland and County Durham. In all his enterprises he displayed great administrative gifts.

His Cathedral Visitations were searching. In his Articles of Enquiry in 1662 and again in 1663, Cosin asked:

> What is become of the lead and wood of the two great broaches [spires] that stood upon the towers at the west end of the Church?

James Green, Minor Canon and Sacrist, added to the replies of the Minor Canons in 1666:

> Mr. Gilbert Marshall, Mr. Gilpin, and Mr. Anthony Smith can best tell what became of it.

Cosin asked repeatedly about the services, furnishings, and poor litany desk.

In November 1662, he conducted a diocesan Visitation. He visited churches in the immediate locality of Durham itself to preach, to catechize and to exhort to baptism; he held a vast confirmation of several thousands of people for two days, to cover the backlog of the last twenty years. Each had to present a note from the parish priest. A synod of clergy was called in Durham and another in Newcastle. Also, he set about gathering like-minded clergy in Durham.

Cosin's Secular Duties

As Lord Lieutenant of County Durham, the King required him to use the local militia to seek out nonconformist conventicles when asked to do so. Cosin's strongly anti-Roman Catholic views were expressed at the time.

He was noted for his business acumen and love of acquiring money; but he spent it on ecclesiastical, charitable and other projects dear to him. He had his faults: wishing to restore the bishoprick to some of its medieval glory, he was violently opposed to the local wish for Parliamentary representation, considering that his own membership of the House of Lords, as Bishop, was sufficient. However, within two years of Cosin's death and during the vacancy of the see before Nathaniel Crewe's episcopacy (1674-1721) a Bill was passed enabling the County and City of Durham to return knights and citizens to Parliament.

Heraldic Visitation of 1662 and Cosin's Coat of Arms

Cosin's replies at the Heraldic Visitation on 4 September 1662, record information about his parents and his own family, with his coat of arms and crest, but it is evident that he knew nothing of his grandparents.

Cosin's coat of arms is *azure a fret or* and was granted probably when he became Bishop of Durham in 1661. The shield is ancient in form but the tinctures are distinctive to Cosin. No one in his father's family appears to have been armigerous, and the design bears no relation to his father's occupation if, indeed, he was a tailor as Smart's gibe inferred, although the fret may be an allusion to weaving. John's brother Nathaniel was a weaver, following his father in one branch of the cloth trade. Other bishops are known to have represented their fathers' occupations in their coats of arms. The College of Arms has no record of the grant, but the herald of the time, Edward Bysshe, was not good at keeping records. Some coats of arms of the period are unauthorized inventions, but Cosin's is obviously genuine, as heralds presided over his funeral in 1672.

Cosin and the Bishop's Manor House at Darlington

This episcopal residence was built about 1164 by Bishop Hugh of le Puiset, with a chapel which still retained features of that period in the late eighteenth century.[23] Bishop Anthony Bek (1284-1311) impaled the park.[24] John Leland (1538) described it as a 'praty Palace'.[24a]

Its site, formerly known as the Hallgarth, was close to the River Skerne, and on the south side of St Cuthbert's parish church, with its park on the east side of the river. It was entered from a courtyard leading from a lane. The Manor House had become ruinous in the seventeenth century, but Cosin restored it and referred to it in his correspondence in his early years as Bishop of Durham. Accounts relating to work done on the Manor House and the Toll Booth are given together, so that it is usually impossible to distinguish the costs separately. A group of local copyholders was responsible for some of the repair costs; but there are items for leading stone, limestone and brick. In 1679 and 1680 further repairs were carried out when the inhabitants of Blackwell township were responsible for leading lime and slates for the Toll Booth and the 'Old Hall'.

Cosin's expectation that the restoration would benefit his successors as a residence was not borne out for long, as the subsequent history of the building shows.

From 1669 Cosin's son-in-law, Charles Gerard, lived there as the Bishop's 'housekeeper'. The Honourable Nathaniel Crewe, who became bishop in 1674, was the last bishop to reside in the Manor House.

The house was neglected in the eighteenth century, when it was sub-let by the life-tenant (the Bishop's 'housekeeper') to the town of Darlington as a poor-house. Ralph Thoresby, the antiquary, visited Darlington on 20 May 1703, and after expressing pleasure at his visit to the parish church, said 'but I was concerned to see the adjoining house of the Bishop of Durham converted into a Quakers' workhouse'. A detailed description of the house exists from the time when it was used as a workhouse.[25] The park at that time was divided into fields and let for terms of years by the See of Durham.[26]

Lady Gerard was said to haunt the house when it was a workhouse, occurrences being before births and deaths. The exploits of the ghost were said to resemble those of the silkies or cauld lads of north country folk lore, partly mischievous, and partly benevolent.[27] The site of the house is occupied today by the Civic Centre.[28]

Cosin's Restoration of Auckland Castle

Cosin seems to have ordered altar plate for Auckland Castle immediately on his appointment as Bishop of Durham. Its speedy execution was, no doubt, because he knew the Master of the Jewel House, whom he had been advising about plate suitable for the Chapels Royal. One of the silver gilt chalices is a slight simplification of the design ordered for St James' Chapel. It has a decorated stem and a base with scalloped edge and matching cover. The pieces were made for Auckland by an English craftsman, and are much more ornate than the chalice presented to him in Paris. For this, in 1660, Cosin commissioned a matching paten which bears the makers' mark IB between laurel branches and a crowned C.

Two ewers or flagons were made also in 1660. One bears a design representing the Resurrection of Christ and the other the Ascension. The designs are by Wolfgang Howzer, a Swiss craftsman who arrived in England about 1657, and it is thought that he decorated but did not make the pieces. Before 1662 two fine, tall silver gilt candlesticks of English craftsmanship were made for Cosin. An alms dish made for Auckland at the same time has a design representing the Last Supper.

Cosin had copies of the Bible and Prayer Book bound in crimson velvet, with silver gilt mounts, and his episcopal coat of arms as a central boss.[29] The Holy Table of Auckland Castle chapel must have looked very splendid with Cosin's plate displayed upon it. The alms dish was placed centrally (instead of the medieval crucifix), flanked by the richly bound copies of the Bible and *The Book of Common Prayer*. These replaced the separate volumes of Epistles and Gospels of medieval times, and emphasized the national character of the Church of England. Cosin's reredos was a tapestry depicting Solomon's meeting with the Queen of Sheba, which the medieval church interpreted as a parallel to the Epiphany - the Manifestation of Christ to the Gentiles.

Cosin inaugurated work on Auckland Castle at the same time as work was proceeding on Durham Castle. Bishop Morton had fled before the Scots; and when church possessions were sold during the Commonwealth, a survey was made of Auckland Castle for Sir Arthur Haslerigg, who bought it for £6,102 8s. 11d. He demolished the two chapels on the east side of the entrance gate. They lay close to a postern in the outer Castle wall south of the Great Hall. He used the stone to make additions to the rest of the building. Isaac Basire speaks of 'two goodly chappels erected there' being blown up by Haslerigg. Sir William Brereton of Cheshire visited Auckland in 1634 and mentions the two chapels, one above the other: the upper chapel was light and airy, but the acoustics were so poor that the voice travelled round and round and could scarcely be heard. For this reason it was used only rarely, and the Sunday services, to which many local people came, took place in the lower chapel.[30]

Cosin remodelled the Great Hall as his chapel. It was built originally in the time of Bishop Hugh of le Puiset, and altered at various times, notably in the time of Bishop Hatfield, when the east and central west windows and those of the sides were changed. The east window has since been tampered with and it is difficult to tell how much of Hatfield's work remains. In common with other medieval halls, there was a central fireplace and louvre (mentioned in Bishop Cuthbert Tunstal's accounts of 1543)[30a] to carry away the smoke. Cosin raised the floor level, had the new floor paved in black and white marble, added a clerestory, and gave the building a new roof.

Both Isaac Basire and Dugdale say that Cosin built the chapel, and Smith says that he built it 'from the foundations'; but a letter from Cosin dated 30 January 1662[/3], giving instructions to Mr Bowser, makes it clear that he was altering the original building; and archaeological and architectural evidence confirms this. Agreements with the masons who built the clerestory, and with the joiners who constructed the new roof, do not appear to have survived; but there is an agreement with the stone carver Richard Herring dated 7 April 1633, and with the glaziers on 13 December of the same year. The outer walls were given a rusticated effect by the insertion of regularly spaced 'brooches' between the ashlars. The work is by John Longstaffe who worked on Cosin's Library in Durham. All Cosin's rain water heads bear dates.

The chapel ceiling was executed probably by James Hall and Mark Todd who worked elsewhere in Auckland Castle. Cosin's coat of arms alternates with those of the See of Durham to give a rich effect. They were painted by John Baptist van Eersell who worked also in Cosin's Library and Durham Castle.

The screens and woodwork are deliberately Gothic in style to emphasize the theological idea of the antiquity of the church. They are the work of John Brasse, a joiner, and Abraham Smith, a carpenter, both of Durham. Their agreement dated 7 March 1663/4 is an example of the instructions given to all the craftsmen:

> to make and erect . . . within the Chappell at Auckland Castle, a skreene . . . eleaven foot high, and of the breadth of the said

> Chappell, and of the same workmanship, according to a modell or draught thereof for that purpose made.

The payment was forty shillings a yard. Smith also wainscoted the chapel and had to execute

> tracery within the pannells of the said wainscott, suitable to the pannells now made on the outside of the skreen in the said Chappell, with a cornish thereon, according to the draught thereof chosen by the said Edward Arden . . .

The paving was by Hendrik de Keyser of Bishop Auckland, probably a member of a Flemish dynasty of workers of the pre-Civil War period. The litany desks are an integral part of Cosin's work. In the centre Cosin provided for his own tomb: his will directs that he was to be buried there. The chapel was at last ready to be consecrated on St Peter's Day, 29 June 1665.

Cosin's work may be seen elsewhere in Auckland Castle. Some of his work however, has been overlaid by the adaptions of later bishops. The oldest part of the medieval manor house, linking the servants' quarters with the Great Hall, is now the hall at the foot of the stairs leading to the Throne Room, is known as the Gentlemen's Hall. Here the window glass is decorated with Cosin's coat of arms.

To the east of the castle lies the Bishop's Park of some eight hundred acres. It had been stocked with wild white cattle and deer, which were extinct at the time of the Parliamentary Survey of the property in 1647. Cosin, however, re-stocked the park with deer, and had park keepers.

Cosin's Restoration of Durham Castle

Durham Castle was in a very bad state of repair when Cosin became bishop. During the Protectorate it was sold to the Lord Mayor of London, who stripped it of lead.

In 1662 a contract was drawn up for building the great stair turret to connect the floors of the north and west wings. The staircase, known as the Black Staircase, and the finest of its period in the country, was planned by Cosin to rise through three upper storeys in a square stair well. The balustrades are carved with thick pierced foliage. The stairs are bonded into the walls and were otherwise originally unsupported. (The present Tuscan columns were added later to bear the weight of an added upper storey.)

Under a contract with Oliphant of Durham dated 22 December 1663, work began on the Great Hall and its pavements; the fireplace and four rooms were added on its west side.

In January 1664/5 the porch before the Great Hall door to the courtyard was constructed in classical style, in front of Bishop Bek's entrance door which was decayed; and buttresses surmounted by cupolas were added at each side. The stone was taken from the Broken Walls Quarry north of the Cathedral's Galilee chapel, where its operation destroyed the medieval defence walls above. (The steep footpath leading to the site from Framwellgate Bridge is known as Broken Walls today.) The building south of the Great Hall is also Cosin's work, bears his coat of arms, and contains a good seventeenth-century staircase.

The Tunstal Gallery and Tunstal Chapel screens also received Cosin's attention, and on 4 January 1664, Van Eersell was instructed to paint the wainscot, screens and coats of arms of the gallery and chapel for seven pounds.

The barbican, leading from the Exchequer Building on Palace Green to the Castle courtyard, was ruinous, and Cosin had it demolished as far as the gatehouse. In July 1664 the east courtyard wall was built with its fountain. He terraced the motte, using turves brought from Elvet Moor, and in his household accounts for April 1666 occurs the item: 'Payd Tho. Miller for two dozen grozier trees [gooseberry bushes] sett in the new walkes under the great Tower in March last, 5s.'. In June 1667 lime was used 'at the orchard, battlement, mount, gallery end, etc.'. What is the 'mount'? It would be surprising if Cosin had not created in his Durham Castle garden a mount and gazebo, so fashionable in the seventeenth century. The remains of a projection in the centre of the false battlements[31] may indicate the position of such a viewpoint over the river banks.

Cosin's Restoration Work in Durham Cathedral

The Dean was John Sudbury, who created a library building from the ruins of the old refectory on the south side of the cloister, an enterprise much in harmony with Cosin's own interests.

As the Cathedral and its precincts are the responsibility of the Dean and Chapter, it is surprising to find the Bishop involved in its restoration. In April 1666 Cosin's accounts show expenditure for twenty wainscot boards 'for the reading desk in the Abbey Church' and for making it.

To Cosin are ascribed the present choir stalls, although some of the work is nineteenth-century. The high pinnacles of the canopies are in Cosin's style. As in a medieval arrangement the choir stalls were originally returned against the screen, and an organ was added above the choir entrance a few years after Cosin's death.[32] Some of the woodwork since removed is now in Norham church, and some of the stalls are in the chapel on Inner Farne.

The massive litany desk was certainly provided by Cosin and bears his coat of arms: perhaps he grew weary of continually asking about the poor litany desk in use. The high-pinnacled font cover and shell font are also attributed to Cosin. The font cover and choir stalls are said to be the work of James Clement, a Durham woodcarver and architect, who was buried beneath the tower of St Oswald's Church in 1691.

Bishop Cosin's Almhouses and Schools

In 1666 Cosin refounded the almshouses which had been provided originally by Bishop Langley on the same site, on the east side of Palace Green. The long building had central rooms, four on each floor, for four men and four women, who were to be natives of either Durham City or of Brancepeth where Cosin was once Rector. The upper rooms were reached by an outside covered stair which existed at the north end until the early twentieth century. The surviving plan and elevation made for Cosin show a central passage, with access to Palace Green on the west end and to a courtyard between the building and the North Bailey on the east. The main doorway was surmounted by a pediment with a foundation inscription and Cosin's coat of arms. The men and women were expected to process in their gowns to the Cathedral to attend services daily. The rooms at either end on both floors were occupied by schools: one was a petty grammar school; the other taught writing and plainsong.[33] The petty grammar school must not be confused with the Cathedral Grammar School on the north side of Windy Gap and facing the churchyard. This was built before 3 July, 1661 by the Dean and Chapter.

By a charter of endowment dated 14 September 1669, Cosin founded also a smaller almshouse at Bishop Auckland for two men and two women of twenty years standing in the parish of St Andrew Auckland. They were allowed each a new gown or cloak every three years, and expected to attend service daily in St Peter's Chapel, Auckland Castle. The original Beadhouses were built on waste land north-east of the Market Place, east of the Bakehouse and adjacent to the Castle gardens and park. The charity was augmented by Sir Gilbert Gerard (Cosin's son-in-law) and Myles Stapylton. Bishop Edward Maltby (1836-56) had the houses demolished and replaced with more suitable ones on the same site.

Cosin's Rebuilding of Durham Guildhall

Cosin, as the first Bishop after the Restoration, resumed the old powers of the Bishop over the City. Under the Commonwealth, the City, as ecclesiastical property, with its rights and privileges, had been confiscated and sold to the Corporation on 18 April 1651. Owing to his resumption of medieval possessions and powers, Cosin's relationship with the City, therefore, was not good. His attitude to the citizens was benevolent if autocratic, but he refused their request for representation in Parliament.

The Guildhall, built originally in 1356, had been rebuilt by Bishop Tunstal in 1535; but it suffered during the Scottish invasion of 1640 and Cosin rebuilt it in 1665. It was much altered in 1752 and in the succeeding years; but the oak panelling of Cosin's time remains with his coat of arms. The Guildhall contains the coats of arms of the city guilds, painted between 1783 and 1785.

Cosin took an interest in the Durham guilds themselves. For example, he granted a charter to the Litsters and Dyers, which is dated 16 November 1664.[35]

Bishop Cosin's Library

Cosin's later years were occupied with founding his library. The library building stands on Palace Green next to the Bishop's Exchequer. It was completed in 1668 at a cost of two thousand five hundred pounds. The main hall is approximately 52 feet by 30 feet and 26 feet high. It was opened in 1669 as the first 'public library' for clergy, gentry and scholars. The door is surmounted by a broken pediment, with his coat of arms, below which is carved the inscription: *Non minima pars eruditionis est bonos nosse libros* (Not the least part of learning is familiarity with good books). The quotation is probably derived from Scaliger.

Between 1670 and 1671 a small room was added, in a space between the main library and the Exchequer Building, to hold maps. It is known today as Little Cosin. It was to have 'a privy door leading to my lord's garden' (known today as the Fellows' Garden), from which the Bishop's garden stair gives access to the Castle courtyard. This door now leads into a passage connecting Cosin's library with the University library buildings on Palace Green.

Cosin, a keen book collector, spent about three thousand pounds in obtaining books; and whenever a new episcopal lease was drawn up, the lessee was asked to give the cost of a book. Cosin's letters to his secretary, Myles Stapylton, are full of reminders. Most of the works are theological, but there are also substantial collections of legal and historical books. There are no copies of some of these in the British Library. Among other treasures, the library has a first folio Shakespeare; the twelfth-century manuscript of Symeon of Durham; the twelfth-century manuscript of Laurence of Durham; and a fourteenth-century manuscript of *Troilus and Cressida*. Cosin's chaplain, George Davenport, later Rector of Houghton-le-Spring, obtained many books for Cosin, and on his death in 1674, bequeathed some manuscripts to the library.

Cosin remarked that books contract mould about November, as winter approaches, and instructed that they must be rubbed once a month before a fire, a practice continued until the 1940s. The library has a great fireplace on its north wall. Thomas Blakiston, grandson of Sir William Blakiston of Gibside, was entrusted with the compilation of the library catalogue; but his dilatory ways caused the Bishop much annoyance. He married Cosin's daughter Frances, the widow of Charles Gerard, and they had one daughter.

Portrait heads, in sets of three over the bookcases, were planned to refer to their contents. Cosin, writing on 17 December 1668, says:

> Hasten on Van Ersell to the finishing of his workes. Everybody that comes to me from Durham speakes highly of the library-room, but say that his picture painting of faces is very ugly and unworthy of the roome: he hath need therefore to goe over the faces again and mend them, that they may not looke like Saracens as all comers say they doe.

The portrait heads, which appear to be copies from engravings, are named in Latin, and from the porch, left, are: St Gregory, St Augustine, St Jerome; St Paul, St Peter, St John; Isaiah, King David, Samuel; John Gerhard, Geo. Callixtus, P. Melancthon; F. Suarez, R. Bellarmine, Tho. Stapleton; J. Scotus, S. Bonaventure, Thomas Aquinas; and on the opposite side, St Basil, St John Chrysostom, St Athanasius; from the gallery stair right to left, and moved here on its insertion: Hugo Grotius, J. Justus Scaliger, Erasmus; Henry Octavus, Charles I, Constantine; Plutarch, Tacitus, Livy; Epictetus, Aristotle, Plato. One set of three appears to be missing. The small adjacent room (now known as Little Cosin) was intended to have a further twelve heads, but Van Eersell left with the work unfinished.[36] The subjects help to illustrate the scope of Cosin's learning.

The library interior is nearly as Cosin left it.[37] His portrait, by an unknown artist in about 1670, shows him wearing a skull-cap over his own white hair, and robed in a bishop's rochet.

The Bishops' Courts

As Prince-Bishop, Cosin had the wide responsibilities, both ecclesiastical and secular, exercised by his predecessors . The Bishoprick courts were modelled on those of Westminster. The Bishops' Courts of Exchequer and Chancery, with rooms for the Receiver and Auditor, were housed in the Exchequer Building adjacent to the Castle on Palace Green. The Court Buildings were formally handed over to the University in 1837, and gradually became part of the University Library; but they continued to be occupied by Court officials for varying lengths of time as the Palatinate was merged with the Crown.

In 1664 Cosin rebuilt the Assize Courts which stood on Palace Green at the north side of Windy Gap. These were replaced in 1820 by the Diocesan Registry whose building is now used by the University.

Last Days

Cosin found the winter months in Durham too hard for his failing health. He suffered increasingly from 'the stone'. He smoked very heavily, believing that it eased his pain, and items for pipes and tobacco recur in his accounts. For example, on 3 September 1665 he bought pipes at 1s. 9d. for half a gross, with a dozen extra for the price; and two pounds and a half of the best Virginia tobacco, which cost eleven shillings. To fulfil his engagements, he continued to travel in his coach on the better roads; but he was unable to bear the great pain caused by jolting, and took a sedan chair on his journeys to be carried over uneven town streets.

To his absences from Durham we owe much of our information about his building and charitable work, for which he gave detailed instructions especially in his correspondence with Myles Stapylton.

After a distressing illness, he died on 15 January 1671/2 in a rented house in Pall Mall, attended by two King's chaplains who were then at Whitehall. Just before his death he was lifted into a chair to receive Holy Communion; and as his head was bound up because he had great pain, he asked that the bandage should be undone before he received the sacrament. In less than half an hour he was laid again in his bed and so died with a prayer on his lips.

His Funeral

The body was embalmed, wrapped in a cere-cloth, and placed in a lead coffin in order to carry out his wish to be buried in his chapel at Auckland Castle. The journey could not be undertaken until April, because of the weather and bad roads.

The Certificate from the College of Arms gives details of the funeral processions in London and Durham. The corpse was carried from the Pall Mall lodging on Friday 19 April in a hearse drawn by six horses, with banner rolls on each side borne by gentlemen of quality, through the Strand and Chancery Lane, to the end of Gray's Inn Lane, with a procession of seventy poor men in mourning gowns, led by two conductors with black staves. Then came his chaplains. Next was the great banner, borne by Myles Stapylton, Esq. After him came Rougedragon, Pursuivant at Armes. Then followed York Herald bearing the crozier, and Norroy King of Armes carrying the mitre; the chief mourner and his assistants all in their gowns and hoods following in coaches. Whence the body was conveyed the same night to Welling, Hertfordshire, and so by several stations to Northallerton in Yorkshire, and on Saturday 27 April to Durham, the greatest part of the gentry, with the clergy of the County Palatine, meeting it at the Tees, and attending on it to the city, into which a solemn procession was made from Farewell Hall, a mile distant. The Mayor and Aldermen stood 'within the West-gate' in their liveries, and followed the procession to the Castle, where a short stay was made. The journey had taken eight days. A short time before Evening Prayer, a new procession was formed to enter the Cathedral in the following order:

Two conductors with black gowns and staves.

The poor of the Hospitals of Durham and Auckland.

The servants of gentlemen.

The Bishop's own servants.

Gentlemen, esquires, and knights, all in mourning.

Clergy of the Diocese in their canonical habits.

Five of the Bishop's chaplains.

Sir Gilbert Gerard, Sheriff of the County Palatine.

The Bishop of Bristol.

The great banner, crosier and mitre, carried as before.

The corpse carried by eight men in gowns under a large pall of velvet supported by four Prebends of the Cathedral. On each side the banner-rolls were carried as before.

The chief mourner and his assistants in close mourning.

The Mayor and Aldermen of Durham with many of the chief gentry.

The choir of the Cathedral in their surplices falling in next to the chaplains at the entrance to the churchyard.

The conductors, the poor of the two Hospitals, the servants 'dividing themselves', remained at the upper end of the central aisle of the Cathedral, the rest proceeding into the Quire, where the corpse was placed in the middle and left until the Monday following.

Then the corpse was carried to Bishop Auckland (seven miles distant) in the same way as it was brought into Durham, and the poor of the two Hospitals were added to the procession on foot from the Market Cross to St Peter's Chapel in Auckland Castle. There, after Evening Prayer, the burial service was conducted by the Bishop of Bristol. The funeral sermon was preached by Dr Basire, before the interment in the tomb which Cosin had prepared for himself in the centre of the Chapel, under a large black marble slab.

The Certificate continues with a long account of Cosin's parentage, the benefices and dignities he had successively occupied, his benefactions during his life and under his will, his marriage, and the inter-marriages of his children.

Cosin's Last Will and Testament

Cosin's will, dated 11 December 1671, was written on ten pages and to this were added two long codicils, the first dated 12 December, and the second, 13 December. The complicated detail of its provisions demonstrates his sure grasp of business; while the lengthy account of how he spent the temporal income of the See of Durham shows the great care in keeping account of his expenditure, not only from year to year, but on each of his prolonged undertakings. The will is worth careful study also for the light it throws on members of his family and his relationship with them.

He instructs that his burial shall take place in the middle of Auckland Castle Chapel; he provides the text of the inscription to be placed upon the memorial slab, with the date 1671, omitting only the day and month of his death (evidently anticipating it was very near); he instructs that the choirmen and choristers of Durham Cathedral attending his funeral, or as many as can be spared to attend, are to receive twenty marks [a mark = 13s. 4d.]; the Doctor or Bachelor of Divinity who preaches his funeral sermon is to receive five pounds and a mourning gown; if the Dean or any Prebendaries are at his funeral, each is to have a mourning ring inscribed *Memorare novissima*; six pounds is to be distributed equally among the almspeople of the two Hospitals he had founded at Durham and Auckland, viz. ten shillings to each of them attending his funeral in their gowns and 'goeing orderly before the Quire to my sepulchre', and if any are unable to attend because of sickness or infirmity they are to have the same allowance as those who attended; immediately after the burial, twenty pounds is to be distributed among the poor people of the country who shall come to ask alms.

Next, Cosin lists building and charitable work he has already achieved and at what cost. He spent about sixteen thousand pounds on repairing and rebuilding his Castles of Durham and Auckland, and the Bishop's House at Darlington; and he has provided plate, books and ornaments for the chapels in his Castles. He has spent other money on his two hospitals: at Durham for four men and four women, and at Auckland for two men and two women; he has rebuilt two schools on Palace Green at Durham, the first founded by Bishop Langley in Henry V's time for two chaplains or schoolmasters but 'laid waste in the time of the late rebellion'. The two schools built at each end of the Hospital cost almost three hundred pounds. He has given to St Peter's College, Cambridge, of which he was Master, one hundred and twenty pounds for re-edifying of the east end of the chapel. He gave three hundred pounds towards the redemption of the Christian captives at Algiers; and five hundred pounds towards relieving the distressed loyal party in England. The sum of eight hundred pounds was expended towards repairing the [river]banks in Howdenshire belonging to the Bishops of Durham. A great part of his temporal estate was spent in founding, building, furnishing, and endowing a public library next to the Exchequer Building in Durham at a cost of about two thousand five hundred pounds.

He founded eight scholars' places at Cambridge University, i.e. five places at St Peter's College, of ten pounds a year each, and three places at Gonville and Caius College at twenty pounds a year each, to be called the Bishop of Durham's scholars 'for ever', and eight pounds yearly to each College for their common chest, and has expended [invested] for these about two thousand pounds.

He explains that he sets all this down as he received nearly twenty thousand pounds for fines and leases, yet took no part of this money for his own use or that of his children, but laid out the whole sum received and a great deal more upon the aforesaid repairs and the pious uses expressed. All these disbursements will, he hopes, acquit him as to his successors' dilapidations and from any opinion or censure that he has enriched himself from his fines; he cannot leave, therefore, to his children and 'allies' any larger gifts than he has already given them, except the few legacies in his will. There follows a list of how he wishes to dispose of the rest or remaining part of his temporal estate.

The bequests to his family are informative, especially as to the marriages and descendants of his own family and his sisters. He begins with 'Mr John Cosin, my lost sonne, one hundred pounds', followed by a statement about his having twice forsaken the Church of England and not sought his father's advice. There are bequests to Sir Gilbert Gerard, and Samuel Davison, his sons-in-law; to his grandchildren Gilbert Gerard, Samuel Gerard, Charlotte Gerard and Mary Gerard, children of his eldest daughter Mary; to his grand-children Richard Burton and John Davison, and Frances Hutton, for whom it appears he has already made arrangements for a settlement on her marriage or coming of age; to his grandchildren John Gerard and Vere Gerard, children of his deceased daughter Frances by her first husband Charles Gerard (brother to Sir Gilbert Gerard); to Sir Gilbert Gerard's two sons and two daughters by his former wife, the daughter of Lord Breereton (i.e. Gilbert, Charles and Elizabeth).[38]

Next he makes bequests to his Norwich family: to his brother-in-law Mr William Hartley, to be distributed among his children; to his nephew Mr Thomas Skinner, a Hull merchant, to buy a piece of plate for his eldest son; to his nephews [blank] Allen of Norfolk, James Rush, Daniel Rush and Thomas Rush of Norwich; to his niece Elizabeth Blackerby, 'lately married to M^{r}. Fairfax, a Physitian in Suffolke', and to Sir Alexander Fraiser and his daughter Elizabeth. Obviously he has kept in touch with the families of his siblings.

He goes on to remember his domestic servants, the first of whom is Mr Myles Stapylton (to whom we owe so much for preserving Cosin's correspondence) and Mr Richard Foorder, if they are in his service at the time of his death on condition of their rendering a true account to his executors; to Mr Richard Laville 'the Groome of my Bedchamber'; and to all his servants an extra half year's wages above the quarterly wages due to them.

The next section expresses his gratitude to those who helped him at the beginning of his career. He asks that the children of Mr John Hayward, late Prebendary of Lichfield and Rector of Coton, near Cambridge, shall be sought out and each given twenty pounds within two years of his death in gratitude to their late father, who 'first placed me with his uncle Bishopp Overall, a prelate of ever honored worth and memory'. Cosin's leases, rents and money owing to him are to provide the necessary monies for his legacies.

He has had an inventory made of all his goods and chattels, dated 9 May 1669, and these are to be sold and the proceeds used by his executors, with the advice and assistance of Sir Gilbert Gerard and his wife, Cosin's daughter Mary, and her sister Lady Burton to pay the funeral expenses, debts, gifts and legacies, the remainder to be divided between his daughter Lady Mary Gerard and Lady Elizabeth Burton.

His daughter Mrs Anne Grenville [*sic*] has had already the capital sum of one thousand pounds as a [marriage] portion and the interest on it, and a lease of property in Howdenshire for herself and her husband, Dr Denys Grenville [*sic*], both settled in the hands of Trustees; but she is now to have interest in a share of the proceeds of the sale of Cosin's goods and chattels. If she survives her husband she is to have more (the conditions are detailed), and if she dies childless the money is to be released equally to the three children of his recently deceased daughter Frances, John and Vere Gerard and Francis Blakiston.

He sets out with great complexity the provisions if these three shall die childless.

Having settled his family affairs he records that he has already given about a thousand books to the library of St Peter's College, Cambridge; and the rest according to a catalogue he has had made, and signed, he has given to his public library in Durham (all his books having cost him nearly three thousand pounds, and care for them over fifty-five years). By deed he has augmented the hitherto poor stipend of the curate of St Andrew, Auckland, from the income from lands forfeited to the King which have been granted to him in his private capacity.

The plate, books, organs and other furniture belonging to his chapels at Durham and Auckland he has given by deed to be kept in those places for the use of his successors. There is a long section securing to the Bishops of Durham the College at St Andrew Auckland 'as a subservient house for diverse offices' to include the use by the families of his successors when they are resident at Auckland.

Lastly he names his executors: Sir Thomas Orby, of the parish of St Paul, Covent Garden, Middlesex, Dr John Durell, Prebendary of Windsor and Durham, George Davenport, Rector of Houghton-le-Spring and Cosin's domestic chaplain, and Myles Stapylton 'my Secretary and Auditor'.

Two codicils were added to the will, each of two sheets of paper, the first dated the following day, 12 December, 1671. He increases his bequest to his 'lost sonne, Mr John Cosin'; and leaves forty pounds to be laid out by Lady Mary Gerard and his executors for a memorial to his late wife Frances Cosin in Peterborough Cathedral; the words to be inscribed are:

MEMORIÆ PRÆSTANTISSIMÆ FEMINÆ FRANCISCÆ COSIN, GENEROSÆ, ET PIENTISSIMÆ CONJUGIS DOMINI JOHANNIS COSIN, S. THEOLOGIÆ

PROFESSORIS, ET OLIM DECANI HUJUS ECCLESIÆ CATHEDRALIS, POSTEA EPISCOPI DUNELMENSIS, QUÆ OBIIT VICESSIMO QUINTO DIE MENSIS MARTIJ, IN FESTO ANNUNCIATIONIS B. MARIÆ VIRGINIS, 1642, ET HIC SUB STRATO MARMORE SEPULTA JACET.

This may be translated:

To the memory of a most excellent lady Frances Cosin gentlewoman and most pious wife of Master John Cosin, Professor of Sacred Theology and once dean of this Cathedral Church afterwards Bishop of Durham who died the 25 day of the month of March on the feast of the Annunciation of the Blessed Virgin Mary 1642 and here lies buried beneath a marble [slab].

Cosin gave also one hundred pounds for a fund to distribute to the poor of Peterborough on the first Sunday of every month in memory of his wife. (Unfortunately the Dean and Chapter of Peterborough failed to carry out the provisions of the will, using the capital to repair the church and making other provision for the poor.)

He goes on to leave one hundred pounds to his grandchild Elizabeth Davison; one hundred marks to his grand-daughter Frances Blakiston, daughter of Thomas Blakiston, by his lately deceased third daughter Frances; forty pounds to William Flower, one of his domestic chaplains if he does not have a better preferment at the time of his [Cosin's] death, but if he has, then he is to have ten pounds to buy a piece of plate; ten pounds or a piece of plate of that value to Mrs Rebecca Lewis who has attended to him during his illness for two years, if she remains in his service until his death; to Sir Paul Neile, son of Richard Neile, Archbishop of York, a mourning ring, with a diamond in it, worth twenty pounds, and to his wife Elizabeth [daughter of Dr Gabriel Clarke, a Durham Prebend] a piece of plate of the same value; and mourning apparel to his four executors and to William Flower, Richard Foorder, Stephen Laville and to other servants whom his daughter Lady Mary thinks should attend his funeral; and mourning rings worth twenty shillings each to be given to twelve Bishops and twelve clergymen and to such of his and her mother's kindred as she shall think fit and who have no other legacies under the will.

The second codicil is dated a day later, 13 December, and provides that if any of his four executors dies before him, Lady Mary Gerard may replace him by any other person she pleases. Lady Mary and her husband Sir William Gerard are to have the oversight of the will and to have twenty pounds each for their trouble.

His brother Nathaniel's widow, of Norwich, is to have forty pounds and her daughter Anne, lately married to Mr William Blacket of Norwich, fifty pounds, or if she dies, to any child of hers, or if there are no children, then ten pounds only to her husband. The children of his sister, Mrs Ward, lately deceased, which she had by Mr Ward, lately Town Clerk of Yarmouth, are to have a piece of plate worth ten pounds given to each of them. If his three nephews, children of his sister Mrs Rush, shall die before receiving the legacies left in his will, then the legacies shall be given to their children, divided equally, and if any of the nephews have no children then their wives are to have each a piece of plate worth ten pounds. The two daughters of his sister Rush are to have ten pounds each over and above the legacies left to their three brothers. To his kinsman Nathaniel Scottow, merchant of London, he leaves twenty pounds or a piece of plate of that value. To his niece, the wife of Mr Robert Barnham of Norwich, a piece of plate of the value of ten pounds. To his grandchild Richard Burton one hundred pounds towards his better education, in addition to the one hundred pounds already left in his will.

All the books in his private library, of which there is a catalogue, are to be given to his grandchild Mr Gilbert Gerard, for the use of himself and his heirs and are to remain at Brafferton House.

To his good friend Mrs Esther Hodges he leaves a piece of plate worth ten pounds.

Then he increases the legacies to Mrs Lewis, and to Mr William Flower, if he completes the alphabetical and classical catalogues of his Durham public library to be transcribed by Thomas Blakiston if he has no better preferment at the time of his [Cosin's] death.

Lastly one hundred pounds is to be distributed among the poor of Durham, Brancepeth and Bishop Auckland by his daughters Lady Mary Gerard, and Lady Elizabeth Burton to whom and in what proportion they please.

Cosin's will shows that he had kept in touch with his family, about whom much can be worked out from its terms. Nathaniel became a weaver, and married Ann Robinson in 1628 at St Stephen, Norwich. Their children were: Prudens, baptized at St Andrew, Norwich in 1629; Elizabeth, baptized at St Andrew, Norwich in 1631; Nathaniel, baptized at St Michael at Plea in 1633; Mary, baptized at St Michael at Plea in 1636; Mary, baptized at St Michael at Plea in 1639; Nathaniel, baptized at St James, Pockthorpe, Norwich in 1642; Francis (a daughter) baptized at St James, Pockthorpe, Norwich in 1644.

John Cosin's sisters married Norwich tradesmen, merchants and professional men: Elizabeth married William Hartlye, a physician, at St Andrew's in 1616; Lidia married John Rickes at St Andrew's in 1623.

Portraits of Cosin

Cosin was appointed Master of Peterhouse on 8 February, 1634/5, and the well known portrait as Master hangs in the Throne Room of Auckland Castle. In the background is depicted the college courtyard and chapel, completed in 1635.

On his own dark hair is a square cap, and he has a moustache and a small pointed beard. He wears a broad white collar over a fur cape worn over a red gown: either the congregation dress of a Doctor of Divinity or the robes of Vice-chancellor of Cambridge University, an appointment made in 1639. The artist is unknown. This portrait was acquired by Auckland Castle in 1815 and was engraved by E. Scriven before that date.

A later portrait of *c.*1665 and by an unknown artist shows him grey haired and wearing a square cap and broad bands, and with a slight beard and moustache. Inscribed on the right are the words: *Epis. Dunelm. 1634* [*sic*]. This is one of a series of over eighteen portraits in the hall of Peterhouse, Cambridge before 1740, but now dispersed in the College.

A portrait by an unknown artist about 1670, and one of a set of full-length portraits commissioned by Cosin, shows him in old age. It hangs in the library he founded on Palace Green, Durham. He wears a skull cap over his own white hair, broad bands, and a red doctor's chimere over a rochet with tippet. In his left hand he holds a book closed round his forefinger; and in his right hand is a staff. A bookcase is shown to the left; and an inscription at the top right reads:

Ioh Cosinus Episcopus Dunelm
Fundator Huius
Bibliotheca.

A copy of this portrait was formerly in Durham Castle but a reduction cut from it in 1968 is now in Durham Cathedral Treasury.

Less well known is a nineteenth-century window in St John's, Briggate, Leeds depicting Cosin preaching there in 1634 when he was Bishop Neile's chaplain.

Peterhouse has three portraits of Cosin, all copies. One is a copy of the portrait in the Throne Room at Auckland Castle. A second, dated 1665, is described above. The third is a copy of a portrait in Durham.

Peterhouse has also a portrait of an un-named young man with the inscription *Aetatis Suae 20 anno 1615*. The Peterhouse archives record no-one in the College of the right age at that date; but John Cosin's age would fit, although he was at Caius. The likeness, especially about the nose and mouth, is remarkable and the young man has the curly hair and attractive appearance ascribed to the youthful Cosin. If it is indeed his portrait, why is it at Peterhouse and who had it painted? It is possible that Cosin may have taken it there when he became Master, leaving it in the disturbance when he was ejected on 13 March 1643/4. The origin of the portrait is unexplained. It seems unlikely that an ordinary young Cambridge graduate of limited means would be able to afford such a portrait. No personal private resources are known, but his family in Norwich was of the prosperous merchant class to which pointers may be found in the details revealed in his will. Is it possible that his mother paid for it, proud of her son, as a modern parent might have a studio photograph taken?

Postscript

A house known as Bishop Cosin's Hall, on Palace Green, Durham, was occupied as a Hall of residence of Durham University from 1851 to 1864. The University was founded by Act of Parliament in 1832 following joint action by Bishop Van Mildert (the last of the Prince Bishops) and the Dean and Chapter of Durham, which endowed it with substantial estates and formed its first governing body. Archdeacon Thorpe became its first Warden. Durham Castle was appropriated to the use of the University in 1837 and became University College.

St Peter's College, Cambridge, known as Peterhouse, where Cosin was Master, was founded in 1284. It has the three-sided Cosin Court, open to the east and completed in 1970, from designs by the prolific Cambridge architect David Roberts (1911-83). It does not form part of the College proper, but contains a series of flats of varying sizes, most of which are let to scholars and their families visiting Cambridge. This large modern building is tucked away unobtrusively behind the buildings in Trumpington Street and Fitzwilliam Street.

NOTES

Printed Books

Basire, Isaac (Archdeacon of Northumberland), *The Dead Man's real speech* (London, 1673)

Church of England, Occasional Offices, *The Manner of the Coronation of King Charles the First of England*, edited by Christopher Wordsworth, Henry Bradshaw Society, 2 (London, 1892)

Cosin, John, *The Correspondence of John Cosin, D.D. Lord Bishop of Durham: Together with Other Papers Illustrative of his Life and Times*, edited by George Ornsby, Surtees Society, 52, 55 (Durham, 1869, 1872)

Cosin, John, *A Collection of Private Devotions*, edited by P.G. Stanwood with the assistance of Daniel O'Connor (Oxford, 1967)

Cosin, John, *The Works of the Right Reverend Father In God, John Cosin, Lord Bishop of Durham*, edited by J. Barrow, Library of Anglo-Catholic Theology, 5 vols (Oxford, 1843-55)

Cuming, G.J., editor, *The Durham Book* (1961)

Hoffman, J.G., 'John Cosin, 1595-1672: Bishop of Durham and Champion of the Caroline Church' (unpublished Ph.D. dissertation, University of Wisconsin, 1977)

Osmond, P.H., *A Life of John Cosin* (1913)

Overton, J.H., 'John Cosin (1594-1672)', in *The Dictionary of National Biography*

Smith, Thomas., 'Vita . . . Johannis Cosini', in *Vitae quorundam Eruditissimorum et Illustrium Virorum* (1707)

Stranks, C.J., *John Cosin Restorer of the Bishoprick 1660-1672* (the text of a lecture given to the Cosin Club, St Chad's College, Durham, 26 June 1978)

Surtees, Robert, *The History and Antiquities of the County Palatine of Durham*, 4 vols (London, 1816-40), I, IV

Manuscripts

Durham University Library, Bishop Cosin's Library, Mickleton MSS.

Durham University Library, Church Commission Durham Bishopric Papers.

Footnotes

1. Letter in Peterhouse Library, Cambridge.
2. John Cosin, *The Correspondence* . . . edited by George Ornsby, Surtees Society, 52 (1869), I.
3. *Francis Blomefield, An essay towards a topographical history of the County of Norfolk* . . . [second edition] IV, 305, 313.
4. P.H. Reaney, *A Dictionary of English Surnames*, edited with corrections and additions by R.M. Wilson, third edition (1991), 375.
5. Information from Norwich Grammar School.
6. *Biographical History of Gonville and Caius College, 1349-1897* (C.U.P., 1897), I, 207.
7. His younger brother Edmund was a friend of George Herbert. According to Isaac Walton's Biography of Herbert, shortly before he died in 1633, he gave a 'little book' to Edmund Duncon, who visited him on his death bed, asking him to give it to 'my dear brother' to be published or destroyed as he pleased.

The 'dear brother' was Nicholas Ferrar of Little Gidding; and Walton says that the 'little book' contained the famous work *The Temple; or, Sacred Poems and Private Ejaculations* which was first published in 1652. Barnabas Oley wrote a new preface to the second edition, published in 1671, in which he says that Edmund Duncon had the manuscript of Herbert's *The Country Parson* (a prose work) and had it published.

8. Cambridge University Archives, Subscriptions 1613-68, 184.

9. P.H. Osmond, *A Life of John Cosin* (1913), 13-14.

10. Part of this house was rebuilt by Dr Fitzherbert Adams (1695-1711), who laid out something over £2000 on the work; it was added to by Dr Hartwell (1711-25), and altered by Dr Haggitt, *c.* 1809.

11. See also the chapter by Patrick Mussett; and Margot Johnson, *Durham historic and university City*, sixth edition revised and with additions (Durham, 1992), 34-7.

12. See note 2, I, xvi. Ornsby gives the marriage date as 13 August 1626, but the original register entry is clearly 15 August. Osmond has quoted Ornsby's mistake. The entry appears correctly in *The Registers of St Margaret's (Durham) . . . transcribed and edited by H. Roberson (1904).*

13. Isaac Basire was the son of Isaac Basire, LL.D. (Rector of Stanhope, 1646, chaplain to Charles I and Charles II, prebendary of Durham and Archdeacon of Northumberland, 1644-76) and Frances Corbett. There were three sons: Isaac, who married Lady Eliza, was at Westminster School and afterwards at St John's College, Cambridge, as was his younger brother Charles, and the youngest of the three, Peter, was also at St John's College, Cambridge.

14. Anne Cosin married Denis Granville when she was eighteen years old. He was brother to the first Earl of Bath. She became unbalanced, and inclined to take too much wine, causing her husband great embarrassment on social occasions. Perhaps he was tempted to marry her because of her dowry; but later Cosin refused to let him have it, knowing him to be a spendthrift, saying that the money was solely for Anne. Acrimonious letters

passed between Cosin and his son-in-law. Granville could not manage money and was often in debt. Apart from this failing Denis Granville had many excellent qualities, became Rector of Sedgefield (1667-71), prebendary of the first stall at Durham, then of the second, and was appointed Dean of Durham on Sudbury's death in 1684. During his time as Dean, he was arrested for debt at the Cathedral as he was leaving a service. No friend or member of the Chapter would offer bail. He refused to take the oath of allegiance to William and Mary in 1688, remaining loyal to James II. He left for France, but, as a staunch Protestant, he was treated coldly by James and the exiled court at St Germains. James nominated him as Archbishop of York (Thomas Lamplugh had died on 6 May) - a hollow gesture. On 25 March 1689 Granville received a licence from Whitehall to travel abroad for the benefit of his health, but as he refused invitations to return and take the oath, he was deprived of his preferments on 1 February 1690/1. Anne Granville was in great distress, and the Durham Chapter granted her a pension in the following December. Denis Granville died in poverty in Paris in 1703 and was buried in the church of the Holy Innocents.

15. The book included a *Table of Feasts and Fasting-days* (which influenced the revision of the Prayer Book in 1661) and Cosin's rendering of the *Veni Creator*, which was included also in the Prayer Book. Five editions were published before Cosin's death.

16. The twenty eight angels which surmounted the medieval choir stalls were gilded.

17. P.H. Osmond, *A Life of John Cosin* (London, Mowbray, 1913), 60, and following pages give a useful summary of the whole affair.

18. Later, when the Puritans had the greater influence, the tables were turned against Cosin, and Smart was released from prison. He died at Baxterwood, just outside Durham, in 1652.

18a. Durham Dean and Chapter Library, MS Hunter 132^{4}; Dean Richard Hunt's Register, part 2, 223.

19. Their history hardly bears out the rumour. The magnificent Jacobean fireplace was formerly in a building now part of

Hatfield College. When it was sold to the University, its former owner, Walter Scruton, Deputy Clerk of the Peace, presented the fireplace to the Corporation, after removing the two portraits. When he died, they passed to his brother-in-law, and after his death they were sold in 1865. At the time it was thought they were by Van Dyck.

20. St John's Briggate, Leeds, is now in the care of the Redundant Churches Fund.

20a. See note 17, 98-102 and references.

21. Dennis Granville, *The Letters* . . . edited by George Ornsby, 2 parts, Surtees Society, 47, II (1865), viii.

22. It was named after the Earl of Savoy and Richmond, who first built here in 1245; but soon it passed into the hands of the Earls of Lancaster. The French King John was imprisoned here after the battle of Poitiers in 1357. In 1381, when it was held by John of Gaunt, Duke of Lancaster, as his London stronghold, it was sacked by the mob during Wat Tyler's rebellion. It remained ruinous until Henry VII restored it in 1507 as a Hospital which continued in existence until the seventeenth century. A print by Wenceslaus Hollar (1607-77) shows it as strongly fortified, and built around two courtyards on the banks of the Thames. Gradually the complex of buildings was demolished, and the name is preserved today in an hotel. The chapel became the parish church of St Mary le Savoy.

23. Robert Surtees, *A History of the County Palatine of Durham* (1818), I, cix, seems mistaken in believing that Bek built the Manor House.

24. W. Hutchinson, *The history and antiquities of the County Palatine of Durham* . . . III (1794), 188.

24a. John Leland, *The Itinerary* [edited] by Thomas Hearne, third edition, III (1768), 72.

25. W.H.D. Longstaffe, *The history and antiquities of the parish of Darlington* (Darlington, 1854), 188-9. In 1834 the building was said to retain 'many traces of antiquity in its low arches, thick walls and long passages'. It was a long building, with windows of all periods from medieval times to the 18th century. An

engraving of the Manor House in the time of George Allan, the antiquary, shows that it originally had a first floor hall, with three round-headed window apertures, in the style of those of Hugh of le Puiset's work in Durham Castle. The drip mouldings of two are visible. Three lancet windows on the street front at the end of the hall indicate the former domestic chapel, which was a chantry dedicated to St James. An adjacent square stone turret may have contained the outer covered stair to the solar end of the hall and presumably to the chapel. In 1548, the Commission (2 Edward VI, 1548) which surveyed chantries recorded Thomas Emerton as its chantry priest. He held also the chantry of St Mary in the parish church and at times references to the two chantries became confused. It was purchased outright from the See of Durham in 1806 under the Act for the Redemption of the Land Tax and was used as the parish workhouse, when a pedimented centre and two wings were added to the south in 1808.

26. See note 25, 71, 336.

27. See note 25, 148, which has a long account of the hauntings and their supposed cause.

28. Peter Meadows and Edward Waterson, *Lost houses of County Durham* (1993), 63.

29. These books and the altar plate are displayed in Durham Cathedral Treasury.

30. The outline of the foundations can be seen in the grass during a very dry season.

30a. Durham University Library, CC Durham Bishopric Clerk of Works account, 190072, f23-24^{V}, 1543-44.

31. On the west side of the Fellows' garden; the medieval wall, which lay well within the present one, had collapsed.

32. The organ case, screen and return stalls were removed in 1842-6 under the influence of Anthony Salvin to provide a vista. The present screen of 1876 was designed by Sir Gilbert Scott.

33. In the nineteenth century both schools had closed; and the University was given these buildings which became lecture

rooms, on condition of building new almshouses which still exist at the top of Owengate.

34. Matthew Richley, *History and Characteristics of Bishop Auckland* (1872), 133-4.

35. A transcript by Dr Christopher Hunter is preserved in Durham Dean and Chapter Library MS Hunter 28[4]. This guild was extinct in 1811.

36. The late David G. Ramage, formerly University Librarian, painted the heads in Little Cosin.

37. David Ramage, 'The Library Buildings on Palace Green, Durham' in *Durham University Journal,* 38, 1 (1945), 94-100. In 1833-4 Bishop Van Mildert built a gallery round the library to house books for the students of the early University. An external turret stair was added on the Palace Green front, but gave no access to the library floor. Corner pillars were added to support the gallery in 1856. The floor was used for undergraduate examinations as shown in a ninteenth-century print. The administration of Cosin's library was entrusted to the University in 1935.

38. The name of the second daughter is omitted.

III

John Cosin: Bishop and Liturgist

Richard J.W. Bevan

Let us begin with a reminder. By the end of his life John Cosin was in an influential position. His path to preferment was due partly to his personal merit and partly to his good fortune in belonging to the right circle. This enabled him early and late in his career to enjoy royal patronage. He endured a long period of exile and straitened circumstances in middle life, and went on to receive well-earned promotion and the King's favour. In his case influential connections and the subject which absorbed his interest combined to lead him from priest to Prince-bishop.

As a liturgical scholar Cosin achieved considerable distinction during his lifetime, and his reputation has remained to this day. It was not his originality but his attention to detail and his diligence which gave him mastery in his chosen field of study. The fact that he was the Bishop of Durham gave him added and weighty authority and status during the years which marked the restoration of the monarchy. His Prayer Books and liturgical notes (in the possession of Bishop Cosin's Library), therefore, are a fascinating part of Anglican heritage and history. Those of us at this Conference can see them for ourselves and may marvel at the intricacy and extent of Cosin's care, attention and thoroughness in carrying out such a wealth of research.

Two thoughts occur immediately. First, at the most critical juncture in his life, the survival of *The Book of Common Prayer* was in doubt. It was certainly, for a number of years, before and right through the duration of the Commonwealth, abolished officially by parliamentary decision. We may say that the fight Cosin put up, and together with him the resistance of countless others, was in no small way responsible for its survival and subsequent rehabilitation by majority consent, when the situation changed. When I say fight, I do not mean physical battle, but simply his courage, determination and unflinching adherence, evident in his exile in Paris, in maintaining the practice of Prayer Book worship and the building up of a strong community, which he led vigorously, and for which he was later commended. To all intents and purposes during those years from 1645-60 the Prayer Book in England was abolished publicly and officially, though used in secret and memorized by the faithful.

Cosin's studies over long years showed the worth of liturgical worship, as he was able to demonstrate in 1662. The period of greatest tension and distress for him and those closest to him was from the fall of Charles I (at least from the end of his absolute rule) until the Restoration - not long as history goes, but very long for those concerned. It must have seemed unbearable and a monstrous deed on the part of the puritan Parliament to forbid and ban the use of the Prayer Book. Largely it was brought about as a result of the Laudian movement, in which Cosin was intimately involved, which to the Puritans was a romanizing, corrupt and dangerously insidious, even treacherous betrayal of evangelical purity and truth, and a plot to overturn the principles of the Reformation. That this was a far-fetched and erroneous interpretation of the intentions of Laud and his followers highlights the misunderstanding of their enemies, and hindsight reveals the *via media* path followed by Laud, Cosin and others. Branded as 'High Church' (and such they were), yet they were true and unswerving Anglicans at heart and to the core of their being. What they practised and professed was mainly to secure decency, discipline, seemliness and orderliness as conducive to reverence.

Secondly, Cosin believed, as was the received notion of the time and of the preceding period, that the Prayer Book was or could be a means of unity by the method of imposing or attempting to impose uniformity. His idea of unity, therefore, was coupled with that of uniformity, and this is the essential reasoning behind the Act of Uniformity of 1559 at the beginning of the reign of Elizabeth I. The Act envisaged 'one uniform Order of Common Service and Prayer, and of the Administration of Sacraments, and other Rites and Ceremonies in the Church of England'. This had been so at the time of Edward VI, and at his death 'repealed and taken away by an Act of Parliament in the first year of the reign of Mary'. Mary was a Roman Catholic. The 1559 Act made it clear that the Prayer Book stood for uniformity, and hopefully for unity:

> Be it therefore enacted that everything therein contained, only concerning the said Book, and the Service, Administration of Sacraments, Rites and Ceremonies contained or appointed in or by the said Book, with the Alterations, and Additions therein added and appointed by this Statute, shall stand and be in full force and effect, according to the tenor and effect of this Statute . .

By this time Elizabeth was on the throne.

Although firmly an Anglican, and opposed, as his writings show, to much in puritanism and romanism, yet Cosin was not bigoted in principle nor in personal relations and endeavours, as his time in Paris reveals, and as his intentions in 1661 at the Savoy Conference exemplify. He had a certain tolerance and hope for the reconciliation of the parties, but he rejected what he felt was not in true catholic order and line of development. So the Prayer Book of 1662 deliberately contained the Elizabethan Act of Uniformity of 1559, itself a reassertion of the Act of Uniformity of Edward VI, but disallowed by Queen Mary, a Roman Catholic. It has been pointed out by more than one scholar that in a nation with different parties and persuasions within it from a religious and political standpoint, yet not a pluralist society in the modern sense, uniformity could in some way achieve unity. It seemed the possible and the obvious way. In the light of history we see the emergence of Free Church or Non-Conformist traditions and the emancipation of the Roman Catholics with their increasing influence. This has sufficiently proved that an imposed uniformity is not possible, and that in any case uniformity is not the same thing as unity. Yet the Act of Uniformity was valuable in enshrining a particular notion of the link between monarchy, the state and the people.

If we think that we have problems now, they certainly had problems then. The Puritans objected to so many things - to bishops, to the notion of church dignitaries, even the simple sign of the cross in baptism, to the ring in marriage. Roman Catholics had basic objections, including that to the liturgy of the Prayer Book itself and to services in the vernacular, i.e. in English. These matters caused dispute, outbursts of revolt, underground murmurings and a groundswell of rebellion and open opposition. We have only to think back to the Smart/Cosin controversy here in Durham, which became nationally prominent, involving the King, the Archbishop, the Bishop and Parliament - and the long-standing struggle which continued up to and after 1662. Cosin devoutly worked for settlement - especially placing his trust in the 1662 Prayer Book to achieve that end.

We may say that for most of the period of his formative years Cosin played a subordinate or ancillary role - very useful and indeed vital. He was regarded with favour or as notorious, however you looked at him. For years, although modestly promoted, he did not fully come into his own. Meanwhile he was struggling with a situation of special intensity beyond his control, and he suffered deprivation and considerable upset in exile. But ahead lay his final years of eminence and recognition. His scholarship, formed in his earlier days, was not to be wasted, but in 1662 was used to the full. Archbishop Laud had been the front-runner for so long, and in 1645 with his execution (he had been sent to the Tower in 1641, and so he endured a long period of imprisonment) Cosin himself was impeached and left for France with his professional career apparently in ruins and seeming disruption. But looking back, seeing that Cosin was never a passive character and never took things lying down (he was an activist, strongly motivated and with strong convictions) - we may apply to him the words: 'They also serve, who only stand and wait'. In France he earned the reputation, so Fuller says, of champion of Anglicanism, and we get the same impression from references in Evelyn's *Diary*. At the Restoration he arrived in England in the company of Charles II and came into his own. His time of waiting, his patient researches, his liturgical expertise, were called into the service of King, country and church. He participated as one of the strongest members of the 1662 Committee in drawing up the new compilation, the 1662 version of *The Book of Common Prayer*.

The very copies of the Prayer Book and the Notes which we know belonged to Bishop Cosin, the liturgical student and scholar, are preserved here in Cosin's Library on Palace Green. They take on, in the light of history, an appropriate importance. They were behind Cosin's role and the part he played in the production of that incomparable part of our heritage - and popularly accepted as such - *The Book of Common Prayer* of 1662. Nor should we ignore the fact that over the preceding one hundred years of our nation's history there had been 'blood, sweat and tears' and much heart and conscience searching on the part of countless famous and unknown persons in what was nothing less than a battle of wills and loyalties, culminating first in the creation of the short-lived Commonwealth and then its replacement by the Restoration.

Let us not forget that there was a strong political bias behind all the happenings between 1640 and 1662. The *via media*, so much part of Anglicanism, was at work in the minds of politicians, to avoid the religious extremes which had brought about polarity, acrimony, grief and persecution after the execution of Charles I. That uniformity was pursued and achieved at least outwardly, but at a cost and under pressure of political unease in the face of religious extremes, may be discerned in the words of the historian of the period, S. R. Gardiner, who wrote in *Oliver Cromwell*:[1]

> It is in the highest degree unlikely that a revolution would ever have taken place merely to restore episcopacy or the Book of Common Prayer. So far as the reaction was not directed against militarism, it was directed against the introduction into the political world of what appeared to be too high a standard of morality, a reaction which struck specially upon Puritanism, but which would have struck with as much force upon any other form of religion which, like that upheld by Laud, called in the power of the State to enforce its claims.

This last sentence is the one which draws our attention to the aspect of politically contrived compromise, lest we suppose that uniformity was an easy and unanimous solution or is the same as, or even conducive to, true unity. Much unhappiness and chagrin may belie outward compliance. On the other hand, there is no doubt that Laud and Cosin believed sincerely that uniformity was in the best interests of all, to preserve catholic integrity and tradition, and that it was the most judicious means of dealing with the problem of differing traditions and allegiances which caused so much heat and burning contention in the minds of worthy people of all ranks. The supposition behind *The Book of Common Prayer* is that it is the Prayer Book of the nation, and indeed this is true of it to an amazing extent.

Addleshaw,[2] points out that there were pressing grounds for the Laudian reforms, with which Cosin was associated. What these grounds were may be seen in the light of a brief historical survey or rather a glimpse of the preceding historical situation. Again we must assert that it should not be assumed that religious uniformity imposed by law was easily sufferable or imaginable, let alone obtainable, even in theory. As it happened, in law it was only just possible. Dom Gregory Dix says:[3]

> The third Act of Uniformity of 1559 (when the Royal Supremacy passed to Queen Elizabeth) was withdrawn for a season after its first introduction, while the government worked upon a dubious House of Commons. It was got through the Commons at a second attempt, and through the Lords by a majority of one, against the vote of every single spiritual peer present. Such was the power of a Tudor government that this faint endorsement was sufficient.

This statement hides what lay beneath the surface. This was the passive and fervently conscientious resistance of numerous dissentients over a considerable period. Gradually, during Elizabeth's long reign and between the time of Elizabeth and Laud, as Dom Gregory says:

> . . . an increasing proportion of countrymen had been passing from acquiescence to acceptance . . . a new generation [which] had never known any other rite than the Prayer Book [was born].

But lest we underestimate or take too low a view of the genuine and commendable aspect (for such it was) of the Puritan objectors, we may pay attention to a strong warning against a purely negative or hostile attitude towards them. Gregory Dix, while not on their side, believed that they possessed 'a strong and lively element, and one to which insufficient justice has generally been done by Anglican historians'. He judged that they stood for less bureaucracy and 'above all a more *religious* organisation and life of the church *qua* church'. They strongly disapproved of the over-interference by the state in the life of the church, making the church almost a state department. He says that:[4]

> In their own ways they were 'high church' movements, and it is the saddest pity that the ancestors of the Anglo-catholics could not possibly have recognised the fact.This was to give the Pritans, who after all sternly opposed Laud and Cosin, their due, although it is not the whole story. Dix himself continues by admitting that:

> Puritans were often exasperating . . . Their objections to the use of the Prayer Book were many of them captious and childishly pedantic . . .

But as we have already seen,[5] one of the adverse elements of uniformity lay in the fact that:

> . . . it [the Church] had legal authority from the Queen [and this continued in subsequent reigns] to compel the puritans to conform to the government's settlement of religion, to which they objected on conscientious grounds.

That the matter of compulsory uniformity by the establishment grew worse is also highlighted by Dix. He continues:

> Nor did its offensively erastian handling of the puritan problem cease in the seventeenth century . . . On the contrary it was intensified by all but one or two of the Laudian divines . . .

The consequence was obvious, if unpalatable to many and a matter of expediency, as Dix comments:

> All this meant - and was intended to mean - that conformity to the official liturgy and not to belief, had to be taken as the Anglican basis.

Those who want further enlightenment as to the actual state of affairs would do well to read the chapter, 'The Reformation and Anglican Liturgy', in *The Shape of the Liturgy*, Dom Gregory Dix's masterly study. It gives a vivid background of the situation in which Cosin grew up and pursued his studies. It also deals with the problem of enforcement of conformity to produce uniformity as the justified means of unity.

The 1662 edition of *The Book of Common Prayer* was the supposed answer to both Laudian and Puritan extremes. I have come across no better summing up of the context of the 1662 Prayer Book revision than that presented by Dom Gregory Dix in the chapter to which I have referred above. It is succinct, accurate, and above all gives a true perspective. With regard to the sweep or survey of the previous century which he had made, Dix goes on to say:

> The situation was certainly different in 1662, in that there were now really three, not two factors in the situation: the church, represented by the Convocations; the newly restored royal executive; and the Parliament which was no longer a royal instrument, but the most powerful factor of the three.

This last remark is indicative of the new powers seized by the political arm of the country during the reign of Charles I, and strengthened during Cromwell's Protectorate. By it the royal power was restricted, and the power of Parliament increased. Gregory Dix states that Parliament, the most powerful of the three factors, that is the Members of Parliament, in the main looked to and insisted upon the 1604 Prayer Book (a revision produced in the time of James I) as providing an adequate and acceptable Service Book,

> . . . not wishing to grant concessions to the lately triumphant puritans nor the innovations of the late Archbishop Laud, who had been unpopular with the squirearchy.

Here Dix adds a most important qualification, which needs to be borne constantly in mind, when we consider the revisions leading to the final version of *The Book of Common Prayer* of 1662:[6]

> The truth is that under cover of a formal consultation of the church the essential process of the Edwardian, Marian and Elizabethan settlements was followed once more in that under Charles II, though with a considerable shift in the balance of the secular power imposing it.

This is a reference to the fact that formerly the sovereign's influence had been paramount, but was now overtaken by the power of Parliament. The statutory authority given to the Prayer Book was not by Convocation but by the King in Parliament. Cosin, and the others who were involved in drawing up the Prayer Book of 1662, had to work within strict limits imposed, rather than recommended by Parliament:[7]

> . . . Parliament . . . throughout insisted on making the Restoration settlement of the church so far as possible a return to the *status quo*. The return to the 1604 liturgy was part of a reactionary policy intended to apply to every aspect of life.
>
> . . . the controller of conscience is no longer in anything but name the personal monarch. It is now the totalitarian Parliament, which had exercised so decisive an influence in the retention of Cranmer's liturgy without substantial change.

Any revision, therefore, in spite of a large number of minor emendations and alterations, had to be strictly conservative.

I referred in passing to Addleshaw's book *The High Church Tradition* . . . Addleshaw refers to the breakdown of Anglican parochial life during the years of the Protectorate, resulting in ignorance on the part of large numbers of people as to the meaning of the Prayer Book and with it ignorance of the principles of liturgical worship.[8] For different reasons Presbyterians, Independents, and Roman Catholics objected to the imposition of *The Book of Common Prayer*. Addleshaw points out that throughout the seventeenth century the Church of England had to defend the use of the vernacular liturgy and expound the principles of worship contained in the Prayer Book. At the same time Laud and Cosin, and the others of that school of thought, although upholders of the catholic tradition, adhered to 'the catholic faith as taught in the Church of England and were averse from all papal and sectariam innovations'. They drew their nourishment from the Prayer Book 'with the Church sanctifying every side of national life and giving society a godward purpose and direction'. Their defence of the Prayer Book was on the ground of its unifying role, its faithfulness to the spirit of worship of ancient times and its magnificence of language in the mother tongue. Addleshaw in his other major book, *The Architectural Setting of Anglican Worship*,[9] points out that corporate worship is clearly presupposed by *The Book of Common Prayer*, otherwise it would not be called 'Common Prayer'. The central feature of corporate or common prayer and worship resides in the participation of those present, and in order that they may take part, they must be able to follow the liturgy with an understanding of its meaning. Sight and hearing must also be possible. A congregation cannot actively share in the proceeding, unless it is possible to hear and see what is going on.

Cosin believed in and acted on this implicitly. As a matter of principle, as well as of practice governing common worship, he urged audibility and visibility, and he assumed the need for intelligibility. The congregation must be able to hear, see and understand what was going on. In Cosin's *Works* in the first series of Notes (the authorship is not absolutely certain, but is obviously in accord with Cosin's own interests) and in the 1662 Prayer Book revision Cosin was strong in upholding this same principle. We find that early in his episcopate in 1662 Cosin held a Primary Visitation of his diocese and cathedral. His Articles of Visitation show similar interests and concerns. His care for those taking part in the Communion Service - not to be separated from the priest at the altar or Holy Table - is a conspicuous example of his concern.

So he asked: 'Is there a partition [screen] between your church and your chancel . . . ?' We may recall the screens erected in St Mary-le-Bow, Durham, Sedgefield and Brancepeth. A screen was similarly erected in Great St Mary's, Cambridge during Cosin's tenure as Vice-Chancellor of the University. Beyond the screen, ornately carved of dark oak, were the chancel and the altar, to which the people withdrew for the celebration of Communion, so that they and the priest were together to share in the service. Again, '[Is there] a desk whereat to say the Litany in the midst of the Church . . . ?' to be near the people and visible from that vantage point. A local report following the Visitation (in the *Mercurius Publicus*) caught something of the Bishop's determination, 'the zeal of God's house and the

Church of England doth even (too truly) consume the good old man'.

Laud, during his imprisonment in the Tower awaiting a thoroughly injudicious and vindictive trial (as far as I can judge) wrote: 'I shall for my part never deny but that the Liturgy of the Church of England may be made better, but I am sure withal it may easily be made worse'. Enshrined in these words is the notion of the legitimacy and hazards of liturgical revision - 'it may easily be made worse'.

This was a principle borne in mind by Cosin, who was conscious both of the merits and limitations of Orders of Service, their compilation and presentation. His judgement of what had to be done in 1662 was afterwards on the whole favourable and expressive of a job well done, or as well done as could be by a committee, albeit a manageable committee of carefully selected men, approved personally by King Charles II. His arrival, together with the restoration of the monarchy, made the whole project possible, acceptable and widely welcomed.

In view of Laud's dictum, it would be hard to say in what respects he and Cosin differed in outlook and method. Laud, of course, was very much senior, more prominent, more prestigious, and in the event, more vulnerable to abuse and calumny, attack, vilification, revenge; but Laud and Cosin, ever since Cosin's early days in the ministry, gave each other great support, especially during the time of supreme influence from the end of the reign of James I up to the beginning of Charles I's decline and downfall beginning in 1640/1. At the time at which Laud was brought to trial, after a tedious imprisonment, no justifiable charge could be found; and even at his trial his defence was so spirited and factual that the guilty verdict, as even Trevor-Roper agrees in his biography, was the concerted one (contrived, as was the guilty verdict on Christ Himself) of a pressure group, which had been boiling up for several years.

Cosin did not escape, but was impeached presently, and was forced into exile in France.

We can learn a great deal about a person from his last Will and Testament. John Cosin was a true son of the Anglican Church. In his last will he had some strong things to say, exhibiting the spirit of the times. For example:[10]

> Whatsoever heresies or schisms heretofore, by what names soever they be called, the ancient Catholic and Universal Church of Christ with an unanimous consent hath rejected and condemned, I do in like manner condemn and reject, together with all the modern fautors of the same heresies - the heresies and schisms, I say, of all these, I also, as most addicted to the symbols, synods and confessions of the Church of England or rather the Catholic Church, do constantly renounce, condemn and reject. Moreover I do profess from my very heart, that I am now, and have ever been from my youth, altogether free and averse from the corruptions and impertinent new-fangled or papistical (so commonly called) superstitions and doctrines, and new superadditions to the ancient and primitive religion and faith of the most commended, so orthodox and Catholic Church, long since introduced, contrary to the Holy Scripture and the rules and customs of the ancient Fathers.

Although Cosin was not the actual author, yet he was a chief collaborator in the 1662 Prayer Book, and we can judge that he was one of the most influential participants in the agreement to its contents, even as he was one of the chief consultants in compiling it. We can detect distinct echoes and tones of Cosin's voice as we read in the Preface:

> And therefore of the sundry alterations proposed unto us, we have rejected all such as were either of dangerous consequence (as secretly striking at some established Doctrine, or laudable Practice of the Church of *England*, or indeed of the whole Catholick Church of Christ) or else of no consequence at all . . . That most of the Alterations were made, either first, for the better direction of them that are to officiate in any part of Divine Service; which is chiefly done in the Calendars and Rubricks: Or

> secondly, for the more proper expressing of some words or phrases of ancient usage in terms more suitable to the language of the present times, and the clearer explanation of some other words and phrases, that were either of doubtful significance, or otherwise liable to misconstruction.

We know that Cosin had a certain measure of charity and ecumenical concern for other traditions. In Paris, for example, he was often found in the company of the Huguenots, and joining in their prayers. So he says:

> For where the foundations are safe, we may allow, and therefore most friendly, quietly and peaceably suffer, in those Churches where we have not authority, a diversity, as of opinion, so of ceremonies, about things which do but adhere to the foundation, and are neither necessary or repugnant to the practice of the universal Church.

Cosin had to face a great deal of hostility during the early and middle periods of his life. Durham Cathedral was one of the places where trouble was stirred up for him. So in his Will, he wrote:

> As for all them who through evil counsel have any way inveighed against, or calumniated me, and even yet do not forbear their invectives, I freely pardon them, and earnestly pray to God, that He also would be pleased to forgive them, and inspire them with a better mind.

In all his endeavours, as a supporter of Laud, as a champion of the high church school, as a liturgist, he had an ecumenical outlook and aim. In his Will this is made clear:

> In the meanwhile, I take it to be my duty, and of all my brethren, especially the Bishops and Ministers of the Church of God, to do our utmost endeavours, according to the measure of grace which is given to each one of us, that at last an end may be put to the differences of religion, or at least that they may be lessened, and that we may follow peace with all men, and holiness.

This is a very brave and noble expression of Cosin, when we consider the strength of opposition which the high church party had to endure from the Puritans in their heyday.

Although of a different stamp, the spirit of Cosin was yet largely the spirit of Laud. One of Mandell Creighton's wisest assessments reflects that spirit in which Cosin undertook his liturgical studies:[11]

> Religious unity was felt by the wisest to be a *political* necessity; no sacrifice was too great to obtain it. The best hope was that the English people would accept the spirit of the changes made under Henry VIII, and forget after a little time the spirit displayed under Edward VI and Mary. If the framework were securely erected things might slowly adjust themselves. Hot blood would cool; opinions would modify one another; the general forms of public worship were such as all men might readily agree to accept; on doubtful points of practice and belief there was a large latitude.

In Creighton's words, at the Reformation:[12]

> they put on one side all the outlying parts of the existing system which were no longer credible . . . and adopted a straightforward system of ecclesiastical organization and worship . . . The services were only simplified, but everything necessary was kept. They wished nothing to be kept in the way of ritual that had no meaning for the people.

I have been looking at the Conference Programme with some care, and I am conscious that there are speakers, who will be dealing with Cosin's life and times, and with his liturgical work. In this preliminary talk, I felt that I would say something about Cosin's *presuppositions*, the basis from which he undertook his meticulous study of the Prayer Book and the 1662 production of which he had the oversight in its printing. He had the mind of an organiser, as is shown in his love of detail. This same interest in detail, which he displayed in his building and restoration projects, the same neat mentality, was exhibited in his careful and almost fussy attention to the printing and publication of *The Book of Common Prayer*, which he saw through the press. He was concerned with the lay-out and look of the Prayer Book. He supervised the proofs and passed them to the printer. His directions, written in his own hand, may be seen on the fly-leaf of his Prayer Book now known as *The Durham Book.* Sancroft, Cosin's former chaplain and a chaplain to the King, was ostensibly the supervisor, and Scatterwood and Dillingham were the proof correctors, but such was the zeal of Cosin, that nothing escaped his penetrating eye:[13]

> Page the whole Booke.
>
> Adde nothing. Leave out nothing. Alter nothing . . .
>
> In all ye Epistles, & Gospels follow ye new translation.
>
> As much as may be, compose soe, yt ye Leafe be not turn'd over in any Collect, Creed, Verse of a psalm, middle of a sentence &c.

These are some of the directions on the fly-leaf. No wonder in a letter from one of Cosin's chaplains, found among Sancroft's correspondence, we read: 'My Lord desires at all times to know particularly what progress you make in the Common Prayer'. The Bishop of Durham was indeed indefatigable in his pursuit of perfection in the production of the new Prayer Book, his pride and joy, to which he had given a life-time of study. Of him it has been said 'he was marked out for a leader in the work of revision'. As we look at Cosin's annotated Prayer Books, we may imagine how he pored over them and used them in committee and consultation, as the 1662 Prayer Book was speedily and efficiently compiled to a deadline, with previous versions at hand, as well as the objections of the Puritans against fixed forms, particularly the high church tradition, which they thought to be idolatrous and pernicious. Cosin's care in the publication of the Prayer Book was in line with his role in the revision of 1662. He was concerned among other things with the careful checking of the rubrics. His aim was that they should be simple, direct, understandable, making for decency and reverence in the ordering of worship. The *Journal of the House of Lords*, XI, May 8th, 1662, reads:[14]

> Whereas it was signified by the House of Commons, at the conference yesterday 'That they found one mistake in the rubric of baptism, which they conceived was a mistake of the writer, 'persons' being put instead of 'children'.
>
> The Lord Bishop of Durham acquainted the House, that himself and the Lord Bishop of Carlisle [Richard Sterne], had authority from the Convocation to mend the said word, averring it was only a mistake of the scribe. And accordingly they came to the Clerk's Table, and amended the same.

The principle on which Cosin and the others worked was to express in the rubrics the essential directions, leaving others unsaid, thus allowing a certain amount of flexibility according to the tradition and practice of the individual in unessential matters. 'The book does not every where enjoin and prescribe every little order, what should be said or done, but takes it for granted that people are acquainted with such common [practices], and things always used already'. This was a sensible ruling, since uniformity did not mean absolute rigidity. Already Cranmer had made it clear in 'Concerning the Service of the Church' in the 1549 Prayer Book, but undoubtedly agreeable to Cosin (in which Cranmer extended the principle of plainness or simplicity to cover the whole liturgy, as well as the rubrics): 'There must be some Rules; therefore certain Rules are here set forth, which as they are few in number, so they are plain and easy to be understood'. With this Cosin concurred, and it was exactly this policy which he had in mind in his own liturgical approach as a leading compiler of the 1662 Prayer Book.

By including the 1611 Authorized or King James version of the Bible for the Epistles and Gospels, with his two Prayer Books of 1619 and 1636, and his three series of *Notes*, Cosin had all the ingredients to form the basis of his expert advice in drawing up the 1662 Prayer Book. His two main liturgical colleagues were Bishop Sanderson of Lincoln and Bishop Wren of Ely. Although it was a long time ago, Cosin still remains a luminary, both liturgical and ecclesiastical, and as such this Conference honours and remembers him. We may recall, as a memorial to him today, his own valiant words in a letter to Sancroft, describing his jubilant reception into the see of Durham:

> the cheerfulness of the country in the reception of their bishop is a good earnest given for better matters which by the grace and blessing of God, may in good time follow here among us all.

Notes

1. S.R.Gardiner, *Oliver Cromwell* (London 1901), 317
2. G.W.O. Addleshaw, *The High Church Tradition: a study in the Liturgical Thought of the Seventeenth Century* (London), 1941
3. Gregory Dix, *The Shape of the liturgy* (1945), 682
4. See note 3, 684
5. See note 3, 685
6. See note 3, 693
7. See note 3, 693-4
8. See note 2, 21
9. G.W.O. Addleshaw and Frederick Etchells, *The Architectural setting of Anglican Worship. An Inquiry into the arrangements for Public Worship in the Church of England from the Reformation to the present day* (1948)
10. John Cosin, *The correspondence . . .*edited by G. Ornsby, Surtees Society, 55 (1872), II, 292-3 (translation from the Latin)
11. Mandell Creighton, *Historical lectures and addresses*, (1904) 167, 151-52
12. See note 11, 151-2
13. G.J. Cuming, editor, *The Durham Book . . .* (1961), 2
14. Journals of the House of Lords . . . vol. XI, p. 450
15. Richard Sterne, later Archbishop of York, consecrated December 2nd, 1660, the same day as Cosin himself

IV

Cosin's Library

J.T.D. Hall

Cosin's Library was founded in 1669 for the benefit of the diocese of Durham by John Cosin, Bishop of Durham (1595-1672). Established during the latter years of Cosin's life after his election as Bishop, the Library which still bears Cosin's name was the crowning achievement of a life-long love of books and libraries.

Cosin was born and brought up at Norwich and it is interesting to note that the first public city library independent of both church and school was established there in 1608, two years before he went up to Caius College, Cambridge. Student days at Cambridge would of course have given Cosin an insight into the value of libraries for scholarship. Further connection with the world of libraries came with his appointment in 1616 as secretary and librarian to John Overall, then Bishop of Lichfield and subsequently of Norwich. Following Overall's death, Cosin returned to Cambridge as Fellow of Caius College, combining this with the post of chaplain to Richard Neile, Bishop of Durham. This in turn led to his nomination in 1624 to the tenth stall in Durham Cathedral Chapter. By 1628 Cosin was resident in Durham and it is perhaps no coincidence that the Dean and Chapter began to take an interest in the reform and restoration of their library from this time. A new donations register was started and gifts to the library are recorded in Cosin's hand. Cosin was in effect the librarian until 1633 when Elias Smith was appointed to the position. But even after this date Cosin was active in the affairs of the Chapter Library. He continued to record donations in the accessions register and was also involved in the checking of the *Magnum Repertorium* of the medieval monastic muniments. In 1635

Cosin was appointed to the mastership of Peterhouse in Cambridge and during his tenure of office the college library was refurbished with new bookcases. The long years of exile in France which followed, when Cosin was chaplain to the Anglican members of the households of Queen Henrietta Maria and Sir Richard Browne, gave an opportunity for acquaintance with the scholarly libraries of Paris, such as the Bibliothèque du Roi, the Bibliothèque Mazarine and the notable private library of Jacques-Auguste de Thou. Cosin's eventual return to Durham as Bishop led to a renewed interest in the Chapter Library as evidenced by various enquiries of Visitations in the 1660s.

The contents of Cosin's Library in Durham also attest to the Bishop's collecting instincts which were cultivated throughout his life. From the evidence of bookbindings it is clear that items in the collection were acquired in Cambridge during the 1620s and 1630s. There are also examples of bindings from an earlier date which were obviously circulating in the Cambridge booktrade subsequently. During the years of exile in France, Cosin's personal library was incorporated into the college library at Peterhouse. Cosin was thus obliged to rebuild his own personal collection in Paris and he received a number of books from friends in England and Holland as well as obtaining very many from France. In 1660, on his return to England, the books at Peterhouse were restored to Cosin. Some were given to the college but the majority of the books which he had acquired before his exile, together with those assembled in France, moved north after his election to the Bishopric.

The closing years of Cosin's life were dominated by his library project. In some ways it is fortunate that Cosin was not much in residence in this period, for the surviving correspondence with his secretary and auditor, Miles Stapylton, gives much detailed information on the creation and development of the Library. Cosin's Library was built on the site of castle stables or outhouses and abuts on to the fifteenth-century Exchequer and Chancery Court building. The main hall was erected by John Langstaffe, a builder and stonemason from Bishop Auckland, with joiners and glaziers employed on other works at Durham and Auckland. A small room, known as Little Cosin, was added in the space between the Exchequer building and the main hall of the Library in 1670 and 1671. The original low-pitched roof was hidden by battlements but these were replaced by the present steep roof and high parapets in the nineteenth century. The entrance to the Library was from Palace Green via a small porch.

The novelty of Cosin's Library lies in its internal arrangement. The English tradition was of the stall system of bookcases placed at right angles to the walls, seen in the college libraries of Oxford and Cambridge, as well as in the older part of Durham's Chapter Library in the Monks' Refectory. Cosin's Library on the other hand was the earliest to be entirely furnished with wall shelving, a continental innovation first seen in England in the Arts End of the Bodleian Library. Cosin's Library, like so many before and since, suffered from space problems and the single cases seen today between the double cases were originally intended to provide seating but had to be converted to shelving during the founder's lifetime.

Each double case is surmounted by three portraits intended to represent the authors shelved below: thus Plato, Aristotle and Epictetus denote the section for philosophers, and Livy, Tacitus and Plutarch that for ancient history. There are antecedents for this type of arrangement both in this country and abroad, such as the library for the manuscripts of Sir Robert Cotton, the presses of which were surmounted by the Roman emperors, together with Cleopatra and Faustina. The portraits in Cosin's Library were the work of Jan Baptist van Eerssell, a painter from the Low Countries who had worked previously at Durham and Auckland. Cosin, however, was dissatisfied with Van Eerssell's work, writing that:

> Everybody that comes to me from Durham speakes highly of the library-room, but say that his picture-painting of faces is very ugly and unworthy of the roome: he hath need therefore to goe over the faces again and mend them, that they may not looke like Saracens as all comers say they doe.

It seems likely that Van Eerssell failed to go over the portraits, just as he failed to paint a shield to be placed inside the Library beneath a portrait over the entrance.

In an account of 1668 Cosin recorded the expenses he had incurred in establishing the Library. The building alone had cost some five hundred pounds and the books contained within it were valued at two thousand pounds. Provision was made for an annual stipend of twenty pounds for the Library Keeper. Cosin's abiding interest in the development and running of the Library is seen in his correspondence with Miles Stapylton. He worried about the roof being weathertight and whether the gutters had been cleaned out properly; he continued to take every opportunity to develop the collection and extracted donations by granting favourable leases to tenants; he was concerned that all the books in the collection be stamped and scolded Stapylton for omitting two books in this process; and ordered that fires be lit in order to prevent the outbreak of mildew:

> I shall also put you in mind that it now beginnes to be winter time, and that the bookes if they bee not all rub'd over before a fire once a fortnight or month at least, they will contract moulding and be in danger to be spoiled: for the better care whereof I have augmented your stipend out of the late bought lands at Dunsforth.

Cosin's Library comprises some 5,500 books and naturally is rich in theology and liturgy, but also has notable holdings of English literature, law, philosophy, history, geography, medicine and science. There is an important collection of French imprints acquired during the years of exile, some of which are of exceptional rarity. The treasures of the Library, of which there are many, include the twelfth-century manuscript of Symeon's *History of the Church of Durham*, a thirteenth-century French Benedictional from the library of Archbishop Cranmer, the first edition of Sir Thomas More's *Utopia* (Louvain, 1516), the celebrated second edition of Vesalius' *Anatomy* (Basel, 1555), the first folio of the *Works of William Shakespeare* (1623) and the 1619 *Book of Common Prayer* with Cosin's precious marginal notes for the revision of 1662.

Cosin's Library was vested in the University of Durham in 1937. It remains in its original building and is substantially as Cosin must have left it in the seventeenth century. The Library is a fitting memorial to the founder and as a library 'for the city and county' embodies the spirit of the motto carved in stone above the entrance: *Non minima pars eruditionis est bonos nosse libros* - Not the least part of learning is familiarity with good books.

Further Reading

On Cosin's Library, see in particular:

The Correspondence of John Cosin, D.D. Lord Bishop of Durham: Together with Other Papers Illustrative of his Life and Times, edited by G. Ornsby, Surtees Society, 52, 55 (Durham, 1869, 1872)

Doyle, A.I. 'John Cosin (1595-1672) as a Library Maker', in *The Book Collector*, 40 (1991), 335-57

Hoffmann, J.G. , 'John Cosin, 1595-1672: Bishop of Durham and Champion of the Caroline Church' (Ph.D. dissertation, University of Wisconsin, 1977)

Northumbrian Documents of the seventeenth and eighteenth centuries, comprising the register of the Estates of Roman Catholics in Northumberland and the correspondence of Miles Stapylton, edited by J.C. Hodgson, Surtees Society, 131 (Durham, 1918)

Whiting, C.E., 'Cosin's Library', *Transactions of the Architectural and Archaeological Society of Durham and Northumberland*, 9 (1939), 18-32

V

John Cosin: The Royal Connection

Richard J.W. Bevan

At the time of Cosin there were considerable problems affecting the monarchy. That a storm was brewing, as we look back, is no surprise. I should like to begin with a quotation from Hutton's *History of the English Church*. It highlights or pinpoints the crucial period in the influence of what I call the royal connection in relation to Cosin's career. Its importance will be seen as we go on in this talk. During the whole of this period the need for toleration and uniformity were the most important considerations. Early in 1629 there was a showdown between Charles I and Parliament. A resolution passed in January 1629 revealed the majority of those in Parliament to be swayed by Calvinist interpretation of the Anglican Articles of Religion. If they were not directly Calvinistic, they were certainly not in sympathy with the High Church party and expressed their opposition: 'We the Commons do reject the sense of the Jesuits and Arminians'. Hutton remarks: 'Arminians had become simply a cant name for refusal to[1]

> accept the whole Calvinistic theology. This famous and revolutionary resolution was followed by attacks on Cosin and Neile, Bishop of Durham. After scenes of wildest excitement Charles dissolved Parliament. It was thus that Charles and Laud stood before the country when the eleven years of personal government began (between 1629 and 1640 Charles ruled without Parliament). It was during these years that Laud was able to work practically unfettered. Church and state went hand in hand. It was enough for him to accept the royal supremacy in the church as it was established by existing law and custom, and, through his own close association with the king, to use it for the great ends which he hoped to accomplish by its means. Thus church and state fell together'.

All the ingredients of Cosin's royal connection are enshrined in these words, waiting to come to fruition in the fullness of time, but the royal connection had already begun for him. When we realize that Cosin had the support and favour of Laud, and through him of the King, the significance of this passage in Hutton will strike us. The connection, small at first, grew in later stages.

John Cosin was all his life what we would call a High Churchman. A perceptive assessment of the context within which he lived is made by one of his biographers, who wrote: [2]

> the union between Episcopacy and the theory of the Divine right of the . . . Crown led to the temporary ruin of both Episcopacy and the Crown . . .Anglicanism fell with a theory of monarchy . . . [this was a reference to Charles I and Laud].
>
> But the Puritan triumph was short-lived; and, with the inevitable reaction, the Anglican party rose to an assured ascendancy. . . [This was with the restoration of the monarchy in 1661.] With this Anglican party, from the very beginning of his career, Cosin ranged himself, sharing its faults and virtues; with this party he basked for a time in the sunshine of royal favour; with this party he suffered persecution and ruin at home, and exile and poverty abroad; and with this party he rose again to power and leading influence'.

This neatly sums up Cosin's career, and now it needs filling in.

The sovereign had played a dominant part in the affairs of the Church of England since Henry VIII. We see it in the reigns of Edward VI and his Protectors, Elizabeth I, James I, Charles I and Charles II. The position of the sovereign was made clear in the Act of Supremacy of Elizabeth's reign, reiterating the position created by her father, Henry VIII. It was no fiction, but it enshrined in those times the deeper meaning of the Crown. It has long since been toned down. The qualification of sovereignty was that the sovereign was not above the law, but was coincident with the law, and must be seen to be the personification of the law. As we know, the most terrible indictment of the abuse of this equation was the condemnation of Charles I by his judges who pronounced him guilty of death, and the 1649 Act abolishing the office of king. The sentence of the High Court of Justice, January 27th, 1649, stated[3.]

> that he, the said Charles Stuart, being admitted King of England, and therein trusted with a limited power to govern by, and according to the law of the land, and not otherwise; and by his trust, oath and office, being obliged to use the power committed to him for the good and benefit of the people, and for the preservation of their rights and liberties; yet, nevertheless, out of a wicked design to erect and uphold in himself an unlimited and tyrannical power to rule according to his will, and to overthrow the rights and liberties of the people, and to take away and make void the foundations thereof, and of all redress and remedy of misgovernment, which by the fundamental constitutions of this kingdom were reserved on the people's behalf in the right and power of frequent and successive Parliaments, or national meetings in Council etc.

In these bitter words we see the culmination of the clash between King and Parliament, which was really a power struggle. Parliament had for years demanded its constitutional rights and privileges and the King acted as though he were absolute, believing in the Divine right of kings. The climax, as a result of the Civil War, was the tragedy, after his utter defeat, of Charles's refusal to acknowledge the authority of the High Court of Justice and his consequent condemnation. His death, although demanded from the start by a pressure group, was by no means a foregone conclusion until his obstinacy proved too much even for those who saw it only as a last resort. The unpopularity and failure of the Commonwealth and the demand for the restoration of the monarchy after so short a time may well be the judgement of history upon the whole sorry, even shameful turn of events in 1649.

The dreadful fate which ended the lives of the Archbishop of Canterbury, Laud and the King, Charles I, although Cosin suffered nothing so drastic or even approaching it, highlights the religious and political agitation and interconnection at the time, and Cosin, an active, scholarly, even notorious, though not at the time a front-rank figure, was involved in some of the more controversial and acrimonious episodes which mark the reign of Charles I. By the beginning of the reign of Charles II he was one of the most highly respected figures among the ecclesiastics.

We have now made it clear that Cosin was a royalist and a High Churchman - both went together - of the school of Laud, of whom for a great deal of his early and middle life he was a close and intimate follower and disciple. It was pre-eminently Laud's leading role in the affairs and fortunes of the King, and Cosin's close link with Laud, which makes the royal connection so important in Cosin's own life and career. Cosin himself was brought by this connection into proximity with the King, as a chosen but not top figure. He was especially recommended to compile the *Book of Devotions* for the Queen's court ladies in 1627, and through his appointment subsequently became a chaplain to the King, although the date of this appointment is not certain. It was probably several years later.

Cosin belonged to the school which accepted that the church, the episcopacy and the monarchy were a unity, bound together in a close and inseparable union. The fortunes of one related to the fortunes of the other - two sides of one whole, church and state. 'No bishop, no King', King James I's adage at the Hampton Court Conference of January 1604, expresses the position at a time when there was also a strong movement away from such an involvement, leading to a Commonwealth for eleven fateful years, which would sever the link between the Establishment and the State, in the 'interests' of both church and state.

Hooker, who wrote in 1594[4] one of the finest works on the nature and position of Anglicanism, and who expressed very much what Laud and Cosin afterwards totally accepted as the comprehensive Anglican teaching on the relation of church and state and the ordering of worship, took for granted the indissolubility of the link between them, the person of the monarch being essentially the focus. Hooker refers to 'this Commonwealth of England'. There was no rupture between citizens of one and members of the other, and the evidence of the unity was in the royal person, 'and in the Royal Person lay also the exemplifying of those laws whereby the wellbeing of Church and State were held in trust and guaranteed - the Laws which were necessary for the right ordering and existence of Church and State unthreatened by anarchy and inordinate individualism'. If the sovereign reflected such lawful existence which guaranteed everyone's rights, privileges and liberty, so the sovereign was 'the rightful and duly hallowed Fount of such lawful existence in his own Person'.

It is late on, right at the close of his volumes entitled *The Laws of Ecclesiastical Polity* that Hooker writes: [5]

> I cannot choose but commend highly their wisdom by whom the foundations of this commonwealth (of England) have been laid; wherein though no manner person or cause be unsubject to the king's power, yet so is the power of the king over all and in all limited, that unto all his proceedings the law itself is a rule. The axioms of our regal government are these: 'Lex facit regem:' the king's grant of any favour made contrary to the law is void; 'Rex nihil potest nisi quod jure potest'. 'The king can do nothing unless [except] that which he can do lawfully'. Our kings therefore, when they take possession of the room they are called unto, have it painted out before their eyes, even by the very solemnities and rites of their inauguration, to what affairs by the said law their supreme power and authority reacheth, Crowned we see they are, and enthronized, and anointed: the crown a sign of military; the throne, of sedentary or judicial; the oil, of religious or sacred power.

In anticipation of the turbulence of Charles's reign and the lack of balance between king and Parliament, Hooker wrote:

> Happier that people whose law is their king in the greatest things, than that whose king is himself their law. Where the king doth guide the state, and the law the king, that commonwealth is like a harp or melodious instrument, the strings whereof are tuned and handled all by one, following as laws the rules and canons of musical science.

Where this balance is not kept, the arbitrary power of the king becomes tyranny. This was almost prophetic in view of what was to come. What Hooker here propounds is an ideal, in practice hard, if not impossible. Nevertheless, the place of supremacy of the sovereign in church and state as the recognized head, binding all together, is consonant with the view held by Laud and his ardent disciple Cosin. It was out of the situation which arose from the reign of Henry VIII, and with Rome demanding obedience and Geneva which denied and deplored the authority of bishops, that the consciousness of Anglican identity of king and sovereign, state and church arose, which was implicit in Hooker, and accepted by Laud and Cosin and others who formed a strong party opposed by the tide of Puritanism in its forms of Presbyterianism and Independancy.

It is of interest that Adams in his book *The Constitutional History of England* refers to the exact principle of monarchy stated in Hooker as being crucial to the popular understanding of the position of the king, or at least the position as seen by Parliament, representative of the people. He writes of the reign of James I, following a chapter entitled 'The Tudor Strong Monarchy':

> It is not at all strange that James became king of England with the determination to go on with the practical absolutism which the Tudors had exercised and indeed with clearer theoretical ideas than they had of monarchy as the natural government intended for mankind and of his own right as the particular monarch divinely selected. Over against the determination of the king was the determination which had slowly been growing in parliament for some years. It would be going too far to say that this was a

> conscious determination that the absolutism of the Tudors should come to an end. It was rather a determination that the king should be held to the law where law existed.

Events shaped themselves in such a way that eventually Parliament asserted itself in the interests of the constitution, and the ensuing conflict brought about the greater dominance of Parliament in the affairs of the nation with the consequent diminution of the power of the monarch. As Adams succinctly says:[6]

> The practical situation was the same as if it had been designed. A square issue was joined between a king determined to go on with a virtual absolutism and a parliament determined that the king should be limited by law.

At his trial in 1644 Laud, the impeached Archbishop, was accused through misconstruction of the evidence, of altering the King's coronation oath, effectively giving the King arbitrary power. Cosin would have taken note of this mistakenness, which placed Laud in an unenviable and unjust position, even in the face of his explanation to set the record straight. It was assumed and asserted that the coronation oath taken by Charles contained a certain significant difference or alteration. The last question to the King was: 'Will you grant to hold and keep the laws and rightful customs which the communalty of this your kingdom have, and will you defend and uphold them to the honour of God as much as in you lieth?' Maitland remarks:[7]

> This form, you will observe, does not assert the right of the people, the community of the realm, to choose its own laws: the king is to hold and keep the laws which the communalty has. Archbishop Laud was accused of having tampered with the oath. His defence seems on this point to be quite sound. He had administered the oath in the terms in which it had come to him, the terms to which James I had sworn, the terms to which Elizabeth had sworn . . . Laud, I believe, successfully showed that he could not be charged with any insidious alterations.

Maitland points out that a more ancient form of oath was so worded that the king undertook to uphold the laws and customs which the community of the realm shall have chosen - '*quas vulgas elegent, les quels la communaute de vostre roiaume aura esleu*'. Is there irony in Maitland's further remark? 'The oaths of Charles II and James II seem to have been just those which Charles I had taken'.

The clue to the attitude Laud and Cosin held regarding the King is to be found in Hooker's words: 'the very solemnities and rites of their inauguration . . . crowned . . . enthronized . . . anointed'. Here we go back to the biblical concept of I Samuel: the anointing of Saul, and again, the anointing of David. So, in one of seven sermons extant of Laud, a sermon on Psalm 122, verses 3-5 Laud said:[8]

> I know there are some that think, that their 'seats' [the bishops'] are too easy . . . yet, and too high too. A 'parity' they would have; no bishop, no governor [no king], but a parochial consistory, and that should be *lay enough* too. They, whoever they be, that would overthrow *sedes ecclesiae*, the 'seats of the ecclesiastical government', will not spare, if ever they get power to have a pluck at the 'throne of David' [the king]. And there is not a man that is for parity, all fellows in the Church, but he is *not for monarchy* in the state.

(This is Laud's way of saying 'No bishop, no king.')

In the previous June (1625), preaching before the King, Laud proclaimed:

> The King's power that is from God: the judges' and the subordinate magistrates' power, that is from the king; both are for the good of the people, that they may lead a peaceable life in all godliness and honesty . . . the King God's High Steward, and they stewards under him.

Laud, in another sermon in 1626, made the strongest possible assertion:

> it is evident that the office and person of the King is sacred; - sacred, and therefore cannot be violated by the hand, tongue, or heart of any man; that is, by deed, word or thought; - but it is God's cause, and He is violated in him. And here Kings may learn, if they will . . . that those men which are sacriligious against God and His Church, are the likeliest men to offer violence to the honour of princes first, and their persons after.

This was prophetic in view of the fate - the sacrilege, as Laud would have it - awaiting both Laud and Charles in the Puritan uprising of the 1640s.

In his sermon Laud stated:

> The King is God's immediate lieutenant upon earth and therefore one and the same action is God's by ordinance and the King's by execution, and the power which resides in the King is not by any assuming of himself nor any gift of the people, but God's power as well in as over him.

Laud, as historians have pointed out, did not invent the doctrine of the Divine Right of Kings. It existed already, and was upheld in order to offset the claim of papal supremacy. As Hutton remarks:[9]

> Its completest expression may be found in words, probably in Laud's own handwriting, written at the culmination of his power in 1640. "The most high and sacred order of kings is of Divine Right, being the ordinance of God Himself, founded in the laws of nature, and clearly established by express texts both of the Old and New Testaments". He denied that there was "absolute power" in the King; and that "he was never yet such a fool as to embrace arbitrary government". . . yet (like others) he was completely favourable to an exalted royal prerogative.

With all this Cosin would agree, and in outlining these points, I am attempting to indicate the importance of the royal connection for Cosin, in its widest and fullest sense of covering that relationship between church and state, church and people, which was ever the conscious and accepted pre-supposition on which Cosin's whole life and work, witness and worship were firmly based. It was an essential part of the coherent picture of the life of church and nation under God, as he would see it.

On 4th July 1627, Roger Maynwaring preached a sermon before the King at Oatlands, in which he said:[10]

> All the significations of a royal pleasure are, and ought to be, to all loyal subjects in the nature and force of a command . . . if any King shall command that which stands not in opposition to the original laws of God, nature, nations and the Gospel (though it be not correspondent in every circumstance to laws national and municipal), no subject may, without hazard to his own damnation in rebelling against God, question or disobey the will and pleasure of His Sovereign.

The sermon caused much heat in Parliament, but its tenor was upheld by the King, who in due course promoted Maynwaring. While it voiced what many felt and accepted, since there was a good proportion of royalists among the populace, there were misgivings and resentment, which later surfaced, when King among and Parliament confronted each other. Wakeman writes:[11]

> Maynwaring, preaching before the King, enforced the duty of obedience as the ordinance of God, and distinctly limited the function of Parliament to that of merely assisting the king in carrying on the government of the nation . . . What wonder was it, that when the Commons met again in 1628 . . . they should indignantly ask themselves if that was the sort of government to which they were required to render a blind and slavish obedience under pain of damnation?

As a consequence, in order to express grievances, Parliament sent to the King a Petition of Right (1628), which contained such complaints as:

> Nevertheless, against the tenor of the said statutes and other the good laws and statutes of your realm, to that end provided, divers of your subjects have of late been imprisoned without any cause showed and when for their deliverence they were brought before your justices, by your Majesty's writs of *Habeas Corpus*, there to

undergo and receive as the Court should order, no cause was certified but that they were detained by your Majesty's special command, signified by the laws of your Privy Council and yet were returned back to several prisons, without being charged with anything to which they might make answer according to law.

The Petition of Right was a lengthy document clearly intimating the need for the King's co-operation with Parliament in dealing with the peoples' rights, but the King's reply was brief and ignored any particular matters. It simply states:

The King willeth that right be done according to the laws and customs of the realm; and that the statutes be put in due execution that his subjects may have no cause to complain of any wrong or oppressions, contrary to their just rights or liberties, to the preservation thereof he holds himself as well obliged as of his prerogative.

Here, while the King is confident of his prerogative, we scent the disquiet, the concern, which before many years flared into open opposition.

For the prime position of the monarch, we may go back to 1559 to the Act of Parliament in the first year of the reign of Queen Elizabeth - The Act of Supremacy,[12] as it is known - an Act restoring to the Crown, after the reign of Mary, a Roman Catholic, the ancient jurisdiction over the state ecclesiastical and spiritual, and abolishing all foreign power repugnant to the same.

That where in the time of the reign of your most dear father of worthy memory, King Henry the eighth, divers good laws and statutes were made and established, as well for the utter extinguishment and putting away of all usurped and foreign powers and authorities out of this your realm and other your Highness' dominions and countries, as also for the restoring and uniting to the imperial crown of this realm the ancient jurisdictions, authorities, superiorities and pre-eminences to the same of right belonging and appertaining . . . That such juris-

> dictions, privileges, superiorities and pre-eminences, spiritual and ecclesiastical, as by any spiritual or ecclesiastical power or authority hath heretofore been or may lawfully be exercised or used for the visitation of the ecclesiastical state and persons . . . be united and annexed to the imperial crown of this realm.

The Oath of Supremacy, required of all archbishops, bishops, and other ecclesiastical officers and ministers, contained the words:

> That the Queen's Highness is the only supreme governor of this realm and of all her Highness's dominions and countries, as well in all spiritual or ecclesiastical things or causes as temporal.

The Oath ended with the words:

> I do promise that henceforth I shall bear faith and true allegiance to the Queen's Highness, her heirs and lawful successors, and to my power shall assist and defend all jurisdictions, pre-eminences, privileges and authorities, granted or belonging to the Queen's Highness, her heirs and successors, or united or annexed to the imperial crown of this realm.

In the same year (1559) in an Act of Recognition the Queen was formally acknowledged as rightfully entitled to the crown and as the highest and most honourable person of the realm. It ended:[13]

> . . . and that your Highness is rightly, lineally and lawfully descended and come of the blood royal of this realm of England, in and to whose princely person, and the heirs . . . after you, without all doubt . . . the imperial and royal estate, place, crown and dignity of this realm, with all honours . . . and pre-eminences to the same now belonging and appertaining are and shall be most fully . . . invested and incorporated . . . as rightfully and lawfully . . . as the same were in the said late King Henry the Eighth or in the late King Edward the Sixth . . . or in the late Queen Mary . . .

This was entirely the position in the reigns of James I and Charles I, and was the position accepted by all good citizens of church and state.

In 1603 in the first year of the reign of James I, Constitutions and Canons Ecclesiastical 'agreed upon with the King's licence, in the Synod of Bishops and Clergy of the Province of Canterbury' were published with the King's authority. The Preface begins with the formula: 'James by the grace of God, King of England, Scotland, France and Ireland, defender of the faith'. Canon I asserts the King's supremacy over the Church of England. It states:

> The duty of loyalty - The Archbishop, Bishops of this Province, all Deans, Archdeacons, Parsons, vicars, and all other Ecclesiastical Persons shall faithfully keep and observe and shall cause to be observed all and singular laws and statutes made for restoring to the crown of this kingdom the ancient jurisdiction over the State Ecclesiastical and abolishing all foreign power repugnant to the same . . . the King's power within his realms of England, Scotland and Ireland and all other his dominions and countries, is the highest power under God: to whom all men, as well inhabitants, as born within the same, do by God's laws owe most loyalty and obedience afore and above all other powers and potentates on earth.

The second Canon condemns 'impugners of the King's Supremacy', and the third Canon states that the Church of England is a true and Apostolical Church and takes a firm stand against 'whosoever shall hereafter affirm, that the Church of England, by law established under the King's Majesty, is not a true and Apostolical Church'. Here again the royal connection is made clear in relation to the established church.

Charles I was equally conscious of his position of supremacy and in 1628, in conjunction with Laud, who had just been promoted Bishop of London, the thirty-nine Articles, which had been authorized in the reign of Elizabeth, were re-issued with an explanatory statement, 'agreed upon in the Convocation holden in London in the year 1562, for avoiding diversities of opinions and for the stabilizing of content touching true religion: Reprinted by His Majesty's commandment, with his Royal Declaration prefixed thereunto'. There follows His Majesty's Declaration, which we know to be not only supported but also largely written by or under the influence of Laud himself.

The Royal Declaration is quite definite about the role and position of the King, and we note that he

> being by God's ordinance, according to our just Title, Defender of the Faith, and Supreme Governor of the Church, within these our Dominions, we hold it most agreeable to this our kingly Office, and our own religious zeal to conserve and maintain the Church committed to our charge, in the unity of true Religion, and in the bond of Peace.

The Declaration continues:

> That we are Supreme Governor of the Church of England: and that if any difference arise about the external policy, concerning the injunctions, Canons, and other Constitutions whatsoever thereto belonging, the Clergy in their Convocation is to order and settle them, having first obtained Leave under our Broad Seal so to do, and we approving their said Ordinances and Constitutions; providing that none be made contrary to the laws and customs of the Land.
>
> That out of our princely care, that the Churchmen may do the work which is proper unto them, the Bishops and Clergy, from time to time in Convocation, upon their humble desire, shall have Licence under our Broad Seal, to deliberate of, and assented unto by us, shall concern the settled continuance of the Doctrine and Discipline of the Church of England now established; from which we will not endure any varying or departing in the least degree. . .

If we examine what happened in the reigns of James I and Charles I, we see that the Roman Catholics were kept in their place, as it were, in spite of secret and not-so-secret machinations, *e.g.* the Gunpowder Plot. The puritans, in spite of overt attempts to gain their way, were also kept within bounds. James and Charles both supported and upheld the

Erastian notion of the church, and Laud gained ascendancy to ensure High Church reformation regarded by the puritans as innovation. With Laud's rise came the opportunity and the occasions for Cosin to come to the fore, but it depended primarily on the royal favour and the royal connection to give private, and indeed public, support to the cause which they both set out to serve and forward conscientiously and whole-heartedly.

In a splendid phrase, Wakeman says of James I that 'in the institution of episcopacy he saw the strongest bulwark of the monarchy'. This is another way of saying, as James did, 'No Bishop, no King'. In other words he meant that the divine right of Kings was reflected in the divine right of episcopacy. Where James and Charles were effectively concerned with the supremacy of the monarchy, bolstered by the church and bishops, the Archbishops, Bancroft and Laud, realized that the supremacy of the church was inextricably linked with the monarchy. Of James I, Wakeman says that the bishops welcomed with adulation a sovereign who looked upon them as the surest support of his throne. This was equally true of Charles I, who soon after his reign began, chose Laud as his chief church link, guide and leading light. This royal connection explains how and why Cosin was 'brought on', as we say, by such an influence through his close personal relationship with Laud.

It was James I who patronized and brought on Laud as a person of influence, and through Laud Cosin also rose; but it was Charles who chiefly personified the royal connection, as far as Cosin was concerned. There was, during this period, what has been called the logic of events. That is to say, Charles on the one hand accepted without question the absolute power of the King as part of the divine right, and in this he was supported by a strong element at court, in the Church and among the populace generally. But it was also the cause of the fatal confrontation between the King and Parliament. This explains everything that happened right through his reign from the time when he held absolute authority to the time when his position was threatened, and on to the time of his downfall and overthrow. Regarding Charles's championing of Laud, and consequently in an ancillary sense of Cosin, the remark of Adams is pertinent when he writes:

> Parliament was interested in two matters: to protect Protestantism against what it believed to be new catholic dangers, and the determination which it expressed in a formal resolution "to discover and reform abuses and grievances of the realm and State".

This is the clue to the hazards which surrounded the actions and attitude of such persons as Cosin, who was one suspected highly of 'furthering these new catholic dangers'. Undoubtedly Cosin received favourable notice from Laud and Charles, who together were the great source of power and influence. Then with their decline of power came Cosin's own deprivation and exile. Subsequently came his return and promotion at the instigation of Charles II on the recall of the monarch and the re-instatement of the monarchy in 1660-1. So the rise and fall and the rising again of Cosin depended on his link with the King, and also on the King's position of power, deposition from power and restored position of power.

Although Charles exercised absolute rule for eleven years from 1629 to 1640, financial exigencies by the end of that time forced him to turn to Parliament, which in turn was enabled to put increasing political pressure on him. Between 1642 and 1646 Propositions were sent by both Houses of Parliament to the King containing various grievances and proposals: 'That your Majesty will be pleased to consent that such a reformation be made of the Church government and liturgy as both Houses of Parliament shall advise . . .' These grew into demands and finally action for the abolition of both episcopacy and the Prayer Book.

Stephens comments:[14]

> Under these circumstances it cannot excite surprise that in 1645 an Ordinance of Parliament (the same which abolished episcopacy) for the taking away of the Book of Common Prayer and for the establishing and putting in execution of the Directory for the Publique worship of God was passed . . . The Lords and Commons in Parliament resolving according to their covenant, to reform religion according to the word of God and the example of the best Reformed Churches . . . do judge it necessary that the Book of Common Prayer be abolished, and the Directory for the Publique Worship of God be established and observed in all Churches within this Kingdom . . .

Force of circumstance did not alter the view and conscience of the King, however much radical changes were totally against his principles, and were offensive to him. Gardiner, referring to the year 1646, remarks that the bishops, in Charles's eye, were not merely 'channels of grace; they were also an effective police for the suppression of anti-monarchical opinions'. He recounts that with a weakened (and non-existent) episcopate and a banished Prayer Book, from then until the King's death the struggle was religious and political - the two were inseparably entwined and interconnected. Those who know Gardiner's volumes on the *History of the Great Civil War*[15] will recall how he traces this struggle to the death. Cosin would have been closely interested in all that went on, although by this time he was in exile in Paris.

The populace in general was never in favour of an out-and-out anti-monarchical lobby. At least there was always a large modicum of genuine sympathy for the King. Those who thought that the King was his own worst enemy and had brought trouble on himself, saw this as the cause of the nation's troubles, but this was no cause for his murder. In Gardiner's words:

> Some, whilst accepting the charge against the King, held that there was no authority in existence which could bring him legally

> to his trial . . . Charles had fallen back on his doctrine of his own indefeasible sovereignity . . .

and Cromwell explained his position in the words:

> If any man whatsoever hath carried on the design of deposing the King, and disinheriting his posterity; or, if any man had yet such a design, he should be the greatest traitor and rebel in the world; but since the Providence of God hath cast this upon us, I cannot but submit to Providence.

Time and space necessitate that I draw towards a conclusion. On January 4th, 1649, the Commons passed a resolution which was fateful in its democratic implication. Its repercussions are to be seen today in our own democratic society. It would have seemed strange and the height of impertinence to Laud and to Cosin.

> That the people are, under God, the original of all just power: that the Commons of England, in Parliament assembled, being chosen and representing the people, have the supreme power in this nation; that whatsoever is enacted or declared for Law by the Commons in Parliament assembled hath the force of Law and all the people of this nation are concluded thereby, although the consent and concurrence of the King or House of Peers be not had thereunto.

King Charles' trial was held before the so-called High Court of Justice. Gardiner's terse summing up of the situation says all we need to know:

> Charles declared that he was King by inheritance, not by election . . . argumentatively, the victory lay with Charles: but it was hard for the Court to acknowledge the weakness of its reasoning.

Let us now imagine the absolutely shattering shock to Cosin caused by the downfall and death of both Laud and King Charles. John Cosin was a liturgical student and scholar who was caught up in events which gave him a prominence he might otherwise never have had. Of him it may be said, as truly as Laud at his trial said of himself (and it was Laud's patronage, which was significant in Cosin's career, if I may use that word of a cleric and divine):

> As for religion I was born and bred up in the Church of England, as it yet stands established by law. I have, by God's blessing, grown up in it to the years which are now upon me and the place of preferment which I yet bear; and in this Church, by the grace and goodness of God, I resolve to die . . . I laboured nothing more than that the external public worship of God, too much slighted in most parts of this kingdom, might be preserved, and that with as much decency and uniformity as might be: being still of the opinion that unity cannot long continue in the Church, were uniformity shut out of the church-door.

I have stressed throughout this talk that the Royal Connection coloured the religious and political scene in Cosin's time to a degree, which in modern times would seem excessive and intrusive. That this was so is a matter of history, and it persists today in a much more nominal and symbolic way.

I should like to end by summarizing the royal connection as it touched Cosin's career, and I can do so by pointing to certain key moments and episodes, since he was subtly influenced indirectly as well as directly from his early ministry onwards.

It was his liturgical interest and study which led to his first being noticed by the King. However, his first two clerical appointments were in themselves fortuitously interconnected with the royal patronage. Cosin was obviously bright, and on leaving Cambridge and after ordination he was offered the work of episcopal librarian by Overall, Bishop of Lichfield. He was virtually the Bishop's secretary and by this means he came into contact with many persons of eminence. Overall had influenced Laud at an earlier time, since he was a leading theologian at the Hampton Court Conference of Puritans and Churchmen, which James I had called to consider Puritan objections to current practices in the church. Overall had written a publication, afterwards known as *The Convocation Book* in support of King James. It upheld the Divine right of

Kings and the antiquity and apostolical authority of bishops. This gave Overall the ear of the King and the sympathy of the young Laud, who was similarly minded regarding monarchy and episcopacy. That Overall inspired Cosin to further his studies, and that these studies were liturgical, and that Overall was *persona grata* with the King had a significance. After his apprenticeship with Overall, Cosin went on to be chaplain to Neile, Bishop of Durham. Neile went on to be the Archbishop of York. When Neile was previously Bishop of Rochester (1608), Laud had been his chaplain. It was Neile who recommended Cosin's own appointment as chaplain to the King, although the date of that appointment is not clear. Laud became interested in Cosin, and so we see the circuitous route involving all these personalities which, when brought together, made up Cosin's royal connection. Neile was Laud's patron. Durham House in London was the headquarters of the so-called Arminians, of whom the leader was Laud. He was to become before many years the invaluable and trusted ally of King Charles I and a great power in the land. Soon after Charles's accession we read:

> Neile, Bishop of Durham, had prevailed upon the King to allow his place as Clerk of the Closet to be occupied temporarily by his friend and protégé, Laud, who had become "as it were, his Majesty's Secretary for all Church concernments".

By now, with his liturgical interests and studies and consequent growing expertise and knowledge, his High Church and anti-Puritan outlook, his close links with Bishops Overall and Neile, an established member of the Laudian circle, the royal connection was a matter of personal relationship as well as of principle and conviction in the mind and life of Cosin.

To Laud and a committee fell the task of arranging the coronation service of Charles, and as Acting Dean of Westminster Laud appointed Cosin as *Magister Ceremoniarum*. Throughout the whole service Cosin directed the ceremonial. Prynne, 'the Puritan historian' stated that 'Popish Master J.C., when the prayers appointed for the Coronation were then read, kneeled behind the Bishops, giving directions to the Quire when to answer'. Cosin's hymn, the translation of the *Veni Creator*, included in his *Book of Devotions*, was printed as an appendix to the copy of the service used by the King himself. Both the King and Laud were anxious that there should be complete correctness of ceremonial, and it was regarded as a compliment to Cosin that Laud recorded in his diary:

> In so great a company and amidst an incredible concourse of people, nothing was lost or broken or dishonoured . . . I heard some of the Nobility saying to the King in their return that they had never seen any solemnity, although much less, performed with so little noise and so great order.

The coronation must have been a highlight of all Cosin's royal connections, and he would remember it all his life as outstanding, as well as a triumph of organisation and ceremonial. Laud was the chief orderer, but Cosin was his lieutenant, who saw that everything was carried out according to plan, and as such the smooth running depended on him, and he must be given the credit.

Shortly after the coronation Cosin was called upon by Laud to act as an assessor in a famous religious dispute or controversy involving Montagu, who had written two books in the reign of James I to contest Puritan claims. He was accused at this time of Arminianism. A consultation was held by order of the King (Charles). Before a body of prelates (including Laud), Cosin spoke in defence of Montagu, partly as a friend of Montagu, partly invited by Laud to assess the writings. One of the charges was: 'Mr Montagu endeavoured to reconcile England to Rome and to alienate the King's affections from his well ordered subjects'. After further consultations regarding the doctrinal questions involved, the Bishops called upon Dr Francis White, assisted by Cosin, who reported in favour of Montagu:

> We do think that Mr Montagu in his book hath not affirmed anything to be the doctrine of the Church of England but that which in our opinion is agreeable thereunto . . . And for the preservation of peace we do concieve [*sic*] that His Majesty do most graciously prohibit all parties any further controversy of these questions.

Since the King was personally concerned, there was a Royal Proclamation to the effect that:

> His Majesty hath thought fit, by advice of his reverend Bishops, to declare and publish his dislike of all those, who, to show the subtlety of their wits, or please their own humours, or vent their own passions, shall adventure any new opinions etc . . . and also to declare that neither in doctrine nor discipline of the Church he will admit the least innovation.

Hutton says here:

> Charles's endeavours to silence contending parties, followed by injudicious promotions, completely failed, and severe aggravation was caused to members of Parliament.

This was the beginning of danger to the King and his circle, but the storm did not break for several years.

We come now to a matter which gave Cosin considerable prominence and added to his reputation as a liturgical scholar. In 1627 he compiled a *Book of Devotions*. This had a direct royal connection. Evelyn's *Diary*[16] gives an account of how Cosin came to be chosen for the task. It was occasioned by the arrival of Queen Henrietta Maria and her French ladies, all of whom were Roman Catholics. The King called Bishop White (of Carlisle)

> and asked whether there might not be found some forms of prayer, that so the court ladies might at least appear as devout as the new come-over French ladies . . . The King commanded him to employ some person of the Clergy to compile such a work, and presently the Bishop naming Dr Cosin, the King enjoined him to charge the Doctor in his Name to set about it immediately. This he did and three months after bringing the book to the King, the

> King commanded the Bishop of London to read it over and make his report. This was so well-liked that the Bishop would needs give it an imprimatur under his own hand.

In 1628-9 the King supported Cosin. The matter was as follows. A sub-committee of the House of Commons drew up a series of Resolutions on Religion, set off by the Montagu case and by Smart's disturbance about events in Durham involving Cosin. In the words of the resolution

> The publishing and defending points of Popery in sermons and books - instance Dr Cosin's Horary (The Hours of Prayer or Devotions) published in 1627. Orthodox Books suppressed; instance in all that have been written against Cosin (for example). That persons who have published and maintained Papistical opinions are countenanced, favoured, preferred.

The comment which I have appended to this information is: 'Disregarded by the King'. Trevor-Roper writes:[17]

> Cosin who had offended the last Parliament by a ritualistic book of devotions was pardoned by the King and promoted.

This happened after a visit to Durham by Charles in 1633. The King was on his progress to Scotland for his belated coronation there. The regulation and ordering of the King's reception and arrangement of the services in the Cathedral fell to Cosin as the expert, and Cosin has left on record in Latin an account of the royal visit. It seems that the King was very gratified by the way he had been treated, and as Visitor he showed his favour towards Cosin by appointing him to the vacant Mastership of Peterhouse, Cambridge, soon afterwards. It was about this time that Cosin, on the advice of Neile, was appointed Chaplain-in-Ordinary to the King, thus cementing the royal connection even further.

In November 1640, Cosin became Dean of Peterborough, held in plurality with his Mastership of Peterhouse, again on the King's appointment. But within months he was in trouble with the politicians. In November 1641, the Long Parliament met, and complaints were lodged against Cosin. His old enemy, Smart, brought charges against him, complaining of Cosin's popish practices, and (strangely) his denial of the royal supremacy. The latter charge was due entirely to a misunderstanding on the part of Smart, and it was fiercely refuted by Cosin. Smart had alleged that at a dinner Cosin had said that the King was not the Supreme Head of the Church, whereas Cosin had said that the exercise of it indeed was under the King, but the power of it only from Christ, and that our kings had never taken any such power upon them. Osmond states that 'Cosin had no difficulty in showing that his views on the Royal Supremacy were perfectly sound'.[18] However, as we might expect, Cosin was deprived of his ecclesiastical preferments. In 1644, he was ejected from his Mastership, accused of sending college plate to the King to support him in kind. Again this was a misrepresentation of the facts. This and his High Church practices, which had outraged the Puritans, now in a position of power, coincided with the fall of Laud and the weakening of the King. Laud wrote in *The History of the Troubles and Tryal . . .*[19]

> . . . and the first charge against me was, 'that I had preferred . . . men popishly affected . . . And . . . they named Dr. Cosin, to be Dean of Peterborough. I named four of his Majesty's chaplains to him, as he had commanded me. And the King pitched upon Dr. Cosens, in regard all the means he then had lay in and about Duresm, and was then in the Scots' hands; so that he had nothing but forty pound a-year by his headship in Peter-House to maintain himself, his wife, and children'.

During his long years of exile in Paris Cosin was, by Order of the King, Chaplain to the Anglicans of the exiled Queen Henrietta's household at the embassy. He was a tower of strength, and held out as the leading Anglican divine. He mourned the death of King Charles I, composing prayers which he said regularly for the departed King during all the subsequent years of his Paris sojourn. Such faithfulness received its due recognition and reward. Fuller, in his *Worthies of England* wrote:[20]

> Since the return of our gracious Soveraign [Charles II] and the reviving of swooning episcopacy, he [Cosin] was deservedly preferred Bishop of Durham.

If I may slightly expand what I have just said for the sake of the record, the period of exile lasted fifteen years. Not only did he keep contact with the Queen, but his loyalty for and love of the King up to and after the King's execution was unfailing. During all the years of the Commonwealth he kept faith with the new King in exile in Holland. He devised a short Office or Form of Prayer which he used in the King's Chapel (as it was called) in Paris on Tuesdays (the day of the week on which the King was beheaded).

At the Restoration he returned to England, and the Mastership of Peterhouse was given back to him as well as the Deanery of Peterborough. There was talk of his being made Dean of Durham, but on December 2, 1660, through the patronage of Charles II, he was consecrated Lord Bishop of Durham.

The royal connection was not over for him. Charles was determined to bring back the Prayer Book as a unifying factor. (Cromwell had abolished it as divisive and introduced the Directory in its place as the means of unity - quite an ironic twist of history.) But first a meeting of the Puritan representatives and the bishops was necessary. In 1661 the Savoy Conference met 'to advise and review *The Book of Common Prayer*'. By the King's choice as well as for his widely regarded liturgical expertise Cosin was a regular and influential attender. Richard Baxter, a leading Puritan, said of Cosin that 'he was more approachable and direct than any of the other bishops'. In the November Convocation (the first since the Restoration) Cosin's proposals were prominent and readily received for the 1662 version of *The Book of Common Prayer*.

Cosin naturally took part in Charles II's coronation. Osmond deduces:[21]

> Cosin's liturgical erudition and his actual experience, gained at the previous coronation, would no doubt be in constant demand during the preparations for the ceremony; whilst throughout the actual sacring, except when receiving and administering the Blessed Sacrament, he was in immediate attendance on the King, supporting him at his right hand.

This is traditionally the place of the Bishop of Durham at coronations to this day.

So in Cosin we see one who, in a time of prolonged religious tension and struggle, found in the royal connection not only a matter of conviction, convenience and principle, but an influence which led to heights and depths of prosperity and adversity, of popularity and unpopularity. But it also enabled him to become a person of importance, and to some extent fame. Anglicanism rose and fell with a theory of monarchy. His biographer remarks:[22]

> With this Anglican party, from the very beginning of his career, Cosin ranged himself, sharing its faults and its virtues; with this party he basked for a time in the sunshine of royal favour ; with this party he suffered persecution and ruin at home, and exile and poverty abroad; and with this party he rose again to power and leading influence.

We can rejoice today in a man of such integrity, and we are indeed celebrating in this Conference 'A Durham Worthy'. I believe that he truly adhered to the royal connection, and that three kings of England had cause to be grateful for his contribution to their cause and for his unswerving support.

Notes

1. W.H. Hutton, 'The English Church from the Accession of Charles I to the death of Anne', in *A History of the English Church* (1903),VI, 76-7.

2. P.H. Osmond, *A Life of John Cosin, Bishop of Durham 1660-1672* (London, 1913), x-xi.

3. Cobbett's *Collection of State Trials* . . . (London, 1809), IV, 1119.

4. Really 1593; see A.W. Pollard, & G.R. Redgrave, *A Short-Title Catalogue of Books printed in England . . . 1457-1640*, second edition (1986).

5. R. Hooker, *Of the Lawes of Ecclesiasticall Politie. Eyght* [really four] *Bookes* [1593], VIII, chapter ii, para. 13.

6. G.B. Adams, *Constitutional History of England* (1935), 265-308.

7. F.W. Maitland, *The Constitutional History of England* (1908, reprinted 1948), 286-7.

8. W. Laud, *The Works,* I, Sermons (Oxford, 1847), 82-83, Sermon preached at the opening of Parliament, February 1625/6.

9. See note 1, 26.

10. R. Maynwaring, *Religion and Allegiance* . . . (1627), 17,19.

11. H.O. Wakeman, *The Church and the Puritans, 1570-1660,* fifth edition (1897), 116.

12. *Select Statutes and other Constitutional Documents Illustrative of the Reigns of Elizabeth and James I,* edited by G.W. Prothero, fourth edition (Oxford,1913), 1-13.

13. See note 12, 21.

14. *The Book of Common Prayer*, with notes legal and historical, by A.J. Stephens, 3 vols (Ecclesiastical History Society, 1849).

15. S.R. Gardiner, *History of the Great Civil War 1642-1649,* new edition, 4 vols (1893).

16. *The Diary of John Evelyn,* edited by W. Bray, 2 vols (London, 1907).

17. H.R. Trevor-Roper, *Archbishop Laud, 1573-1645* (Oxford, 1940, reprinted 1962), 91.

18. See note 2, 64-5.
19. 'The History of the Troubles and Trial . . . of William Laud' [edited by James Bliss] in The Works of . . . William Laud . . ., Library of Anglo-Catholic Theology, 7 vols (Oxford, 1847-60), IV 292, 293-4.
20. Thomas Fuller, *The History of the Worthies of England.* Endeavoured by Thomas Fuller . . . (1662), [part 1] 296.
21. See note 18, 167.
22. See note 18, xi.

VI

Cosin and Smart: Using Musical Evidence to Untangle some Historical Problems

Nick Heppel

Religious developments in the decades before the Civil War were experienced on several levels. On the higher plane, matters of theology were the preserve of the universities, the court and the Parliament; these debates, and the importance which should be attached to them, have become the subject of heated argument among historians, with some keen to stress the conflict of ideologies, and others emphasizing the extent of consensus, within the English church.[1]

The dispute which preoccupied English divines surrounded the teachings of the Dutch theologian Arminius, in particular his doctrine of grace available to all.[2] This was seen as an implicit and fundamental challenge to Calvinist predestinarianism, the more extreme interpretations of which saw men divided arbitrarily and permanently into the elect and the reprobate. This division was ordained by God before the beginning of time, and thus an individual had no control over his own destiny: no amount of sinful or virtuous behaviour could alter one's fate as determined by the Almighty.

While accepting the concept of a system of election and reprobation, Arminius challenged the notion that the elect could, in no circumstances, fall from grace; similarly, he suggested, the reprobate could redeem themselves through good works. Thus, according to Arminius, God's grace or damnation was not a foregone conclusion at birth, but a commodity that was, in part at least, deserved by one's actions and thoughts. It was the degree to which an individual had influence over his own fate which caused the acrimonious disputes within the churches of Holland and England.

Ordinary people, on the other hand, came face to face with this debate more directly through liturgical and ceremonial change. In England, regular reception of the sacraments came to be seen by a group of divines as the most important means of obtaining salvation, and this was the cue for a tranche of Eucharistic thought which had its most visible effect in liturgical and ceremonial innovation during the 1620s and 1630s.[3] This group, of which John Cosin was a prominent member, has become known as the Laudians.

It was largely on behalf of ordinary people that Peter Smart, prebendary of Durham Cathedral, launched his bitter attack on the innovations being pursued there by John Cosin, Augustine Lindsell and several others. When Peter Smart mounted the pulpit of the Cathedral on 7 July 1628 to preach his notorious sermon, one of the most celebrated disputes within the English church in the early seventeenth century was about to begin. Not until the 1640s was the case resolved, having passed through a series of ecclesiastical courts and parliamentary committees.

Apart from the importance of the events themselves, the proceedings also spawned Smart's voluminous writings, which must be counted among the most colourful in the religious history of the period.[4] His vitriolic attacks on John Cosin and his associates, from the sermon in 1628 to the *Cantus Epiphalamicus* of 1643, have frequently been quoted by historians as examples of the intensity of feeling aroused by liturgical developments in the decades before the Civil War.

Yet while Smart's accusations are frequently employed in the present historiographical debate over Laudianism,[5] it is perhaps not so freely noted that Cosin was able to answer most or all the detailed charges eventually brought against him in the Commons in 1640.[6] So cogent were Cosin's responses that not even a hostile Parliament felt that further action could profitably be taken against him; indeed, Smart's 'forward, fierce and unpeaceable' manner during the proceedings began to be something of an embarrassment to his supporters, his own counsel stating that he was 'ashamed of him, and could not in conscience plead for him any longer'.[7] When one reads Cosin's measured replies, one is left wondering, with Kippis, 'at the weakness of Dr Cosin, for inventing and pressing the observance of such ceremonies and insignificant things: . . . so, on the other hand, who can be sufficiently amazed at the confidence of P. Smart, in charging the Doctor with things he could so easily disprove?'[8]

If, then, Cosin was able to sweep aside the allegations of liturgical experimentation, to what extent can Peter Smart be regarded as an accurate witness of practices at Durham Cathedral in the 1620s and 1630s? The nature of the latter's prose has led commentators to take a somewhat sceptical approach to the *minutiae* of his argument; on the whole, however, the fundamental accuracy of his case has rarely been called into question. What evidence do we have with which to assess the validity of Smart's claims?

With the exception of the stone altar erected by Dean Hunt, and the cope donated by the King to the Durham Chapter in 1633, any alterations made by Cosin before the Civil War to the fabric of the Cathedral were either destroyed during the wars, or replaced by him at the Restoration; and it might be thought that the veracity of Smart's attacks was largely a matter of his word against Cosin's. There survive, however, nearly thirty witnesses to the controversy which have rarely, if ever, figured seriously in modern writing on the subject, witnesses who possibly sat in the choir stalls throughout the 1630s, and whose outward appearance bears many of the hallmarks of the 'beauty of holiness': the musical manuscripts still surviving in the Dean and Chapter Library.[9] While their importance from a musical point of view has long been recognised, they have not attracted the attention of religious historians.

This paper will seek to use the evidence of the musical sources at Durham to analyse some of the claims made by Peter Smart. Firstly, his accusations about the role of music within the liturgy will be considered in the light of this evidence; then the sources will be examined for evidence relating to Smart's other, non-musical claims; and finally some more fundamental ideas not mentioned specifically by the inveterate controversialist will be discussed.

Musical Manuscripts at Durham Cathedral

Ever since the 1920s, when Edmund Fellowes discovered the only surviving source for large sections of Byrd's *Great Service*, the inestimable importance of the Durham manuscripts has been recognised by all musical historians. Given the paucity of musical documents to survive the ravages of the Reformation and the Civil Wars, quite apart from the normal wear and tear of daily use, the part-books housed in the Dean and Chapter Library represent one of the most complete and wide-ranging sources of English church music of the sixteenth and seventeenth centuries. Apart from major works such as the *Great Service*, there are many other *unica* in the books; and several composers would be completely lost to us if the Scottish soldiers held captive in the Cathedral in 1651 had come across the manuscripts in their search for fuel.

Of the six sets of part-books recorded in a post-Restoration inventory, we possess members of five.[10] Most impressive are the large books containing festal psalms for the six main feasts of the church year, together with several elaborate services and settings of the preces and responses.[11] Only one member each survives from two sets of books of service music designed for more general use.[12] The two other groups of part-books are devoted to anthems, the first set being mainly ferial [non-festal] anthems,[13] and the second containing a highly ordered collection of pieces written for specific feasts.[14] In addition to these books there survive a number of singletons probably copied for individual churchmen; one of these, the Dunnington-Jefferson manuscript, is thought to have belonged to John Cosin himself.[15] Five organ books also remain from this period, containing outline scores of a large proportion of the overall repertoire of the part-books.[16] Completely missing are the sets of manuscripts described in the inventory as containing music for men's voices; while these might well have given us insights into music of the immediate post-Reformation period, during which such music flourished, the remaining books allow us a relatively full picture of the working repertoire of the Durham Cathedral choir in the 1630s.

It is more than likely that some of the earlier sets of books were copied in the late 1620s as replacements for older, dilapidated manuscripts,[17] and as such they cannot be considered as evidence for the deliberate cultivation of polyphonic music by the Cathedral authorities. Copying musical manuscripts was a costly business, as Cosin indirectly admitted in his *Answers* to Parliament. So concerned was Cosin to refute the figure of two thousand pounds for the new altar at Durham, he inadvertently reveals the extent of financial support given to this activity by the Chapter in these years:

> In the furniture or alterations (besides necessary repairs) of the church there was not expended, between defendant's coming in to be prebendary and Mr. Smart's sermon, above 200*l.*, which was chiefly laid out in procuring books for the quire . . .[18]

By about 1630 the amount of music at Durham would have probably been sufficient for most provincial cathedrals, yet the researches of Dr Crosby have shown that music was being copied into the part-books throughout the 1630s and almost up to the collapse of services in the 1640s.[19] These books contain a substantial quantity of music by local composers, although the books are dominated by Chapel Royal composers of the early seventeenth century. The inescapable conclusion here is that the repertoire of the choir was being augmented in a systematic manner during the 1630s; by the intervention of the Civil War, the choir had a repertoire of over two hundred anthems and about sixty services, not including the contents of the lost sources. This variety was matched by the difficulty of some of the music; clearly, the choir was able to perform on a regular basis music in six or more parts, and it is quite likely that at this time Durham was almost the only provincial choir capable of rendering the Byrd *Great Service*, which requires up to ten separate voice parts.[20] The testing nature of this repertoire had a parallel in the encouragement of indigenous composing talent - William Smith, Henry Palmer, Richard Hutchinson and John Geeres - to produce a vibrant musical scene at Durham during the 1620s and 1630s. Indeed there were probably more composers active in Durham at this time than at any point before or since.[21]

Beyond their purely musical value, these manuscripts have an importance which has hardly been noted by mainstream historians. They represent documentary evidence of the workings of a prestigious ecclesiastical establishment during the height of Laudian influence on the English Church, and as such they deserve closer inspection from the angle of the religious historian. In particular, it is the set of books containing festal anthems, together with the singletons, which have much to tell us about John Cosin and his associates.[22]

In contrast to most contemporary sources of church music, which distinguish pieces on the basis of the number of separate voice parts required,[23] the anthems in the later Durham books are grouped according to purely liturgical rank. The connection between liturgy and music in Cosin's thought is clearly shown by the fact that the anthems are arranged by feast, and that the order of the feasts is almost precisely the same as that given for the collects in *The Book of Common Prayer*. Seasons such as Advent and Lent combined in chronological order with feasts specific to Christ come first, with the cycle of saints' days following. Cosin's fascination with the ranking of feasts in the Sarum liturgy is seen in his Prayer Book annotations, and his influence on the organisation of these musical manuscripts is unmistakable. Furthermore, the non-festal anthems which make up the latter sections of the books are more or less ordered by theme: praise, prayer and penitence.[24] The arrangement of these books made them simple to use and must have given the choristers and lay clerks a tangible sense of the rhythm of the church year.

As has been mentioned, this degree and type of internal organisation is extremely uncommon in English sources of the period, and, with new anthems arriving almost continuously, difficult to maintain. Yet detailed forward planning is visible in the fact that spaces are left between each feast for later additions, the larger gaps expecting anthems for the more important feasts. The measures taken to ensure that the rapidly expanding repertoire was manageable could be said to be a matter of common sense; looked at another way, they reflect the workings of an acute liturgical mind.

Not only was there sufficient foresight in the planning of the books to cope with the influx of new materials, great care was taken to ensure that the music was beautifully presented. There are relatively few staves per page, and the great majority of the pre-Civil War hands in the books were admirably clear and precise, easier to read, in fact, than some of the additions made in the late seventeenth century. Beyond these sensible precautions, there was an attempt made to beautify the manuscripts further; indeed, they were to be as elaborately ornamented as they were strictly ordered. Room is left at the beginning of every anthem for a large illuminated initial; and although these never materialised, the intention is clear. The leather covers, ornamented by gilt tooling, show that the manuscripts were designed to be durable performing materials.

Durham has been described as a model diocese of Laudianism, which would have influenced later developments across the country, had not the Civil War intervened.[25] As with liturgical and ceremonial innovations, so with music. In their outward appearance and their internal organisation, these books bear the stamp of Laudianism; many features of Laudian church policy - attention to detail and a love of order, hierarchy and beauty - may be seen reflected in the pages of the Durham manuscripts.

Cosin, Smart and Music in the Liturgy

The style and extent of polyphonic music within the liturgy was significantly pared back during the middle decades of the sixteenth century, with the exuberant and highly melismatic idiom of the pre-Reformation replaced by a broadly syllabic and more restrained manner for the English rite. There was a similar reduction in the number of opportunities for choral music, with the removal of, among other things, the sung *Sanctus* and *Agnus Dei* in the 1552 *Book of Common Prayer.*[26] Although Elizabeth I did what she could to encourage polyphonic music - by overlooking the recusancy of some of her most prominent musical employees and by reinstating the non-liturgical anthem to the end of both Morning and Evening Prayer[27] – a combination of economic reality and theological change meant that she had little success outside the Chapel Royal and the related institutions.

The rapid rise in inflation in the late sixteenth century was responsible for a corresponding fall in the standard of living of lay clerks, whose salaries were fixed by cathedral statutes, thus making such posts unattractive to talented young composers; and dissemination of Calvinist doctrine during the Elizabethan period also accounted for a less approving attitude to elaborate church music from cathedral authorities.[28]

By the early seventeenth century, the church composer could write settings of the morning canticles (*Venite, Te Deum* or *Benedicite, Benedictus* or *Jubilate*), the *Kyrie* and Creed at

Communion and the evening canticles (*Magnificat* or *Cantate Domino, Nunc dimittis* or *Deus misereatur*), with some optional extras such as the preces and responses and festal psalms. Finally there was the anthem, the texts for which were often selected or compiled by the composer himself; the Psalms were the most common source of anthem texts, in either metrical or prose forms, although other areas of scripture were also explored.

Music was one of the most contentious issues at Durham during the 1620s and 1630s, not only between Smart and Cosin, but also between Bishop Howson and the Laudian contingent in the Chapter. That Bishop Laud, and even the King himself, became involved in the latter dispute (caused by Howson's attempt to support Smart's allegations during his Visitation of 1631), is a measure of the importance which they attached to liturgical music.[29] Peter Smart's writings (and documents surrounding the Visitation) are concerned as much with music as with the now more prominent dispute over the replacement of the Communion table with a stone altar. Four pages of the *Sermon*, nine of the twenty points in the *Short Treatise* and three of the paragraphs in the *Briefe Narration* are concerned with music.

It should not be inferred from this that Smart was against music *per se*. On the contrary, he stood in the mainstream of Calvinist thought on music in that he supported the singing of Psalms by the congregation. It was only when the prescriptions of *The Book of Common Prayer* were exceeded that Smart protested. What Smart perceived was a professionalising of divine worship, with the musical portions taken almost exclusively by the choir, and with congregational involvement severely limited. Smart's (and most other Calvinist critics') primary objection to polyphonic music was that it contributed little, if anything, to the edification of the people: the densely interweaving lines of much of the music contained in the part-books obliterated the text being sung, and thus prevented the promulgation of God's word:

> . . . those books I say [*The Book of Common Prayer*, the *Articles of Religion*, the *Injunctions and Homilies*], appoint, and command, all the service to be said and sung so as the people may understand all, and be edified therby. But our new fangled reformers of Durham, Cosin himself, &c. have within these five years brought into this Church such a strange change of Services that the greater part thereof, can no better be understood, then if it were in Hebrew or Irish.[30]

Any move towards increasing the extent of music within services would, therefore, have struck Smart as suspicious. One of his most bitter attacks was on the replacement of congregational metrical psalms with anthems sung by the choir:

> Why forbid they singing of Psalmes in such a tune, as all the people may sing with them . . . How dare they in stead of Psalmes, appoint Anthems to be sung, which none of the people understand, nor all the singers themselves.[31]

The exact dating of the alteration is unclear: alongside the accusation in the *Short Treatise* is printed in the margin 'since the year 1627';[32] the text of the *Treatise*, however, states that the 'singing of Psalmes in the vulgar tunes within these five years . . . hath quite been banished out of Durham Church' and, since the *Treatise* bears the date 1629, this would appear to mean 1624, the year of Cosin's arrival at Durham. As with most of his claims, Smart blames Cosin as ringleader of the Durham Arminians. In response, Cosin is at the very least disingenuous:

> The singing of metre psalms was never forbidden by him or any other (that he knoweth) in that church, where he used daily to sing them himself (as in other places his custom is to do) with the people assembled at the six o'clock morning prayer. But as to the singing of them before and after the sermon (which is there always preached in the quire) the use was long before his coming

> thither, and is so still, afore the sermon to sing the Creed, (as the Book of Common Prayer by law established doth appoint), and after the sermon to sing an anthem or hymn, which that the people might the better know what was at any time sung, was always publicly declared by one of the quire-men, out of what psalm (being many times a metre psalm) or other part of Scripture, or the Book of Common Prayer, the same was taken.[33]

Such an explanation would hardly have satisfied Smart, because it was the very fact that the congregation was no longer singing the Psalms that infuriated him.

Cosin admits here the practice of singing anthems after sermons (presumably as well as at the normal point at the end of Matins and Evensong), and the evidence of the musical manuscripts bears him out. Firstly, there is the sheer size of the anthem repertoire with over two hundred being copied in the years after 1625.[34] Many of them are festal, and their use would be restricted to the feast day for which they were intended. A large number (indeed an entire set of books is devoted to them) are for ferial use, perhaps performed on a weekly rota system.[35] Many of the anthems are in fact taken from metrical psalms, although the Durham composers themselves do not seem to have been particularly keen to set such texts.[36]

Part of the demand for new anthems may be explained by a desire on the part of the Laudians at Durham to have as many feasts of the church year as possible decorated by settings of proper texts, and this desire would seem to have its incarnation in the set of books for festal anthems. Yet non-festal anthems continued to pour into the books at a similar rate, and it is this trend which appears to point to new opportunities for performance of anthems within the liturgy. One of the more likely places for such performance would indeed seem to be either side of the sermon at Communion, or the second service; certainly the number of anthems provided for some major feasts would seem to suggest that more than one anthem was performed on those days.

Valuable evidence for this practice is seen in a letter from Cosin and Lindsell to their colleague Eleazor Duncon which dates from the 1631 Visitation by Bishop Howson. The letter recounts the attempts made by the new bishop to turn back the liturgical clock:

> . . . we understand well what the difference is betwixt an Anthem sung by the Quire (when it is part of a singing psalme) and the singing psalmes themselves, as they be sung by the whole multitude of people in the common tunes of parish churches. After this manner is our practice now, and not after that other . . . Upon the fourth Sunday he [Howson] sent a messenger to the Chantor . . . commanding him so to order the service . . . that after the Creed so read, he should begin a psalme for all the people to sing before the Sermon, and after Sermon sing another, as they use to do in parish churches . . . because 2 psalmes, one before and another after Sermon, seemed to take up too much time, it was then ordered, that the common psalme shold only be sung after the Sermon (in stead of the Anthem before in use).[37]

It would seem, then, that the practice of choir anthems after sermons was current at Durham before 1631, although it is not possible to state precisely when it started. Following this brief interlude of congregational Psalms, performance of anthems resumed, since Howson was forced by Laud and Charles I to retreat from his stance at the Visitation, and the only regular opportunity for popular involvement in music was eradicated.

A parallel and equally disturbing trend was noticed by Smart: the substitution of said prayers by choral settings of the same texts. This again had the effect of confusing the congregation and alienating them from the 'sacred actions' being performed. Only one instance of this practice is given by Smart in the *Briefe Narration*, although the practice as a whole is condemned in his 1640 Articles against Cosin:

> He converted divers prayers in the Book of Common Prayer into hymns, to be sung in the choir, and played with the organ, contrary to the ancient custom of that church.[38]

The occasion which Smart singled out was at Easter in 1628:

> On the fast day after Easter last, he commanded the last prayer at the end of the Communion, to be sung with the Organes as an Anthem, so that no man could understand one word, in so much that the people rising up and sitting when it began to bee sung, Mr COSENS call'd to them that sate neare about them [him?], saying, you must kneele, you must kneele, it is a prayer: then all the congregation kneeled downe, and prayed very devoutly they knew not what.[39]

The prayer referred to at the end of such a commination service would be *Turn thou us, O good Lord*, and indeed there are two settings of this text in the Durham books. The 1640 Articles imply, however, that this was not an isolated occurrence, and the Prayer Book texts normally said by the minister were regularly given a polyphonic rendering by the choir. One set of texts which may have been performed in this way are the festal collects. There are twenty-three feasts from the church calendar which are provided with settings of collects in the part-books, and the contribution to this repertoire by the local composers is striking: nearly half of the outputs of William Smith and Henry Palmer consists of collect settings, a proportion far higher than in the work of the major composers of the era.[40] It can only be assumed that the Durham musicians were responding to an incentive to compose music for these prayers. Provision of polyphonic settings of collects was a means of giving musical expression to the hierarchy of feasts in the church year; and it is possible that the authorities went a step further by ordering the replacement of the said text by the sung version. As has already been mentioned, several feasts were supplied with three, four or even more anthems, one of which would usually be a setting of the collect, and an efficient use of this material would be to use the collect setting as a prayer and use one of the other items as the anthem proper.[41] To these festal collects may be added two other pieces which may be referred to in the Articles; both of them are settings of Communion collects: *Prevent us, O Lord*, by Byrd, and *Almighty God, the fountain of all wisdom* by Tomkins. Richard Hutchinson, Cathedral organist at the time, reveals in his testimony that, on four days of the week the order of service was: the Ten Commandments, Epistle, Gospel, Creed, anthem and collects;[42] these two items may have been acquired specifically for these services.

Although we cannot be certain as to the use of all these pieces, there is a substantial body of music which would seem to support Smart's claim that prayers offered by the minister on behalf of the people were regularly replaced by choral versions of the texts. There are two important aspects to this issue. Firstly, this would appear to be an example of the professionalising of worship which Smart feared; such changes would have enhanced the role of the choir and brought them into contact with a new repertoire, much of it home-grown; there may well have been an element of commissioning of new anthem settings of collect texts by the Cathedral authorities; with a growth in opportunities for choral music went a corresponding reduction in the portions of service understood by the congregation.

The second aspect involves the choice of collects in particular for choral performance. These were the texts which gave each feast its special commemorative character, and it is probable that the motivation for obtaining settings of as many festal collects as possible was to have music which would distinguish feasts from one another, and also feasts from ferial services. We have already seen Cosin's interest in the ranking of feast days under the Sarum liturgy reflected in the internal organisation of the part-books, and this fascination may have extended to a desire to express the hierarchical structure of the church year in polyphonic music. Certainly the choir would have been aware of each passing feast or season, even if the congregation was denied the opportunity of hearing the collect which explained its importance.

Another of Smart's musical criticisms which may be assessed from the evidence of the part-books is the singing of the Nicene Creed by the choir, as opposed to the 'normal' practice of the congregational Apostles' Creed. It is one of his most consistent and emotive themes:

> . . . hee enjoynes all the people to stand up at the Nicene Creed, (a Ceremonie which your Church enjoynes not) which he commands to bee sung with Organs, Shackbuts, and Cornets, and all other instruments of musicke, which were used at the Consecration of NABUCHADONOZERS golden Image, (unfit Instruments for Christian Churches where men come for to pray, and not for to chaunt, or heare a sound or consort of they know not what).[43]

This claim is relatively easily verified by an examination of the creed settings intended for choral use. All of them take the Nicene Creed as their text, with some minor alterations in a few cases. This would presumably have been considered by Smart a regressive move of the greatest importance, since the regular rehearsal of the principal tenets by the people was designed by sixteenth-century reformers as a major element in their edification. It is not surprising, therefore, that Smart was so enraged by its removal to the distant choir.

The performance of music 'at the very time' of the administration of the sacraments was nothing short of scandalous to Smart. It seemed to him to alter the very essence of the Eucharist:

> That is a time of mourning, a time of sighing, a time of weeping and lamenting, a time of confessing, and begging pardon, it is not a time of piping and singing . . . What hath musick to do with mourning? or a song of mirth, with a day of the greatest sorrow, which is the Passion of Christ . . . Our eares must attend the word of truth, not delicious tunes of musicall melody . . .[44]

The expression 'the very time', used frequently by Smart, is somewhat vague: it could mean any time from the commencement of the canon, or it could mean music to cover the actual administration of the bread and wine. Either way, Smart's claims indicate an extension of the role of music at this point in the service beyond the limits of the Prayer Book. The remarks also indicate that it was vocal, as opposed to purely instrumental music (organ voluntaries, for example) which was performed at this point, and so it is again to the part-books that we must turn for guidance. Three areas of possible performance practice need to be addressed in this connection: the use of music as sanctioned by *The Book of Common Prayer*; the unsanctioned use of polyphony; and musical items which may be considered for performance during the administration of the sacraments.

From the preface onwards, the only text permitted to be sung by post-1552 Prayer Books was the prayer of thanksgiving or *Gloria*, although remarkably few settings of the text survive from the early seventeenth century. The Durham part-books contain several such settings, but although we know the composers of these works - Child, Foster and Loosemore - to have been active before the Civil Wars interrupted cathedral music, the scribal hands in which they are copied into the books seem to date from the Restoration. The last few pages of the Dunnington-Jefferson manuscript (DJ), however, offer us significant further evidence on this issue, for they contain two settings of the *Gloria* in a hand which almost certainly predates the Civil War.[45] Both pieces are left unattributed (extremely rare in these books) which may mean that the first is by William Smith, as it follows his anthem *I will wash mine hands* without a further ascription. More important (in the context of this discussion) than the authorship of these *Gloria* settings is the probability that they were in the repertoire of the Durham Cathedral choir by about 1640. The acquisition of these items at a relatively late stage would have been an important addition to the scope of choral polyphony, given the role and position of the text in the liturgy. The *Gloria* represented the last opportunity for choral music in the Communion ritual, and as such it would have lent a sense of musical wholeness to the latter stages of the service; as we shall see, music played a part in the preparation and the administration of the sacraments, and it may have been felt that music should be found or commissioned to round off the high point of the liturgy. Once again, a crucial text - the prayer of thanksgiving uttered by the minister on behalf of the people - was being transferred to the choir. The later acquisition of the settings by Child and Loosemore, as well as the indigenous efforts of Foster (who became organist at the Restoration) may thus be seen as an attempt to expand the repertoire of *Gloria* settings just before the collapse of choral services in the 1640s or just after the Restoration.

Despite the fact that Durham was probably one of only a very small number of establishments to require polyphonic settings of the *Gloria* in the decade before the Civil War, this activity is not necessarily surprising, since it falls within the regulations of the Prayer Book. More wide-reaching is the suggestion that two items of the Communion liturgy, whose choral performance had been effectively banned since 1552, were being sung to polyphony at Durham by the late 1630s. Two settings of the *Sanctus* are to be found in the part-books, both of them paired with the above-mentioned settings of the *Gloria* in DJ.[46] In addition to this musical evidence for the performance of the *Sanctus*, the testimony of the organist Richard Hutchinson, written in defence of Peter Smart, seems to put the issue beyond doubt:

> And for the order of the Communion, when they come first to the Communion table, at the entering of the door every one doth make a low congie to the altar, and so takes his place. . . And then the priest goeth up to the Table and beginneth the Exhortation, and goeth on until he cometh at *Lift up your hearts*, that he

> singeth, and the quire answereth, singing in strange tunes so far as the priest and answer goeth: then for the rest, one of the priests reads some part of it at the end of the table, and after the prefaces, the priest begins, *Therefore with angels and archangels*, until he comes to the three Holies, and then the quire singeth until the end of that: so in order doth he administer the Communion . . .[47]

Between those of Tallis (*c*.1552) and William Child (who seems to have had close connections with Cosin during his Peterhouse years) settings of the *Sanctus* by English composers were extremely rare; the change in the 1552 Prayer Book rubric seems to have had its desired effect, if the number of new settings is anything to go by. Not so at Durham, where polyphonic settings of the *Sanctus* were apparently revived during the 1630s and 1640s. Since the restoration, among other things, of the sung *Agnus Dei* during the administration of the sacrament was one of the proposals in *The Durham Book*,[48] it is not difficult to detect the hand of John Cosin behind these changes at the Cathedral.[49]

Even rarer than *Sanctus* settings were versions of the Communion responses, the only one recorded in Daniel and Le Huray's index being in the Peterhouse part-books, for which Cosin was responsible.[50] Hutchinson's statement shows that the responses were sung at Durham in his time (i.e. the 1630s), and one pre-Civil War setting is to be found in the Durham books (A3 and DJ).[51]

There are two anthems which have close connection with the Communion liturgy. Byrd's anthem *Have mercy upon us* is given the superscription 'at ye Communion' in MS A1.[52] On its own it seems to be an all-purpose setting of Psalm 51. 1-3; however it is part of a set at the back of the DJ manuscript containing the Communion responses and the second *Sanctus*, a grouping which suggests a more specific place in the liturgy; similarly, William Smith's work *I will wash mine hands* is part of the Communion Day music in DJ, along with the first

Sanctus and *Gloria*. The text of this anthem seems to make it particularly appropriate for use here:

> I will wash mine hands in innocency, O Lord, and so will I come to thine altar.

If we take the ambiguous phrase 'at ye Communion' as meaning during the distribution of the elements, these two pieces, together with the two Communion collects mentioned above, seem to be plausible candidates for regular performance at this time in the Communion ritual.

Though so much of the evidence rests on the difficulties of dating music copied by mid-century scribes, it is probable that by about 1640 the polyphonic sequence of Communion responses - *Sanctus* - Communion anthem - *Gloria* - was a feature of Communion services on major feast days at least. As such it would represent the greatest concentration of polyphony in the liturgy, not surprising, given the weight attached to the sacraments by Cosin. Equally, it is in the area of music for Communion that Cosin is revealed most clearly as as innovator, this sequence being unmatched anywhere else in the country, based on the surviving evidence. One interpretation of the sources is that, having seen to the expansion of the anthem repertoire in the early 1630s, Cosin was concerned in the years just before the Civil War to enhance the role of music at Communion time. It would be remembered, of course, that Smart made his accusations as early as 1628; and while he could be referring simply to the performance of anthems during Communion, it is probable that the extent of Communion music was increased in the following years. The choral versions of the responses meant that the last opportunity for congregational participation before the administration of the sacrament was forfeited. The preparation for receiving the bread and the wine must have appeared a purely professional affair. Indeed, with the sung *Kyrie*, Creed, responses, *Sanctus* and *Gloria*, together with an anthem, the casual onlooker at

Durham in the 1630s could, perhaps, have been forgiven for thinking that the only aspect of liturgical worship to have changed since the Reformation was the language in which it was delivered. Three of the major polyphonic items of the pre-Reformation festal mass had reappeared, with only the *Agnus Dei* missing.[53]

We still know very little about the realities of the performance of liturgical music at English cathedrals and churches in the early seventeenth century. The ambiguous rubric for the role of the anthem and the decline in church music generally perceived by contemporaries, combined with a severe lack of reliable evidence on performance practice, means that we are still only scratching the surface of musical traditions passed down from generation to generation. Yet it is possible to see at Durham in the 1630s an attempt to extend the scope of polyphonic music, especially in terms of the number of opportunities afforded to it in the daily liturgy. A vast source of anthems and service music was built up, and local composers were encouraged to provide music for parts of the services not previously set to music. Particularly interesting are the many connections between features of their work (settings of collects and Communion music, for example) and Cosin's liturgical thinking, as seen in his Prayer Book annotations. Anthems were employed to replace both Psalms, on a regular basis, and prayers less frequently. The array of service music shows that polyphonic performance of the canticles was the rule and not the exception, and that the Nicene Creed was sung by the choir. Smart was correct in perceiving a professionalising of divine worship, with the opportunities for congregational participation gradually eroded. These moves were part of a programme of musical changes and, as we have seen, its originators could be certain of support from higher quarters if their plans were challenged.

Non-Musical innovations Reflected in the Musical Sources

The innovations described thus far involve merely the choral performance of texts which would previously have been spoken, the *Gloria* and *Sanctus*, the Creed and some prayers. On one level the actual service texts remained largely intact, with the mode of delivery being changed. While these moves were bound to strike Smart as sinister, it is possible that more drastic changes to the liturgy were being implemented, which allowed more opportunities for music. In particular Smart objected to the division of the morning service into two distinct liturgical units, Matins and Communion, causing 'such a confusion of the fore-noone Liturgie'.[54] He seems to suggest, furthermore, that it was precisely in order to encourage music at the Cathedral that this step was taken:

> He hath divided the Morning Service into two parts, the 6. of clocke Service which was used to bee read onely, and not sung: hee chaunts with Organs, Shackbuts, and Cornets which yield an hydeous noyse, and makes that Service which was scarce one quarter of an houre long before, one houre and an halfe at least: and this hee calls Mattens. The second Service at 10. of the clocke hee calls Masse, which consists of Epistles, and Gospels, the 10, Commandments, and the Nicene Creed, which are onely to be read on Sondayes and Holydayes, by the order in the Common Prayer Booke . . .[55]

> *David*, that renowned Prophet of God, devised many instruments of musick, and he taught the Levites sing and play hymnes to the Lord, *per Sabbathorum dies aliasque solennitates*: at the solemnities of Festivall dayes and Sabbaths. Therefore not every day in the week, nor thrice every day: they did not turn the houres of prayer into solemne services, with piping and chanting, morning, and evening, and mid-day, as our new-fangled ceremony-mongers of late most audaciously attempted to do in this Church of *Durham* . . .[56]

The early morning service, which had, according to Smart, been until about 1625 a brief prayer meeting designed mainly for students, was now extended into a full Matins and followed by the outline of the Communion service, although we do not know how often the Eucharist itself was distributed. Cosin denied that it was he who had authorized the decision, and even went as far as to say that he had been responsible for restoring the former service:

> . . . at his first coming, he found the 6 o'clock morning prayer (said to have been usually read in former times in a part of the cross-isle) removed into the quire, which was done (as he can prove) by a capitular act, whereunto Mr. Smart gave his assent, divers years before defendant became prebendary there. Was so far from taking the old morning prayer quite away, as alledged, that during his abode in Durham, he did constantly frequent the same, as well when it was for divers years read, as when for a small time it was (by appointment of the late Dean) sung in the quire. And whereas, at his first coming, he found it removed from the accustomed place of the church, it was, by defendant's special instance brought back to the same place, wherein it hath been read at 6 of the clock in the morning there 11 or 12 years last, without any alteration except the addition of the first lesson to it, according to law, which had been in former times neglected and omitted when Mr. Smart was prebendary.[57]

Having examined mainly the anthem repertoire for material for the previous section, evidence on this issue comes from the books devoted to service music. As with the anthems, the Durham part-books are among the most complete sources left to us, and it is unlikely that any other institution (except perhaps the Chapel Royal) possessed a comparable number of canticle settings. Particular attention has been paid to balancing the number of settings for each service; there is a roughly equivalent quantity of Matins, Communion and Evensong music, with some composers supplying the missing sections to other composers' settings. A logical conclusion to be drawn from this evidence is that the number of occasions on which each service was celebrated was approximately similar, which would support Smart's charges. This does not prove, however, that it was Cosin himself who was responsible for the alterations, although Nicholas Hobson, ageing lay clerk, was in no doubt as to the identity of the driving force behind the liturgical changes: 'I say, that Dr. Cosins was the principal man that made the alteration mentioned in the morning prayer'.[58] More information on this matter comes from the outputs of the two most prolific composers at Durham at this time. Both Henry Palmer and William Smith arrived there in about 1627, and analysis of their work shows that their only contribution to ferial service music was for the second, or Communion service. Since it is possible to see in their outputs the influence of new trends at Durham, there is a strong likelihood that the Communion service was being celebrated more frequently from about 1627 onwards.[59]

While Smart's objections relate largely to gradual developments, he occasionally cites specific events, such as the celebration of Candlemas. This feast was of great importance to the Laudian party, since it marked the anniversary of the coronation of Charles I, and Smart was clearly incensed by Cosin's ostentatious celebrations:

> On Candlemas day last past: Mr. COSENS invenuing [renewing] the Popish Ceremonie of burning candles to the honour of our Lady, busied himselfe from two of the clocke in the afternoone till foure, in climbing long ladders to sticke up wax candles in the said Cathedrall Church: The number of all the Candles burnt that evening, was 220. Besides 16. Torches: 60, of those burning tapers standing upon, and neare the high Altar.[60]

While Cosin refuted these claims, stating that the number of candles in the choir was only sufficient for the proper and dignified celebration of divine service, they are backed up by other sources, including Joseph Mead at Cambridge, who noted that:

> Mr. Cosins was so blind at evensong on Candlemas day that he could not see to read prayers in the minster with less than 340 candles, whereof 60 he caused to be placed round about the high altar. Besides, he caused the picture of our Saviour supported by two angells, to be sett in the quire upon Bishop Hatfield's tombe.[61]

We can only imagine the impression made by the chancel of the Cathedral decorated and illuminated in this way; possibly nothing like it had been seen there since the Reformation.

No mention is made of music for the feast, but the part-books reveal three anthems designed for use on Candlemas Day. Surprisingly, they all use the same text, the collect from *The Book of Common Prayer*, this being almost the only example of such duplication in the festal anthem repertoire:[62] while some feasts have several proper anthems, none has two collect settings. Stranger still is the fact that two of the anthems are by the Durham composers, William Smith and Henry Palmer. The other setting, by Thomas Tomkins, may derive from the fact that the composer was responsible for most of the music for the coronation in 1625. It is difficult, however, to explain the existence of both the Smith and Palmer anthems, especially since there is no other example of such overlap in any of their surviving works. Their existence at least highlights the symbolic importance of the feast in the Laudian calendar, and the performance of all three anthems on the same day (either in the usual liturgical position or as a replacement for the spoken text, or both) is not implausible, regardless of the accuracy of Smart's claims about the number of candles used at Evensong.

Beyond this single occurrence there is the wider question of 'royal' music in the Durham sources, an issue which has several facets. First there is the importance of Chapel Royal composers, such as Byrd, Gibbons and Tomkins, in the books. While significant contributions from such men are a feature of most sixteenth- and seventeenth-century sources, the size of the Durham repertoire makes their role even more conspicuous.

Interestingly, Durham seems to have been the only establishment to have acquired several pieces by major composers of the period. Much of this music is among the most elaborate written since the Reformation - the services by Byrd and Weelkes, for example - and considered by some commentators beyond the scope of provincial choirs at this time.

A closer look at the details of the repertoire shows a substantial sub-group of anthems composed not just for the Chapel Royal, but for the monarch himself: anthems praising him or praying for his speedy recovery from illness and so on. In one sense, there was little need for these pieces to be used outside the Chapel Royal, for which most, if not all, the anthems and services were composed. Many of them are occasional pieces which would not be performed once the immediate context for them had disappeared. Since the performing materials associated with the Chapel Royal have been almost entirely lost, Durham is now the only source containing many of these anthems.[63] The most likely explanations for the survival of such a large and specific repertoire almost exclusively at Durham is the political outlook of the new generation of churchmen drafted into the Cathedral in the mid-1620s, and this is a point which Smart picked up:

> But now I come to their maine argument, which they think quite overthrows all that I have said concerning Altars and Ceremonies. *The King's Chappell,* say they, *hath an Altar, and all furniture belonging thereunto: Dare you disallow in ours, what the King hath in his? It is little better then treason,* as one said . . . what have we doe with imitation of the Court? May we be so sawcy, as to imitate the King in all things? Is it not treason? . . . The King commands us to obey his lawes, which binde Cathedrall Churches as well as the rest; none are exempted, none can be dispenst withall.[64]

The sheer number of anthems specified for The King's Day (the anniversary of the accession) is revealing and is more than for any other feast. The feast was also marked by singing from the Cathedral tower, for which the choir received an extra payment, and Gunpowder Day was another celebration for which special anthems were imported. All told there are about a dozen anthems making direct reference to the monarch and his family, and while their arrival at Durham may perhaps be explained by royal visits in 1617 and 1633, their copying into the repertoire and the inclusion of the two feasts in the liturgical ordering is a reflection of the allegiance to the monarch felt by the Laudians at this time.

The most conspicuous feature of the Laudian programme was the erection of stone altars at the east end of the chancel to replace the wooden Communion tables which had previously stood in the body of the church. In a new theology which saw the sacraments as more important than the sermon in terms of gaining salvation, the altar took on a renewed significance, and the Laudian altar was, typically, railed off and provided with plate and candles, all of which was designed to inspire respect and veneration. Such adulation could be expressed through frequent bowing and by facing east for the recital of the Creed. Taken to extremes, these ceremonial alterations were an obvious target for Puritan pamphleteers such as Prynne and Burton.

There is clearly no need to turn to the musical sources to prove the erection of a stone altar at Durham, since Dean Hunt's altar of *c.*1620 is one of the early examples of the practice. However the 'beauty of holiness' surrounding the altar is reflected in some of the music in the part-books. The musical settings for use during the Communion added an extra dimension to the adoration of the sacraments themselves. They intensified the most symbolic moments of the Communion service. The William Smith anthem quoted above is especially significant for its use of the term 'altar', a word to which Smart objects throughout his writings:

> I will wash mine hands in innocency, O Lord; and soe will I goe to thyne Altar, for I have loved the habitation of thy house and the place where thy honor dwelleth.

All the five voices combine at the word 'altar', making it the most audible word of the entire anthem, although how much importance should be attached to this is not certain. Nor should it be forgotten that William Smith was no mere musician simply reacting to pressure from his superiors, as may be the case with some of the other composers working at the Cathedral. He was a minor canon of the Cathedral who held the post of Precentor for several years, in addition to his benefice of St Mary-le-Bow, Durham. Most significantly of all, perhaps, is the fact that he was educated at Cambridge during the 1620s, a period in which the debate surrounding Arminianism preoccupied the university.[66] Smith would, therefore, have been well aware of the significance of the word 'altar', and of the ideology behind the programme of altar building.

Unease at liturgical trends at the Cathedral was not limited to Smart. As we have seen, the organist Richard Hutchinson took the perhaps unusual step of supporting the old prebend in the detail of some of his accusations against Cosin. Hutchinson's career at Durham was, to say the least, eventful, including a sojourn in jail for repeated inebriation and assaulting a lay clerk. Although the Chapter was keen to retain the services of a talented organist, relations between it and Hutchinson were strained for long periods. Some of Hutchinson's unease at the new ideas being promulgated at Durham is reflected in his anthem *Lord, I am not high minded.* Hutchinson appears to be a rare example of a musician finding it hard to work for an institution implementing policies which included the promotion of his own art:

> Lord, I am not high minded: I have noe proude looks: I doe not exercise myselfe in great matters which are to[o] high for mee. But restraine my soule and keep it lowe like as a Childe that is

weaned from its mother. O Israel trust in the Lord from this time forth for evermore. Amen.

Conclusion

Detailed analysis of the musical sources at Durham from a variety of viewpoints tends to justify the majority of Peter Smart's charges against Cosin; indeed, closer inspection of them reveals liturgical experimentation which not even Smart noticed. Music was a powerful element in the Laudian programme, and the composition, copying and performance of liturgical music was supported and encouraged at Durham in a number of ways. Congregational involvement in music through chanting of the Psalms was replaced by its musical antithesis, choral polyphony; understanding of the service by the ordinary people was reduced by transferring some texts from the minister to the choir, and by giving the rehearsal of the fundamental tenets of all true believers to the professional musicians; the most symbolic moments of the Communion ritual were adorned with polyphonic music; the accepted pattern of daily worship experienced by several generations was interrupted, with a consequent increase in the amount of choral music performed each day. When all these points are considered, Cosin's place as one of the most controversial innovators of the era can hardly be disputed.

For all that the manuscripts appear to support Smart's accusations, several important questions remain to be addressed. Most mundanely, perhaps, how did Cosin escape parliamentary censure (and worse) in 1640, if the remaining evidence seems to condemn him so comprehensively? To what extent was Cosin operating autonomously at Durham during the 1620s and 1630s? What did Laudians see in choral music which motivated them to support its performance with substantial sums of money? Finally, how much scope is there for further examination of musical sources for evidence of more general historical interest?

The dismissal of Cosin by Parliament seems all the more surprising, given the weight of evidence which we can see against him. In part, it must be credited to Smart's excessively vindictive conduct during proceedings, behaviour which clearly upset members and alienated the natural support for him which must have existed in the Commons. In contrast to his opponent, Cosin's replies suggest a complete control of the materials, and an ability to rebut the charges brought against him without calling upon the emotive language to which Smart was all too prone. The skill of Cosin's answers lies in his emphasis on the corporate nature of some of the decision-making which led to Smart's accusations, and in particular in implicating Smart himself in some of the 'innovations' of which he was later to complain. Wherever possible, Cosin stresses the fact that any changes to worship were necessarily passed by resolution of the Chapter. His opponents would have had to have brought action against all the surviving members of that body, and the value of such an exercise must have been questioned. Significantly, where Cosin is willing to reveal personal intervention in liturgical matters, he is keen to portray himself as a conservative, trying to reverse potentially controversial decisions made by the Chapter. With Cosin, as with Smart, the only way to justify action is on the basis of precedent, and the restorative nature of, for example, Cosin's moves on the issue of Matins is emphasized. From all that we know of Cosin's liturgical outlook, he was indeed a conservative, not of the type he wishes to appear by his answers in 1640, but a radical conservative, aiming in many ways at the resuscitation of the 1549 Prayer Book.[67] The detailed nature of many of the charges brought by Smart, obscured both by the quality of the old man's prose and the passing of nearly twenty years, may have caused Parliament to hesitate before pressing forward with the legal action. Apart from the additional testimony of Richard Hutchinson (and that of the ninety-two-year-old lay clerk, Nicholas Hobson)[68] the case rested solely on the veracity of the two protagonists' statements, as was the case concerning Cosin's alleged denial of the royal supremacy,[69] remarks which must have seemed at the time to be far more interesting to Parliament than the minutiae of liturgical worship at Durham Cathedral in the 1630s.

Where Cosin was in overt control of an institution, as at Peterhouse, the personality behind liturgical change was clearly visible; it is more difficult to discern how far Cosin was personally and solely responsible for all that occurred at Durham, and to what extent he was following a course of action agreed by others. Our best guess must be that, given the quality and independence of his liturgical thought from an early stage in his career, and the connections between the detail of the musical sources at Durham in the 1630s and Cosin's recommendations for the 1662 Prayer Book, he was largely in charge of developments. As a key member of the Durham House group, he arrived at Durham just as that party began to establish its grip over the monarchy and the patronage system, and he seems to have taken advantage of the new freedom of operation in his activities at the Cathedral. Indeed, it was here that Cosin was at his most radical and controversial; his later experiences, according to Dr Cuming, tended to tone down some of his more extreme opinions.[70]

It needs to be stressed however that Cosin could perhaps not have survived unscathed without the backing of a substantial group of Laudians within the Durham Chapter. Any divergent voices were presumably silenced, and the frustration of several years of impotence in the face of the new recruits is borne out in Smart's sermon. Equally important was the support Cosin knew he could rely upon from Bishops Laud and Neile. When a challenge came from a more high-profile source - Bishop Howson in 1630/1, for example - he was clearly guaranteed support from London and Winchester. It is less likely that either Laud or Neile were behind any of the specific innovations of the 1620s and 1630s (apart from the erection of the high altar) described here; these are, it would appear, almost entirely to be pinned on Cosin the liturgist.[71]

Music was a small but significant part of a much wider set of policies which embraced all aspects of liturgical worship, and which derived from a view of the regular and dignified reception of the sacraments as indispensable for a man's salvation.[72] It has been said of the Arminians that they were largely practical men, who did not enter into the big ideological controversies of the times,[73] and the same could be said of their attitude to music. Despite the large sums of cash which Neile, Cosin and Laud were prepared to spend on new organs, on the copying of musical manuscripts and so forth, none has much to say on the position of polyphonic music in their thought. Although it might be said that music was merely a matter of local tradition and practice, and that as such, little needed to be recorded about it, it is difficult to find any remark in their writings which could be seen as justifying those amounts of money. As a result, any comment on Cosin's motives for his encouragement of liturgical music during his time at Durham and Peterhouse must remain speculative.

There are two main possible sources of reasoning: the first relates to the full and proper implementation of the requirements of both *The Book of Common Prayer* and of Cathedral Statutes. These were taken as rigid instructions, whose minimum regulations were not to be transgressed. Cathedral Statutes laid down the number of lay clerks and choristers to be employed by the Chapter and to be present at services; any attempt to reduce that number would have been seen as challenging the legitimacy of the Statutes. The members of the choir were a professional body, a layer of the hierarchical structure of the Cathedral establishment, who had distinct and clearly defined responsibilities within the worship, namely the singing of those parts of the liturgy suggested by *The Book of Common Prayer*. Centuries of the practice of polyphonic music in the liturgy were not to be swept aside because of a passing phase of unpopularity.

These are arguments merely for the maintenance of levels of musical provision, not for the expansion of the role of the choir. Clearly polyphonic music had an important role in distinguishing the chancel of the cathedral from the nave, a division which was to be further emphasized by repeated bowing to the high altar on entering and leaving the choir; music enhanced the special atmosphere necessary for that part of the building housing the high altar. The physical separation of the clergy (and the musicians) from the people increased the status of the former, but was bitterly condemned by Smart, who saw the relegation of the Cathedral's font to the west end of the building as a related issue:

> Why is the Altar lifted up to the top of the Sanctuary or Chancell, and the Font not admitted so much as to the bottome? It is not suffered to stand in the wonted place behinde the quire dore, why is one preferred as holier then the other, being Sacraments of equall dignity.[74]

> Why are not the like comely gestures [bowing, etc.] used at the Altar of the Font, when the Sacrament of Baptisme is administered? Is not Baptisme as comely a Ceremony, because so many legs, and curches [curtsies], no not one at all is made to the Font.[75]

Given the resurgent clericalism within the Laudian polity and the potential of choral music to enforce this at service time, it is not perhaps surprising that levels of provision were, apparently, increased. The prestige of music-making would also have been enhanced by the participation of a number of clergy, including William Smith and Cosin himself. Smart, conversely, saw this activity as a lowering of the clerical estate:

> And still he [Cosin] aspireth, and climeth higher, never thinking himself sufficiently rewarded for his great learning, and service of God, in sitting at Church three times a day, to heare men pipe, and chaunt, and chaunt himselfe where he listeth . . . St Paul saith, *I*

> *was not sent to baptise,* (much lesse to sing in a quire) *but to preach. And woe to me,* saith he, *if I preach not the Gospell:* he saith not, *woe to me, if I observe not the canonicall houres of devotion in singing.*[76]

Music also contributed significantly to the creation of an atmosphere of mystery surrounding the sacraments which was encouraged by Laudian thought, the stylized ritual having its musical equivalent in elaborate polyphony. It was perhaps music's power to inspire a sense of divine mystery in the common people which led to the support given to its practitioners by the Laudians during their period in power; and, while Cosin's only comment on the aesthetics of music in church apply to the chanting of prayers, they could be said to sum up the reasons why he was in favour of extending the role of polyphonic music within the liturgy at Durham:

> . . . this is the reason that in places where they sing, all our prayers are sung in a plain and audible tone. Reading hath not the force to affect and stir up the spirit, which a grave manner of singing has; and singing, if it be not tempered with that gravity, which becomes the servants of God in the presence of his holy angels, is fuller of danger than edification.[77]

The musical manuscripts surviving at Durham are, as much as is possible with working documents, a reflection of the period of Laudian dominance at the Cathedral. They have been used here to assess some of Peter Smart's Articles against John Cosin, and it is hoped that this paper has shown the value of approaching them from the point of view of the mainstream historian. Clearly the expense of copying and the fact that some are intended for everyday use has an impact on the appearance of musical sources; yet the liturgical - and, by inference the theological - preoccupations of each age are reflected in them in some way or other. Musical manuscripts (where their provenance and date can be ascertained) can represent, therefore, a valuable source of evidence on those aspects of liturgical practice which have otherwise disappeared.

NOTES

1. The principal texts of this controversy are: N. Tyacke, 'Puritanism, Anglicanism and Counter-Revolution', in *The Origins of the English Civil War*, edited by C. Russell (1973); and N. Tyacke, *Anti-Calvinists: the Rise of English Arminianism c. 1590-1640* (1987); P. White, 'The Rise of Arminianism Reconsidered', in *Past and Present*, 101 (1983); W. Lamont, 'Comment: The Rise of Arminianism Reconsidered', in *Past and Present*, 107 (1985); P. Lake, 'Calvinism and the English Church 1570-1635', in *Past and Present*, 114 (1987); Tyacke and White locked horns in: 'Debate: The Rise of Arminianism Reconsidered', in *Past and Present*, 115 (1987). It should be clear from this paper that, on the whole, the present author finds Tyacke's interpretation of the role of religion in the decades before the Civil War the more convincing. The term 'Laudian' is used throughout to describe the programme of liturgical and ceremonial ideas conceived by a group of English divines in part from the doctrines of Arminius. Whether or not it is correct to devote the name of this set of policies to William Laud, is less important in the context of this discussion, than the view that the ideas were indeed a package, and had intimate connections with Arminian theology. For these connections, see the conclusion to Tyacke's *Anti-Calvinists*, 245-47, and A. Foster, 'The Church Policies of the 1630s', in *Conflict in Early Stuart England*, edited by R. Cust and A. Hughes (1989), 210-17.

2. Jacobus Arminius, *Writings*, translated by J. Nichols and W.R. Bagnall (Grand Rapids, 1956).

3. For the connections between theology and liturgy in the outlooks of Laud, Wren, Cosin and others, see H. Davies, *Worship and Theology in England 1603-90* (Princeton, 1975) and *The Durham* Book, edited by. G.J. Cuming (1961); see also note 1 above.

4. Peter Smart, *A Sermon preached in the Cathedrall Church of Durham, July 7, 1628* (Edinburgh, 1628); *A Short Treatise of Altars, Altar-furniture, Altar-cringing, and Musicke of all the Quire* (1629); *A Briefe, but True Historicall Narration of some*

Notorious Acts and Speeches of Mr. John Cosin (1641); *A Catalogue of Superstitious Innovations* (1642); *Canterburies Crueltie* (1643); *Cantus Epithalamicus* (1643).

5. For example, K. Sharpe, *The Personal Rule of Charles I* (1992), 376-77; N. Tyacke, *Anti-Calvinists* (1987), 109-110, 116-19.

6. Reprinted in *'The Acts of the High Commission Court within the Diocese of Durham'*, edited by W.H.D. Longstaffe, Surtees Society, 34 (1858), Appendix A, 197-250.

7. See note 6, 243, note c.

8. See note 6, 215.

9. Durham, Dean and Chapter Library, MSS A1-3, 5-6; C2, 3-11, 14, 16, 18; E4-11a. In addition there is the Dunnington-Jefferson part-book (York Minster Library, MS M29 S and referred to hereafter as DJ).

10. Durham University Library Special Collections, Durham Cathedral Post-Dissolution Muniments: Miscellaneous Charter 7116.

11. Durham, Dean and Chapter Library, MSS E4-11a.

12. See note 11, MSS C8 and 18.

13. See note 11, MSS C4, 5, 6, 7, 9 and 10.

14. Durham, Dean and Chapter Library, MSS C2, 3, 7, 14. MSS C11 and 16, and DJ are organised in a very similar way to these books.

15. If so, John Cosin was a bass! See W.K. Ford, 'An English Liturgical Part-book of the Seventeenth Century', *Journal of the American Musicological Society*, 12 (1959).

16. See note 11, MSS A1, 2, 3, 5 and 6.

17. One of the sets of service books was replaced by order of the Chapter in June 1629. Durham University Library Special Collections, Durham Cathedral Post-Dissolution Muniments, Chapter Act Books, II, *f.*80*r*.

18. See note 6, 217, J. Cosin, Answer 1 in 1640.

19. Brian Crosby, 'Durham Cathedral's Liturgical Manuscripts *c.*1620-*c.*1640', *Durham University Journal*, New Series, 35 (1973-4); and *A Catalogue of Durham Cathedral Music Manuscripts* (1986).

20. Part-books containing the *Great Service* are also in the libraries of York Minster, Pembroke College and Peterhouse, Cambridge.

21. Dr Crosby's research has uncovered several other dimensions to the musical scene at Durham Cathedral in these years, including the use of cornetts and sackbuts to augment the choral sound.

22. See note 14.

23. For example, *The First Book of Select Church Musicke*, edited by J. Barnard (1641).

24. The index to Dunnington-Jefferson MS, York Minster Library, MS 29 S, uses these descriptions explicitly.

25. Hugh Trevor-Roper, *Anglicans, Catholics and Puritans* (1987), Chapter 2.

26. The standard text on the impact of religious trends on church music remains Peter Le Huray, *Music and the Reformation in England,* second edition (1978).

27. *1559 Injunctions*, reprinted in *Visitation Articles and Injunctions of the Period of the Reformation*, edited by W.H. Frere and W.P.M. Kennedy, Alcuin Club Collections, 14-16 (1910-).

28. British Library, MS Royal 18, B XIX.

29. Much important evidence on this case is to be found in the letters between Cosin, Laud, Howson and Duncon in *The Correspondence of John Cosin*, edited by G. Ornsby, Surtees Society, 52 (1868), 200-10.

30. Peter Smart, *A Short Treatise*, 8, section 9.

31. Peter Smart, *A Sermon preached, 19-20.*

32. See note 30, 7, section 8.

33. See note 6, *The Acts of the High Commission Court*, 224-25, Answer 6 to Smart's Articles of 1640. Cosin's concern to make the anthem texts known to the congregation is seen in the annotations in some of the part-books describing the derivations of the texts.

34. This is established by the Byrd anthem with the original title, *O Lord, make thy servant, Elizabeth* being amended for use in the reign of King Charles. See also note 63.

35. Durham, Dean and Chapter Library, MSS C4, 5, 6, 9 and 10.

36. Only one of William Smith's seven anthems, and none of Henry Palmer's eight, are settings of metrical texts.

37. See note 29, 200-1. One of the interesting features to emerge from this letter is the role music was felt to play in the distinction between cathedral and parish churches, which was emphasised in other areas of Laudian policy.

38. See note 33, 225, note c.

39. Peter Smart, *A Briefe, but True Historicall Narration*, section 9.

40. Of Byrd's seventeen English anthems, only *Prevent us, O Lord* is a collect; less than ten per cent of Tomkins' much larger anthem output falls into this category.

41. Examples include: Easter Day (four anthems), Ascension (four), Whitsun (three), King's Day (seven).

42. 'Testimony of Richard Hutchinson', reproduced in *Hierurgia Anglicana* . . . revised and considerably enlarged by V. Staley, new edition, 3 vols (London, 1902-4), III, Part II (1903).

43. See note 39, section 8.

44. Peter Smart, *A Short Treatise*, 18, section 19.

45. York Minster Library, Dunnington-Jefferson MS 29 S, *f*.338, 339.

46. See note 45.

47. See note 42, 227.

48. *The Durham Book*, edited by G.J. Cuming (1961), 175-76, 291.

49. The manuscripts which contain settings of both *Gloria* and *Sanctus* almost all have intimate connections with Laudian institutions such as the Chapel Royal, Ely Cathedral, and at Cambridge, Pembroke College and Peterhouse.

50. R.T. Daniel and P. Le Huray, *The Sources of English Church Music* (1972).

51. Durham, Dean and Chapter Library, MSS A3, *f. 10-11;* C4, *f.* 92; C5, *f.* 92; C7, *f* 314; C10, *f.* 86.

52. Durham, Dean and Chapter Library, MS A1, *f*.78-80.

53. The restoration of the sung *Agnus* is, unsurprisingly, another of Cosin's recommendations in *The Durham Book*, 176.

54. Peter Smart, *A Short Treatise*, 8, section 9.

55. Peter Smart, *A Briefe, but True Historicall Narration*, section 7.

56. See note 54, 5-6, section 7.

57. See note 33, 220-1, Answer 3 to Smart's Articles of 1640.

58. See note 42, 226, Third Article, 'The Answer and Examination of Nicholas Hobson, singing-man of the Cathedral Church of Durham, aged about 92 years'.

59. The testimony of Richard Hutchinson gives the details of the bipartite morning service. It is also interesting to note in this connection that no fewer than six settings of the Litany were copied into the part-books for Peterhouse, some of them apparently commissioned for Cosin. See note 50, 163.

60. See note 55, section 4.

61. See note 6, 'Letter to Sir Martin Stuteville', 1628, 197-8.

62. There are also two settings of the Easter anthem *Christ rising,* by Byrd and Juxon, along with the two versions of *Turn thou us, O Good Lord,* by Batten and John Tomkins.

63. Byrd's anthem *O Lord, make thy servant, Elizabeth our Queen* (amended to *O Lord, make thy servant, our sovereign King Charles* in later sources) is a rare exception, being one of the most popular works of the period. See also note 34.

64. Peter Smart, *A Sermon*, 32-33.

65. Brian Crosby, *A Catalogue of Durham Cathedral Music Manuscripts* (1986), 245.

66. N. Tyacke, *Anti-Calvinists* (1987), Chapter 2.

67. *The Durham Book*, edited by G.J. Cuming, Introduction.

68. See note 42.

69. See note 55, section 1.

70. See note 67.

71. See note 61, 198. During his Durham years, Cosin seems to have been the dominant partner in his relations with Neile: 'A great part, if not most of the evil of our church, at this present, is supposed to proceed from him [Cosin], and those he wholy ruleth, as my Lord of Durham, who admireth him'. From a letter written in 1628 by Dr Joseph Mead of Christ's College, Cambridge.

72. S. Doran, and C. Durston, *Princes, Pastors and People* (1991), especially Chapters 2 and 3.

73. A. Foster, 'The Church Policies of the 1630s' in *Conflict in Early Stuart England*, edited by R. Cust and A. Hughes, (1989), 214.

74. Peter Smart, *A Sermon*, 17.

75. Peter Smart, *A Short Treatise*, 12, section 14.

76. See note 74, 21.

77. *The Works of John Cosin*, edited by J. Barrow, Library of Anglo-Catholic Theology (Oxford, 1843-55), V, 54.

VII

John Cosin and Music

Brian Crosby

What can be said about John Cosin and Music? In terms of personal involvement, very little. There is no evidence that he composed anything or that he played a musical instrument. There is no evidence either that he had a particular ability as a singer, though in the arrangment of the table of contents to the Dunnington-Jefferson MS there is a pointer to him having a bass voice.[1] Even the phrase, 'John Cosin, Patron of Music', used in the literature relating to this Conference, is misleading. Normally such a description is used of those of noble families who provided a base and finance for budding musicians. Although one musician associated with Cosin did go on to enjoy a limited fame,[2] the individual singers and instrumentalists he made use of were possibly of only tertiary importance to him. Even music itself was but a means to an end, for Cosin would have readily concurred with the assessment, made at Durham in June 1390, of the part which music could play:

> . . . let both musical harmony and [ceremonial] be had in the choir as much as for [enhancing] the dignity of divine worship [as for] inspiring the devotion of the people . . .[3]

Music and ceremonial may have been in favour at Durham in monastic times, but since the 1560s worship at the Cathedral had been under the control of those of reforming Genevan persuasion, and, consequently, devoid of any trappings.

Some idea of what worship was like then is conveyed by William Whittingham, Dean of Durham from 1563 to 1579. Whittingham was a writer of hymns and co-translator of the Geneva Bible. In a letter to Cecil, the Queen's Secretary, in

December 1563, he described the ordering of worship at Durham in these terms:

> First in the morning at six of the clock, the grammar school and song schole, with all the servants of the house, resort to prayers into the church; which exercise continueth about half-an-houre. At nyne of the clock we have our ordinary service; and likewise at thre after none. The Wednesdays and Fridays are appointed to a general fast, with prayers and preaching of God's word. The Sundaies and holydays before none we have sermons and at after none the catechisme is expounded.[4]

But it was not all prayers and metrical psalms, for, reformer though he was, Whittingham did value the contribution that music could make, and

> was very carefull to provide the best songs and anthems that could be got out of the Queen's chapell to furnish the quire with all, himselfe being skillfull in musick.[5]

It was into this setting that John Cosin came in 1619, first as chaplain to Richard Neile, Bishop of Durham. He was then aged twenty-four. Five years later, on 4 December 1624, he was appointed Prebendary of the tenth stall.

By 1628 the innovations introduced into worship at Durham had so incensed and exasperated Peter Smart, the dour Senior Prebendary, that on 27 July he publicly gave vent from the pulpit, preaching on the text, 'I have hated them that hold of superstitious vanities'.[6] This outburst, and his refusal to retract what he had said, led to his expulsion, degradation from Holy Orders, and imprisonment, though in the end he was vindicated, and Cosin impeached.[7]

An element of discretion prevailed in the sermon in that Smart named no names, though the reference there to 'our young Apollo' clearly pointed to Cosin.[8] In *A Short Treatise of Altars* . . . (1629) Smart did go further, naming as the targets of his displeasure Bishop Neile and his chaplains Cosin, Augustine Lindsell, Francis Burgoine, Eleazar Duncon, and [Ferdinand]

Moorcroft.[9] Not only Cosin but all the other chaplains were Smart's fellow prebendaries. Again, in one of his private notebooks, Smart has this to say:

> If the house of God were ever made a theatricall stage for the people to heare and see playes acted therin, the Cath: church of Durha~ is such an one at this tyme, especially when the sacraments are admynistred, w[ch] if St Jerome were now alyve to heare and see, when Mr. Burgoyne, Mr. Cosyn, Smyth, and Leonards in theire Babalonish and pybald vestments are the Actors with theyr glittryng picturs, and histronicall gestures, with all the confused voyces of the singing-men and quoristers with a multitude of melodious instruments, no doubt but Jerome would say, that the wicked spiritt cast out of Saule is entred into Cosyn and his fellow-singers, pipers, *tobacconists and drunkards* [*sic*] . . . [The words in italics are crossed out in the manuscript.][10]

Where this extract ranges over what Smart considered to be the beguiling accretions of worship, the sermon and his other writings, including the charges laid before Parliament, are more expansive about particular aspects. Referred to again and again, and regarded as dangerous as the music of the Sirens in diverting the earthly traveller from his goal, is the part played by music in the services. Typical of such references are three taken from the sermon and one from *A Short Treatise of Altars* . . .

> 7: Seventhly, he hath divided the Morning Service into two parts, the 6, of clocke Service, which used to bee read onely and not sung: hee chaunts with Organs, Shackbuts and Cornets which yield an hydeous noyse, and makes that Service, which as scarce one quarter of an houre long before, one houre and an halfe at least: and this hee calls Mattens. The second Service at 10, of the clocke hee calls Masse, which consists of Epistles and Gospels, the 10 Commandments, and the Nicene Creed, which are only to be read on Sondayes and Holydayes, by the order of the Common Prayer Booke.[11]
>
> 8: Eightly, hee enjoynes all the people to stand up at the Nicene Creed . . . which he commands to bee sung with Organs,

> Shackbuts, and Cornets, and all other instruments of Musicke, which were used at the Consecration of NABVCHADONOZERS golden Image, (unfit Instruments for Christian Churches where men come for to pray, and not for to chaunt, or heare a sound or consort of they know not what) . . .[12]
>
> 9. Ninthly, hee hath turned most of the Service into Piping, and singing, so that the people understand it not no more then they doe Greeke or Hebrew: . . . Hee will not suffer so much as the holy Communion to be administered without an hydeous noyse of vocall and instrumentall Musicke (the tunes whereof are all taken out of the Masse-booke:) . . .[13]
>
> 11. Neither rest they contented with the horrible prophanitation of the Lords Supper, with immoderate chaunting, and Organ-playing, and with other superstitious vanities; but the Sacrament of Baptisme also, they will not suffer it to be administred, without an heideous noise of musick, both of voyces and instruments . . . In the meane time [on 7 September 1628] while one of the Prebendaries baptized the child, which is a principall part of Divine [Evening] Service,[14] two Prebendaries remaining in the Quire, commanded the Organist to play, and the Quire-men, and boyes to sing the rest of the Service, at the same instant that the Sacrament was administered, with such a noise, that they could not heare one another at the Font . . .[15]

Although the manner in which Smart made his original attack cannot be condoned, and although how one reacts to Smart's point of view will depend upon one's own churchmanship, yet the scene he depicted was accurately portrayed.

The installation of the new organ to which Smart refers was on 15 November 1621 described as 'lately begunne'. Its cost, alleged by Smart to be 'at least 700li',[16] was met not by Chapter but by Dean Hunt. Chapter, however, on 16 March 1621/2, did grant the Dean the lease of Bywell St Peter for twenty-one years so that its revenue could be offset against 'buyledinge the newe organe at my onley charge'. Just over two months later, on 27 May, the Bishop was granted 'one of ye lesser Organes in the Church and he to make choice of the said organe'.[17] Richard Hutchinson, adjudged in the 1690s by Mickleton - or rather by the sources he relied on - to be a brilliant organist, responded to the challenge offered by the new instrument, so much so that added to those remunerated in the Treasurer's books was 'a boy at the hand of the organist'. A Chapter Minute for 3 April 1627 makes it clear that this youth was responsible for 'turninge over the orgaine booke, upon Mr Hutchinson playeth on the orgaines'.[18]

Until a few years ago it was supposed that the role of the cornetts and sackbuts was to double the treble and bass parts played by the organ. It is now appreciated that this would have resulted in a bare hollow sound, and suggested that the cornetts played the treble and counter-tenor parts, and the sackbuts, the tenor and bass.[19] This is particularly thought to apply to the verse anthems of the period, where the four-part texture of the accompaniment of the solo sections seems hardly to have been written with just the organ in mind.

That there were cornetts and sackbuts is confirmed by the Treasurer's books for 1632-3, 1633-4, and 1635-6: they pay George Barnfather and John Hawkins as cornett players, and Miles Atkinson and William Sherwin as sackbutters. In view of the wealth of information the books contain, the pity is that the period from September 1617 through to September 1632 is bereft of such records. The triennial Visitation schedules for 1618, 1621, 1624, 1627 and 1630 partially compensate for this by including the names of the singing members of the choir. However, they do not list the instrumentalists because they were not members of the foundation as constituted in 1541. The instrumentalists are further mentioned in a Chapter Minute of 22 November 1633. It enjoins their presence at all services, and states what fines absence would incur on weekdays and on Sundays. Moreover, Smart himself in one of his notebooks records that:

> John Watkins, one of the~ that had a stipend to play every day on a shak=but in the quire, kept a book of all the alterations wch day by day Mr : Cosin and his fellows made in Durha~ church.[20]

That Cosin approved of the instruments at this time is evident from Chapter's collective reply to the Articles of the 1665 Visitation. In the margin is the comment:

> the Bishop likes them very well having been established when he was a Prebendary heretofore.[21]

Elsewhere in his writings Smart does mention a wider variety of instruments, but his statement may be nothing more than an instance of hyperbole:

> 5: . . . especially the horrible profanation of both the sacraments with all manner of musick, both instrumentall, and vocall, so lowde that the Ministers could not be heard, what they said, . . . with fluits, and bag-pipes; with tymbrells and tabers . . .[22]

There are no references to viols in the Durham muniments, nor for that matter in any of the contemporary local parish registers, wills or inventories which have been examined. The Cathedral Register does record the burial on 12 April 1627 of Robert Greenwell, a lutenist, but there is nothing to associate him with the music of the Cathedral. When John Foster, Hutchinson's successor as master of the choristers and organist, died some fifty years later, in 1677, he had an organ, three virginals, a dulcimer, two bass viols, two violins, and a 'Cittraine'. The organ and the virginal apart,[23] however, there is no way of determining whether he had received instruction on any of those instruments whilst a chorister in the 1630s.

Smart's criticisms were not confined to the instruments of music. Also incurring his displeasure were the members of the choir and the nature of the music sung during services. In one of his notebooks he says about the former:

> As for some of our quire-men of Durham more notable drunkards then whom no Cath. church of England hath, they sitt night and day quaffyng and carousing in Alehouses and tavernes . . . Silly

> person among such, renowned John Cosyn delytess Is to be, with his tobacco-pipe, and to chant with them all day long, in comparison of whom he cares not for preachers, for he sayd before his Lord and many others, that he had rather goe 40 myles to a good service then 2 myles to a sermon.[24]

Such an account calls to mind the description of the vicar choral in *Microcosmographia*, published by John Earle in 1628.[25]

Smart's various attacks and charges reveal much about the music sung in the Cathedral. About it he says:

> Lastly, why forbid they the singing of Psalmes in such a tune [i.e., in metre],[26] as all the people may sing with them, and praise God together, before and after Sermons, as by authority is allowed, and heretofore hath been practised both here and in all reformed churches? How dare they, in stead of Psalmes, appoint Anthems (little better then prophane Ballads some of them) I say, so many Anthems to be sung, which none of the people understand, nor all the singers themselves . . .[27]

> 6: For prohibiting Psalms to be sung in metre, and procuring songs and anthems to be sung of the Three Kings of Cullen [Cologne] . . .[28]

> 9: He hath brought meere ballads and Jigs into the church, and commanded them to bee sung for Anthems: and, among many others, the three Kings of Colen [Cologne], IASPER, MELCHIOR, and BALTHASE . . . On the fast day after Easter last, he commanded the last prayer at the end of the Communion, to be sung with the Organes as an Anthem, so that no man could understand one word . . .[29]

For Smart then the singing of the Psalms in metre by all the people was more satisfying than the far from intelligible renderings by the choir. For him the Creed at Communion and the collects were parts of the service designed to be said and not offered up as anthems. As for what was a legitimate anthem, he had strong views about that too, feeling that its text should be drawn from the Bible, hence his objections to the 'Three Kings of Cologne'.[30]

Such was Smart's position. Cosin, for his part, in his defence claimed that:

> The singing of the metre psalms was never forbidden, by him or any other (that he knoweth) in that church, where he used daily to sing them himself (as in other places his custom is to do) with the people assembled at six o'clock morning prayer. But as to the singing of them before and after the sermon (which is always there preached in the quire) the use was long before him coming thither, and is so still afore the sermon to sing the Creed, (as the Book of Common Prayer by law doth appoint), and after the sermon to sing an anthem or hymn, which that the people might the better know what was at any time sung, was always publickly declared by one of the quire-men, out of which psalm (being many times a metre psalm) or other part of Scripture, or the Book of Common Prayer, the same was taken.[31]

As for the particular anthem mentioned by Smart, Cosin replied that:

> The anthem the Kings of Colen (as in the impeachment it is called) was never sung, since defendant came to be prebendary, nor (as he hath been informed) in the memory of man before, and it is not like to be sung hereafter, for at his first coming to be chosen treasurer (about 14 years ago) [i.e., *c.* 1627] he caused the said anthem to be razed and cut out of the old song book belonging to the quire, and the common school of the choristers, where it had remained all the time Mr Smart had been both schoolmaster and prebendary before. Defendant hath frequently shewed his dislike of singing any anthem which is not part of the Scriptures or a hymn publicly allowed by authority.[32]

In view of Cosin's alleged action, it is not surprising that that anthem is not to be found in any of the music manuscripts. All one can do is query whether its text might in any way have been related to the following six lines which are recorded in the private notebook of Elias Smith (minor canon, 1628-76):

Three kings unto the king of kings 3 gifts did bring
Myrrhe, incense, gold, as unto man god king
Three holy gyftts be like wise given by thee
To Christ, even such as acceptable bee.
For Myrrhe bring teares, for Frankincense impart
Submissive prayers, for pure gold a pure hart.[33]

On the page in question Smith states: 'These verses are extant in y[e] principall Church of y[e] citty of Collon', and he gives them in Latin as well as in English. Speculation that they may even be the text of the anthem is increased by the inclusion in the notebook of 'The Blessed lambe' (p.105), another non-Biblical anthem. Edmund Hooper's setting of this text as an anthem is still extant in the survivors of a set of Durham part-books dating from the 1630s.[34] That Smith was transcribing the text of this anthem and not just that of a religious poem is confirmed by the inclusion of the words 'vers' and 'cho:' at the appropriate points.[35]

Although no book survives from which the anthem 'Three Kings of Cologne' might have been cut, the Cathedral does hold one of the major collections of early seventeenth-century music manuscripts. Included in them are choral settings of some of the Psalms, of the Nicene Creed, and of many of the collects special to each Sunday and Feast Day of the church's year. All of these items, which were detested by Smart, adopted the popular contemporary Baroque format of extensive sections for solo voices, with short, often recapitulative, sections for the full choir. Conspicuous among the writers of these 'verse' anthems are Richard Hutchinson (the organist), John Geeres and Henry Palmer (lay clerks), and William Smith (minor canon).[36] Of these, Hutchinson stands apart, for he did not set any collects, and his anthems are of a personal contemplative nature. The other three, however, clearly responded to the impetus injected by Cosin, and William Smith particularly so. A former chorister and lay clerk, and an expert keyboard exponent,[37] Smith copied nearly all of his compositions onto the first forty-one pages of organ book MS A1. Even a cursory examination of the compositions there prompts the feeling that Smith's musical activities could well have been upmost in Smart's mind, for Kyries, Gospel Sentences and Creeds, Preces and Festal Psalms, and the most extreme of verse anthems with collects as their texts, are all there. Smith's second setting of the Nicene Creed must have been particularly offensive, for probably only the final 'Amen' was sung by all the choir.[38] But Cosin's defence is also true in the case of Smith's compositions, for the texts of all his anthems were drawn from either the Psalms, the metrical psalms, other parts of the Bible, or *The Book of Common Prayer*. In the case of Candlemas, the First Sunday in Lent, Ascension and the Conversion of St Paul, Smith made use of the collects for the day.

Cosin had also indicated earlier that Smart's statement about the musical content of services was exaggerated. In a letter dated 16 January 1630/1 and sent to Eleazar Duncon, a fellow Prebendary, Cosin and Lindsell stated that the Creeds and Anthem-psalms were not sung apart from on Sundays, and then not on every Sunday. Adding their names in support of this, were William James (another Prebendary), William Smith (described as Sacrist), and Richard Hutchinson (described as Organist).[39]

It has been mentioned that Durham has one of the major holdings of early seventeenth-century liturgical music manuscripts. In fact, five organ books and twenty-four part-books survive. Twenty of the part-books may be divided into five sets, the other four being composite volumes of anthems or services. Each set originally had ten members.[40] Eight books (MSS E4-E11) remain of the set of services designed to be used on the six major feast days of the church's year, one (MS C18) of the set of verse services, and one (MS C8) of the set of full services for general use. Six books (MSS C4, C5, C6, C7,[41] C9, and C10) survive of the set of books having full anthems and verse anthems for general use, and four (MSS C2, C3, C7,[42] and C14) of the set having verse anthems for all the feast days of the Anglican church's year. This last set also has a section of verse anthems for general use.

Three of the sets - those with anthems for special occasions, those with services for the six major feast days, and those with full services for general use - I have long regarded as being inspired by Cosin. This feeling partly stemmed from the statement at the end of the Minute for 2 June 1629 that the copyists

> shalbe rewarded and paid for there paines by the treasurers for the tyme being accordinge to that agreement wch Mr. Cosin shall make wth them for the same.[43]

Also lending support is the notation used in the sets. Where the slightly earlier set of anthems for general use and MS C18 employ round notation, the three sets in question abandon this in favour of the older square notation. In the case of MSS E4-E11, which measure an impressive 500 x 300mm, this may be seen as a deliberate attempt to imitate the manuscripts of the later monastic period. Indeed, a comparison with British Library Add. MS 30520, which includes a fragment of Durham Cantor Thomas Ashwell's *Missa Cuthberti*,[44] makes one wonder whether that manuscript is of Durham origin and, if so, whether it was still in Durham in the early seventeenth century.

The set of books with anthems special to the feast days groups in its last two sections anthems for the fifth of November and for the King's Day. Both of these were royal occasions, and included because the monarch was the head of the Anglican church. The former commemorated the deliverance of James I from the Gunpowder Plot, the latter the anniversary of the accession of Charles I. The anniversary of the accession of Elizabeth I and James I had, during their reigns, been marked by bell-ringing and bonfires, and during the reign of James I, the fifth of November was similarly remembered.

During the reign of Charles I the seeds of another tradition first took root. That was the tradition of the choir singing three anthems from the top of the Cathedral tower. It used to be supposed that this tradition originally commemorated the victory at the Battle of Neville's Cross, fought in 1346, but that after 1660 the date was changed to 29 May to commemorate the Restoration of Charles II. The attempt to validate the tradition found no shred of evidence to support any association with the Battle of Neville's Cross, but the commemoration of the Restoration was confirmed by muniments from at the latest 1672 - the records from 1660 until then are somewhat lacking in detail - through to 1969.[45] It also emerged from the three surviving Treasurer's books of the 1630s that the choir sang from the tower top on 5 November 1633, 25 March 1634, and 5 November 1634 but not in March or November 1636. These dates are significant, and point to Cosin being responsible for the custom, for the reason why the choir did not sing from the tower in 1636 may have been because by then Cosin had been rewarded with the Mastership of Peterhouse, and as a result the scene at Durham no longer had his undivided attention.

The set of books with anthems special to the feast days also bridges the gap between Durham and Peterhouse, for there is a further manuscript in the same hand and with the same anthems and more.[46] Known as the Dunnington-Jefferson MS (MS M29S) it is now in York Minster Library. The link is in the arrangement of the table of contents of the MS, for unlike the Durham books which group the anthems under the various days, it divides them according to their mood, and has sections headed 'Of Praise', 'Of Prier', and 'Penitentiall Anthems' [*sic*]. This conjunction of the Durham repertoire and the table headings of the Peterhouse music books leads one to suppose that the Dunnington-Jefferson MS was used by Cosin himself, and that as it contains the bass parts, Cosin was possessed of a bass voice.

The impact Cosin had on music at Peterhouse is many-stranded. In the first place, he took with him from Durham to be the college organist Thomas Wilson who had but lately ceased being a chorister at Durham. He also drew heavily on Durham's musical repertoire. That the indebtedness was this way round, and not the other, can be gathered from the fact that in the set of Peterhouse music books known as 'The Former Set' the handwriting of no fewer than eight adult members of the Durham choir has been detected.[47] In most instances they were responsible not for single pages but for corpora of considerable extent, whilst in a few cases Durham seems to have sent on, either in error or because the work had gone out of fashion, items no longer represented in the Durham books.[48] A further indication that it was Peterhouse borrowing from Durham, and not the other way round, may be drawn from the fact that none of nineteen items composed by Wilson at Peterhouse found its way back to Durham.

Unlike the Durham manuscripts those at Peterhouse include works in Latin. These include a *Te Deum* and *Jubilate* composed by William Child 'for the right worshipful Dr. Cosin', and the indications are that *In manus tuas* by John Geeres, lay clerk of Durham, was also written for the Peterhouse choir.

Such was the prominence given to music at Peterhouse that one of Cosin's critics suggested that it and not academic prowess was the key to entry to the College:

> Instead of Aristotle's *Organon*
> Anthems and organs did I study on . . .
> I cousen'd Dr. Cosin and ere long
> A Fellowship obtained for a song . . .[49]

In October 1660, after spending many years in France in exile with the royal household, Cosin was elected Bishop of Durham. In the years that followed he is said to have expended a considerable sum of his own money on repairs to his palaces at Auckland and Durham and to the Cathedral. One small item among this expenditure was the provision for the Cathedral in June/July 1661 of a little organ obtained by Cosin for eighty pounds from London. This was tuned for use by John Nicholls and James Smart, two of the lay clerks.[50] It was intended only as a temporary measure, its purpose to make it possible for choral worship quickly to be resumed. Nor was the organ the only instrument to be heard in the Cathedral, for by the time Cosin was enthroned on 2 December 1660, two unnamed boys had been found to play the cornetts.[51] As the cornetts had not been played at Dean Barwick's installation on 1 November 1660, and as four choristers progressed to the cornetts and sackbutts when their voices broke during the financial years 1663-64,[52] it is possible that the presence of the cornett players at Cosin's enthronement was to please him rather than a step in the re-establishment of the musical tradition.

Cosin also set about providing for the music in his chapel in Durham Castle and in that in his palace at Bishop Auckland.[53] Boys there certainly were in the Auckland choir, for Cosin's household account for 2 October 1665 includes the detail,

> for washing the 2 singing boys, 2s. 3d.[54]

and there are several references to 'George the singing-boy'; they tell of him being provided with a new suit and also with a hat.[55]

Whether the Auckland establishment boasted any men is not known. The entry for 15 September 1665,

> Pay^{d} M^{r}. Forster, organist for the 16^{en}. services he prickt for Awckland Chapel, 16s.[56]

offers no indication, neither does the payment on 22 December 1665 to Elias Smith, the Durham precentor,

for makeing and pricking of songbookes, £1. 8s. 8d.[57]

The household account for 15 September 1665 also has the entry,

> Pay^{d} him [M^{r}. Foster] and M^{r}. Nicholls for a journey for tuneing the organ at Awckland. 5s.[58]

John Foster was not Cosin's organist but the Master of the Choristers and Organist at Durham. John Nicholls, one of the Durham lay clerks, was evidently a useful and conscientious person - 'a diligent painfull man' is how Bishop Cosin described him.[59]

Nicholls and Foster are mentioned again on 16 October 1669 in a letter from William Flower, the Bishop's chaplain, to Miles Stapleton, the Bishop's secretary:

> speake to M^{r}. Nicholls and M^{r}. Foster, Organist of Durham, to see if they can prepare a boy to play well on the organ against my Lord comes down into the country . . .[60]

Whether the two musicians did not attend promptly to the matter, or whether there was a problem in communication, cannot be ascertained, but in another letter dated 22 February 1669/70 Cosin complained to Stapleton:

> Nor doe you tell me whether M^{r}. Nichols or M^{r}. Foster hath provided me a new organist boy since Francke ranne away . . .[61]

The reason why Nicholls is named first in these later entries is that since 1667 he had been master of the 'petty' school, an appointment which Bishop Cosin erroneously supposed was in his donation.[62] As for Frank, his identity emerges from Bishop Cosin's Household Book. In the London sections of the accounts it names Francis Forcer, a former Cathedral chorister (1661-65), as the Bishop's organist from 3 February 1665/6, when he received four pounds in respect of 'halfe a years wages ending at Christmas last' through to September 1667.[63] Although the book shows that salary payments were far from prompt,[64] it does reveal that Cosin was prepared to pay for his young organist's continuing musical education. On 21

September 1667 Forcer was given one pound 'to pay his M^{r}. [Master] M^{r}. Hinkston for a mo~. ending now'.[65] At the time John Hingeston, who had been a member of the York choir and private musician to Oliver Cromwell, was a member of the Chapel Royal musical establishment and a viol player of some distinction.[66] From this it may be concluded that Forcer, also known for his instrumental compositions, did not run away to London to seek his fame and fortune, but left Durham House, the Bishop's residence in London, without giving notice, for a position presumably affording better prospects. That position could well have been at Dulwich College, for he was elected Fourth Fellow or Organist there on 25 October 1669.[67]

An examination of the scene after 1660 might lead to the conclusion that much of Cosin's involvement was of necessity, that whoever had been Bishop would have had to attend to the same problems. To this it should be countered that some of Cosin's actions could only have been carried out by one who valued the contribution that music could make to worship, for how many other Bishops had choirs in their private chapels? Of the value of Cosin's contribution to music in the 1620s and 1630s, however, there can be no doubt. Without the changes he introduced into worship at Durham several sets of music books would never have come into being, and had it not been for him the Caroline part-books at Peterhouse would never have been produced. As all the surviving books at Durham and those at Peterhouse represent about a twelfth of the extant liturgical music manuscripts of the period 1560 to 1640, it can rightly be claimed that without John Cosin the heritage of English church music would be much poorer.

NOTES

DCD = Durham University Library, Durham Dean and Chapter Muniments.

DCL = Durham Dean and Chapter Library.

DUL = Durham University Library, Mickleton and Spearman MSS.

SS = Surtees Society.

"p." and "pp." have been omitted for printed books but used in the case of manuscripts.

1. A bass part-book, now in York Minster Library (MS M29S). Its contents are substantially the same as those of Durham Music MSS C2, C3, C7 (first fascicle), and C14, and it is in the same hand. See note 42.
2. Francis Forcer; see notes 61, 63, 65 and 67.
3. DCD, Locellus XXVII, no.35, dated 10 June 1390.
4. 'Life of Mr. William Whittingham', edited by M.A.E. Green, in Camden Society, *Miscellany VI*, 23, n.1 (taken from J. Strype, *Parker*, 3 vols (1821), I, 267-68).
5. See note 4, 22-23.
6. Psalm 31, v.7 (v.6 in modern psalters). Smart, a prebendary since 1609, had previously been headmaster of the grammar school (1597-1609).
7. It is surprising that the contemporary Act Book of the Dean and Chapter is devoid of any reference to the altercation.
8. Peter Smart, *A Sermon preached in the Cathedrall Church of Durham, July 7, 1628* (1628), 24.
9. Peter Smart, *A Short Treatise of Altars* . . . 1629 (1641), Preface [2, 8], and Bodleian Library, MS Rawlinson D.821, ff. 4, 5, 6, 108.

10. M.S. Rawlinson D.1364, *ff.* 8-9^{v}. Leonard and Smith were minor canons. Leonard had been brought from Windsor on account of the quality of his voice (see British Library Harleian MS 6853, f. 525). Smith, a chorister at Durham from 1613 to at least 1618, was active in the 1620s and 1630s as a composer. His Preces and Responses are still widely sung today.

11. *A Briefe, but True Historicall Narration*, DCL, I.VII.87.(2), p. [3]. (Other copies of the *Sermon* may not contain this addition which seems not to be by Smart himself.) Compare *The Acts of the High Commission Court within the Diocese of Durham*, edited by W.H.D. Longstaffe, SS, 34 (1858), 220.

12. DCL, I.VII.87.(2), p. [4]; compare *A Sermon*, 19, and *The Correspondence of John Cosin*, edited by G. Ornsby, SS, 52, 55 (1869,1872), I, 183, Item 16.

13. DCL, I.VII.87.(2), p. [4].

14. It took place after the second Lesson. See *The Correspondence of John Cosin*, I, 182, Item 15.

15. *A Short Treatise*, 9.

16. The Correspondence of John Cosin, I, 167, Item 9.

17. For the three references to the organs see DCD, Act Book 2, *ff.*10, 17^{v} and 23.

18. See note 17, *f.* 49^{v}.

19. For more about these instruments see notes 51 and 52.

20. M.S. Rawlinson D.821, *f.* 98^{v}.

21. DCL, Hunter MS 11, gathering 83.

22. See note 16, I, 165.

23. These instruments are mentioned in the Minute (DCD, Act Book 2, *ff.* 86-87) which deals with Hutchinson's partial deprivement in May 1627.

24. M.S. Rawlinson D.1364, *ff.* 8-9^{v}; compare *The Correspondence of John Cosin*, I, 185, Item 17.

25. The Dean and Chapter Library has a manuscript copy, Hunter MS 130, dated *c.* 1636. It gives the date of the work as 14 December 1627.

26. The bracketed insertion is Smart's.

27. *A Sermon*, 19-20; compare *The Correspondence of John Cosin*, I, 183-84, Item 16, and 166, Item 8.

28. *The Acts of the High Commission Court*, 224, Article 6 sent from the Commons to the Lords in 1641.

29. *A Briefe, but True Historicall Narration*, DCL, I.VII.87.(2), p. [4], section 9.

30. There was a tradition that the Wise Men set out from Cologne in their search for the infant Jesus. According to *A Description or Briefe Declaration of all the Ancient Monuments, Rites, and Customs belonging to, or being within, the Monastical Church of Durham, before the Suppression* (known as *Rites*), edited by J.T. Fowler, Surtees Society, 107 (1903), 47, the scene was depicted in monastic times in the central light of a window in the west wall of the Galilee chapel.

31. *The Acts of the High Commission Court*, 225-26, Cosin's reply to Article 6 before Parliament in 1641.

32. See note31.

33. DCL, Hunter MS 125, p.133.

34. DCL, MSS C2, C3, C7 (first fascicle), and C14.

35. This has been checked against DCL, MS C1, pp.104-6, a Medius (= treble) part-book.

36. Elias Smith has been disregarded as he was not sworn as a minor canon until about a week after Smart's *Sermon*. His solitary anthem, 'How is the gold become dim', was inspired by the execution of Charles I and consequently does not belong to this period.

37. DUL, MS 32, *f.* 52.

38. DCL, MSS A1, pp. 6-9; C8, pp. 192-93; C13^{v}, p. 89 and E11 A, p. 336.

39. *The Correspondence of John Cosin*, I, 200-2.

40. DCD, Miscellaneous Charters 7116-17.

41. DCL, MS C7, second fascicle.

42. DCL, MS C7, first fascicle.

43. DCD, Act Book 2, *f.* 80^r.

44. Ashwell was Cantor from 1513 to at least 1525.

45. There were, of course, minor breaks. In 1969 the date was changed to the Sunday nearest to 29 May, and in 1986 to Ascension Day.

46. That a few anthems are missing is a pointer to their being added at Durham after Cosin had gone to Peterhouse.

47. Minor canons John Todd (died 1631), William Smith, Elias Smith, and James Green; and lay clerks Henry Palmer, Toby Brooking, John Geeres, and probably John Gaydon.

48. A few of these items, however, may have been in the set of books of anthems and services for men's voices, a set still in use in 1665 but of which no member has survived.

49. Peter Le Huray, *Music and the Reformation of England 1549-1660* (1967), 50, quoting Dom A. Hughes, *Catalogue of the Musical Manuscripts at Peterhouse, Cambridge* (1953).

50. The purchase and tuning of the little organ is referred to in *Rites*, 163-64.

51. For the information about the cornettists, and the build-up of the choir after 1660, See DCL, Hunter MS 125, pp. 221, 223, 225, 232-33.

52. Robert Arrundell (buried 23 March 1695/6) and Matthew Ridley (buried 30 December 1697) (cornetts), John Wilkinson and Alexander Shaw (sackbuts). The latter two were replaced some time between September 1672 and September 1673, the former two continued until their deaths.

53. *The Correspondence of John Cosin*, II, 334-35 (Durham), 332 and 338 (Auckland).

54. See note 53, 333.

55. DCL, Sharp MS 163, p. 21.

56. See note 53, 332.

57. DCL, Sharp MS 163, p. 34 as in *The Correspondence of John Cosin*, II, 337.

58. See note 53, 332.

59. See note 53, 203.

60. See note 53, xxxvi.

61. See note 53, 232.

62. He clearly was not aware of DCD, 3.3. Pont. 10, the deed whereby Bishop Cuthbert Tunstal handed over to the newly-founded Dean and Chapter the entire running of the chantry schools founded by Thomas Langley in 1414. The deed is dated 31 May 1541, just nineteen days after the re-foundation of the Cathedral.

63. DCD, Treasurer's account books, pp. 44, 133.

64. See note 63, pp. 70, 150.

65. See note 63, p. 133.

66. *The New Grove Dictionary of Music and Musicians*, edited by S. Sadie (1980), VIII, 588-89.

67. I am grateful to Robert Ford for this information. By 1684 Forcer seems to have teamed up with Sadler. From 1697 to 1699, with James Miles, he leased Sadler's Wells, then a pleasure garden and spa in Islington (*The New Grove Dictionary*, VI, 704).

VIII

Some Aspects of Church Furnishings in Cosin's Time

Pat Mussett

Buildings and furnishings by Cosin and his associates survive in at least fourteen places. This paper discusses only the church furnishings, and not all of those, because they survive to a greater or lesser extent at Bishop Auckland, Brancepeth, Durham Cathedral, Easington, Egglescliffe, Elwick, Haughton-le-Skerne, Ryton, Sedgefield, Kirk Merrington, Aycliffe and St Helen Auckland, with strays on Farne and at Norham. There used to be similar furnishings at Bishop-wearmouth, and at St Mary's Gateshead, until it became the custom of vandals to set fire to that church every few years.[1]

It is worthwhile reminding ourselves of the liturgical context of the church furnishings commissioned by Cosin and his associates. In pre-Reformation England the ordinary postures for the laity in church were standing or kneeling. Many parish churches had almost no seating in the nave; and no medieval nave seating seems to have survived in County Durham. Pulpits, although they had become much more common in the fifteenth and early sixteenth centuries, were not universal; sermons were not rare but they were not very long.[2]

Reformed worship made for less frequent celebration of the Eucharist, which was monthly in most English cathedrals; the norm for most parish churches eventually became about four times a year, with more frequent and longer sermons. Consequently, pulpits and seats for the congregation became highly desirable.

In 1566 Archbishop Parker ordered all choir screens to be retained, but the rood lofts above, with their crucifix and attendant figures of St Mary and St John, to be removed. The Ten Commandments were to be put up on the east wall of the chancel. The Communion Table was to be placed against the east wall when not in use but moved westwards (into the nave if necessary) for celebrations of Holy Communion. A seat for the minister to read the service (when there was no celebration) was to be set where he could best be heard, just outside the chancel or further west if more suitable. So the church remained divided in two, as in the middle ages; instead of one area for the laity and one for the clergy, the normal arrangement was that the chancel was used for the Communion service (when all communicants moved there, while non-communicants departed) leaving the rest of the church for other services.[3]

Canon 82 of 1604 ordered the Communion Table to be located in either nave or chancel, so as to allow the minister to be heard and to let sizeable groups of people approach for communion. The Canon, in fact, accepted the practice of placing the Table east-west in the middle of the chancel, and it did not forbid putting seats around it. The same Canon ordered the Ten Commandments to be displayed at the east end of the church, and Cosin's *Visitation Articles* of 1662 ask whether the Commandments and other sentences of Scripture are well placed.[4] It is noticeable that nowadays we do not find, in most of the 'Cosinesque' churches that I have seen recently, Brancepeth being the exception, any trace of the Commandments being displayed. This is one reminder that even where we find a great deal of seventeenth-century furniture preserved, as at Brancepeth and Sedgefield, this is no guarantee that all is exactly as it was originally.

From 1620 or so Anglicans began to quarrel about the location of the Communion Table. To have it in the middle of the chancel made it easy to receive Holy Communion in a sitting position, as Calvinists did, instead of kneeling as *The Book of Common Prayer* prescribed. Most bishops disliked seated Communion, and they could see that to have a celebration with the Table against the east wall made seated Communion difficult while protection of the Table against irreverent use was easier. Choir screens seem to have remained, or to have been replaced if necessary, until *c*.1700. The latest 'Cosin-esque' screen is probably the one at Kirk Merrington where, in 1682 John Sudbury, Dean of Durham, paid Thomas Browne for one hundred and three yards of wainscot in the chancel, for side and end seats, for the rails above the step and Table, and for the screen.[5]

Canon 82 specified a seat in which the minister was to read the service. George Herbert gave the church of Leighton Bromswold (which was attached to the Lincoln prebend he held from 1626) a matching pulpit and reading desk, to left and right of the chancel arch, 'like early Christian ambos'.[6] At Croscombe, Somerset, a re-furnishing of 1616 produced matching desks left and right in front of the choir screen, plus a pulpit one bay to the west on the north side. St Mary-le-Bow, Durham, was given matching desks at some point in the seventeenth century. The earliest dated three-decker pulpit is at Kedlington, and is of 1619.[7] Three-deckers, the great English invention in liturgical furnishing, sometimes incorporate existing pulpits, as does the seventeenth-century example at Salle, Norfolk.

The commonest arrangement for an English parish church before 1700, quite irrespective of whether or not Cosin and his associates had anything to do with the place, was the pulpit and reading desk at the east end of the nave, with the font at the west end of the nave or of the north or south aisle. The screen was kept in place and the chancel left empty except for the Holy Table against the east wall, and a few seats at its west end.[8] Although a minority of churches had the pulpit and reading desk roughly half-way down the nave, it may be that rather more had this arrangement than we imagine. The seventeenth-century seating plans preserved at Brancepeth and Sedgefield show the pulpit and reading desk against piers of the nave arcades one or two bays west from the screen and not, as they are now, at the extreme east end of the nave.

The standard 'Cosinesque' layout in a parish church, therefore, includes a choir screen with almost-identical square pulpit and reading desk just west of its north and south ends, the font at the west end of the nave, perhaps with a canopy, the Holy Table against the east wall of the chancel, a reredos, Communion rails, and stalls on either side of the chancel in college-chapel or monastic-choir fashion. Sometimes the ensemble includes nave benches, and in some places a chancel ceiling. At the present day the parish churches of Sedgefield, Brancepeth, Ryton and Haughton-le-Skerne all preserve much of this plan. Addleshaw and Etchells are quite sure that the chancel stalls at Brancepeth are primarily for communicants.[9] At Brancepeth, the flat chancel ceiling is decorated as a tester or canopy and panelled in squares arranged diagonally with bosses or angels at the junctions. Over the sanctuary, angels bear shields with inscriptions praising God.[10] Similar treatment was given to the ceiling above the sanctuary at both Sedgefield and Haughton-le-Skerne, but neither has survived.

Both the elaborate ceiling and the Communion rails help to make the sanctuary visually distinct and important, while the use of a screen with doors emphasises the specially sacred nature of the chancel, besides providing greater protection for the sanctuary. The Brancepeth screen has a pair of carved wooden doors set beneath the elaborate pinnacle work of the chancel screen.[11]

A reredos, tapestry, or coloured window could add to the visual impact and symbolism associated with the Holy Table. Sedgefield, Haughton-le-Skerne and Brancepeth each have a reredos; and in Auckland Castle chapel, in Cosin's time, a tapestry depicting Solomon's meeting with the Queen of Sheba served the same purpose. This motif was a familiar one: Solomon's generous display to her of his wealth and wisdom on the occasion of her visit was regarded as a type (or symbolic foreshadowing) of Christ's mission to the Gentiles. The Brancepeth reredos is made up of re-used fifteenth-sixteenth-century carved panels from Durham Cathedral.

Sedgefield is a particularly spectacular and difficult 'Cosinesque' church. The screen is thicker and more three-dimensional than even that of Brancepeth: the pinnacles are very plump octagons. The polygonal uprights at either side of the doors have a pattern of incised lozenges similar to those on the Romanesque piers of Durham Cathedral, while Brancepeth has a chevron pattern in the same area. The Sedgefield screen has doors, which can be locked only from the western side. The solid lower part of this screen is so high that it was difficult for anyone in the nave to see into the chancel without standing. This problem is now solved by the simple (though hardly cheap) expedient of setting the whole nave area two steps higher, so that anyone walking westwards out of the chancel descends one step at the choir screen and then ascends two full steps from the crossing into the nave (Sedgefield has transepts). This makes it a difficult and dangerous church in which to conduct a marriage service. These steps are modern; in the church is a painting (which is probably of the early nineteenth century) showing the crossing without them. If the nave is intended to be used for Morning and Evening Prayer and the chancel for Communion services then a visual separation between the two areas may have been immaterial when it was planned. Perhaps, therefore, it did not matter that it was hard to see through the choir screen.

The organ at Sedgefield is now on the north side of the choir, but it used to be in a western gallery. The chancel has seats for twenty-eight, with flat roofs to the stalls to keep off the draughts. At each side of the chancel just west of the screen there are box pews. One on the south side was originally a churching pew, and another on the north was reserved for the parson's wife.

Sedgefield has lost its seventeenth-century pulpit and reading desk. It is interesting that they may not have been a matching pair and they seem not to have been placed just west of the choir screen. In the church is a pew plan of 1669, which shows the reading desk against the north-east pier of the nave and the pulpit against the south-east pier. The pulpit is shown as having steps on its east side, while the reading desk has none. From documentary evidence, the Sedgefield woodwork seems to date from the late 1630s and so could conceivably have been moved and altered by 1669, yet this was only one year after the death of Joseph Naylor, who was rector of Sedgefield when the 'Cosinesque' woodwork was put in.

The Durham Cathedral woodwork also presents problems. The font canopy is magnificent, but the bird at its lofty summit is rather a dull creature, and it seems odd to emphasise the font so strongly in a Cathedral. Ely Cathedral had a font, of the late seventeenth century and generally similar in style to that of Durham, but without an imposing canopy. (This font has been removed and is now in a parish church a few miles away.) Moreover, a long look at the Durham font canopy suggests to me that its top and bottom date from the seventeenth century while the middle is medieval. The choir stalls and the screens between choir and aisles are of a splendid late-Gothic style, but they are all in remarkably good condition. At Scott's refurbishment of the choir in the 1870s, nearly half the stall canopies appear to have been renewed to replace those destroyed in 1848,[12] and one bay of the screen between the choir and the north aisle carries the coat of arms of a nineteenth-century bishop. If the Durham choir stalls are compared with the well-known late-medieval sets at Beverley, Carlisle or Manchester then they can be seen to represent progress in avoiding the heavy string-courses elsewhere.

The former choir screen at Durham Cathedral seems at first sight to present another problem. Was it of Cosin's time or is it a little later? Or was it basically a Cosin screen, altered in the 1680s to carry the new organ? The west side of the screen, as it is displayed at the west end of the nave, is of a different style from the stalls and looks later in date, but bears Cosin's coat of arms. The east-facing side of the screen had eight return stalls, four on each side; all are now in the chapel on Inner Farne.

Cosin had been used to a choir screen in the 1620s and 1630s and would have encouraged the Dean and Chapter to instal one if the original had been destroyed.

East of the choir stalls, the Cathedral had a 'Cosinesque' pulpit, which is now at Norham; whether it had a matching lectern is not clear. In 1668 Cosin recorded having provided for the Cathedral 'a faire carved lecterne' and made no mention of a pulpit. Was this lectern the pulpit now at Norham?[13] The Cathedral once had 'Cosinesque' communion rails, which seem to have been removed in 1850 as being 'of a bad age and in a corrupt style'; in June 1943 the Dean and Chapter tried to find them, and thought they might be in the University's possession.[14]

It is always interesting to look for antecedents of an architectural style. For the 'Cosinesque' woodwork I gladly follow Pevsner's suggestion about the Neville altar-screen at Durham Cathedral. One of the interesting things about it is that it is now the only surviving medieval English stone altar screen surmounted by canopies. So far as is known, no more than two other such screens ever existed: one at Exeter, and one at Cosin's other Cathedral, Peterborough. The Exeter screen has gone, leaving only very slight traces; but the vanished Peterborough screen is depicted in an engraving in Symon Gunton's *History of the Church of Peterborough* (1686), which shows the medieval screen drawn by a seventeenth-century draftsman.[15] It is difficult to know how far this style continued to influence Cosin, as he did not become Dean of Peterborough until 1640. St John's Church in Leeds has a lovely set of 1637 furnishings, which demonstrate what the 'Cosinesque' churches of County Durham might have looked like without the Gothic influence.

Cosin is undoubtedly the most important of the clerics associated with these County Durham furnishings, but it is worth remembering that until 1660, Cosin was a major canon of the Cathedral and a parish priest, but had no jurisdiction of his own within the diocese. The 'Cosinesque' furnishings at Bishopwearmouth, Easington, Gateshead, Ryton and Sedgefield, as well as at Cosin's own parish of Brancepeth, all certainly date from before 1640; and of these the Brancepeth furnishings do not seem to be the earliest.[16] By the time we get to the Durham Cathedral furnishings of the 1660s we are on much firmer ground. It is not necessarily and generally true that a bishop involves himself with refurbishments of his Cathedral, but Cosin's agreement with the Dean and Chapter in September 1665 that they would add no 'skew doores of unhansome work to the new chaire-quire-work' suggests close involvement on Cosin's part, and his 1668 list of expenditure on buildings and other charitable purposes includes 'a faire carved lecterne, and a Litany Desk for the use of the Quire there'.[17]

NOTES

1. H.L. Robson, 'The Cosin Furniture in Durham Churches', in *Antiquities of Sunderland*, 24 (1969), 1-12.

2. G.W.O. Addleshaw and F. Etchells, *The Architectural Setting of Anglican Worship* (London, 1948), 16.

3. Nigel Yates, *Buildings, Faith and Worship. The Liturgical Arrangement of Anglican Churches 1600-1900* (Oxford, 1991), 31.

4. *The Works of John Cosin*, edited by J. Barrow, Library of Anglo-Catholic Theology (Oxford, 1851), IV, 507.

5. Durham University Library, Durham Dean and Chapter Muniments, Post-Dissolution Loose Papers, Box 25, *sub anno* 1682.

6. N. Pevsner, *Bedfordshire and the County of Huntingdon and Peterborough*, The Buildings of England, 34 (1968), 282-83.

7. See note 3, 34.

8. See note 3, 35.

9. See note 2, 115.

10. The concept, familiar in the seventeenth century, of a monarch holding court beneath a canopy or tester, and separated from others by a rail, is carried here into the idea of God's majesty, with his throne represented by the Communion Table. [Editor's note.]

11. See note 1, 7-8, quoting a letter to Cosin of 20 April 1638 and citing *The Correspondence of John Cosin*, edited by G. Ornsby, Surtees Society, 52 (1869).

12. Ian Curry, *Sense and Sensitivity: Durham Cathedral and its Architects*, Durham Cathedral Lecture 1985, 24 and note 99a has a statement along similar lines, but I cannot now trace my own source.

13. *The Correspondence of John Cosin*, Surtees Society, 55 (1872), 172.

14. Durham Dean and Chapter Office, Durham Dean and Chapter Muniments, Chapter Acts, 12 June 1943.

15. See the engraving reproduced in *Medieval Art and Architecture at Durham Cathedral*, British Archaeological Association Conference Transactions for 1977 (1980), 92.

16. See note 1, 12.

17. See note 13, 137, 172.

IX

John Cosin: A Collection of Private Devotions 1627

Daniel O'Connor

'Next to the various versions of the Prayer Book itself . . . the most important Anglican liturgical compilation since the Reformation' - thus wrote a leading American liturgical scholar some forty years ago, of Cosin's *Collection of Private Devotions*, and I guess that is still the case.[1] The *Devotions* has the added distinction of being the only extended liturgical text completed by Cosin alone. It is also an immensely interesting and richly attractive work, and so I appreciate this opportunity to turn to it again. If I can be personal for a moment, my own work on the *Devotions*, a dissertation for this [Durham] University,[2] followed by a share in the preparation of the only twentieth-century edition, lay way back at the beginning of my ministry; since then, my life and interests have taken me to a whole series of wonderful pastures new, including, incidentally, lecturing on some of Cosin's opponents and their fascinating attempts during the Commonwealth period at an indigenous, thoroughly English liberation theology, and yet I want to testify to the sheer delight entailed in a return to this little masterpiece, still, as when it was first published, a 'Jewel of great Price and Value'.[3]

The immediate occasion of the compiling of the *Devotions* in the later part of 1626 and early in 1627 is described in an entry in the diary of John Evelyn, after he had visited the exiled Cosin in Paris in 1651. Cosin told him that:

> . . . the Queene [Henrietta Maria] coming over into England, with a great traine of French ladys, they were often upbraiding our English ladys of the Court, that, having so much leisure, trifled

> away their time in the antichambers among the young gallants, without having something to divert themselves of more devotion; whereas the Ro: Catholick ladys had their Hours and Breviarys, which entertained them in religious exercise. Our Protestant ladys, scandalized at this reproach, it was complained of to the King. Whereupon his Majesty called Bishop White to him, and asked his thoughts of it, and whether there might not be found some forme of prayers amongst the antient Liturgys proper on this occasion . . . [and] immediately commanded him to employ some person of the Clergy to sett upon the work, and compose an Office of that nature. The Bishop presently named Dr. Cosin, (whom the King exceedingly approv'd of) . . . [4]

The relatively young John Cosin, in his early thirties, already making his mark both as a career churchman and as a liturgist, was an obvious choice for the task, and he plainly went about it with energy and urgency for it was completed in three months, the book being licensed by the Bishop of London on 22 February 1627.

Cosin makes no reference in his Preface to the occasion of the compilation of the *Devotions*. Instead, he gives four very general reasons why such a collection of 'DAILY DEVOTIONS AND PRAYERS . . . after the . . . manner and DIVISION OF HOURS' should at this time be published:

> 1. The first is to continue & preserve the authority of the ancient *Lawes*, and old godly *Canons* [customs] of the Church, which were made and set forth for this purpose, that men before they set themselves to pray, might know what to say, & avoid, as neer as might be, all extemporall effusions of irksome & indigested Prayers . . .
>
> 2. The Second is to let the world understand that they who give it out, & accuse us here in ENGLAND to have set up a *New Church*, and a *New Faith*, to have abandoned *All the Ancient Formes of Piety and Devotion* . . . doe little else but betray their owne infirmities . . .
>
> 3. The Third is, That they who are this way already religiously given, and whom earnest lets & impediments do often hinder

> from being partakers of the *Publicke*, might have here a Daily & Devoute order of *Private Prayer* . . .
>
> 4. The last is, That those who perhaps are but coldly this way yet affected, might by others example be stirred up to the like heavenly duty of performing their *Daily* & Christian *Devotions* to Almighty God . . .[5]

In fulfilment of his commission, there lay to hand for Cosin to develop an entire tradition, namely that of the Primer, the traditional Western book of private devotion, 'the fruit of generations of accretion and selection . . . [with] a tradition of flexibility and adaptability'.[6] The *Hours* of the French ladies at the Court were, of course, unreformed Primers. There is plenty of internal evidence in the *Devotions* that Cosin was familiar with a number of these, but he is careful on his title-page to make clear that his particular models are taken from the reformed primers of the Church of England; the title-page reads: *A COLLECTION OF PRIVATE DEVOTIONS . . . CALLED THE HOURES OF PRAYER. As they were after this manner published by Authoritie of Q.Eliz.1560* . . . published as he emphasizes in his Preface, 'by high and sacred authority'. There is not time on this occasion to look at this interesting tradition, or at the Elizabethan models that Cosin used, but simply to note what he made of the tradition, how he used and modified it in the light of his own gifts and knowledge, and of his own Laudian churchmanship and conviction.[7]

The core of the *Devotions*, then, is Cosin's version of the Offices for the seven canonical hours of prayer as these had evolved chiefly in the Primer, though the Breviary is also influential here and there. His first Office, 'THE MATINS, *OR* MORNING PRAYER . . . ' is very substantial, a good deal longer than Morning Prayer in *The Book of Common Prayer*, though following it in general arrangement. His prayers at the Third, Sixth and Ninth Hours, and 'PRAYERS AT THE VESPERS, OR TIME OF EVENSONG', all follow a much simpler pattern, with the Third very distinctively an Office of the Holy Spirit, the Sixth of the Passion, and the Ninth emphasising the Passion as a revelation of the divine love and mercy. Compline is followed by a set of 'FINAL PRAYERS TO BE SAID BEFORE BED-TIME', not in the form of an Office but plainly intended to be a provision for the seventh of the canonical Hours.

Accompanying these Hours is a considerable amount of other material, as was the case of course with the earlier Primers. A preface, calendar and various tables, and a collection of catechetical material, corresponding to what was usually known as the 'A.B.C.' or 'Articles of the Faith' in the earlier Primers, precede the Hours. Typical Primer elements following them include the Seven Penitential Psalms, the Litany, a set of Collects, another of Eucharistic devotions (much fuller and more formal than was usual), prayers for the sovereign in the form of a votive Office, Embertide prayers (as in one of the Elizabethan Primers but here, seemingly uniquely, in the form of an Office), Offices for the sick and the visitation of the dying, and a concluding set of 'Prayers and Thanksgivings for Sundry Purposes'.

Almost the entire form of the *Devotions*, then, follows the precedent of and stands firmly in the Primer tradition. We are bound to ask therefore what is its originality? There are four main aspects to this.

First, there is the sheer richness and quality of so many of the prayers, from the delicate beauty of the very brief 'At the washing of our hands' to the grandeur and dignity of the 'Prayer and Thanksgiving for the whole estate of Christ's Catholic Church'. Cosin uses the entire armoury of rhetorical devices to capture what he calls in his Preface 'the grave and pious language of Christ's Church'. The sources are immensely varied, but perhaps most striking is the bold and ample use of the Scriptures; the prayer for the Ember Week in

September, to take one example, includes eight allusions to the Psalms and the New Testament.

Next, two features of the prayers deserve to be noted separately. One of these is the stress upon the Passion. Where in the original of a prayer we may find 'that precious death', or 'Thy Passion' or 'His blessed passion', Cosin will expand these into 'this Thy most precious death', 'that blessed Sacrifice which once Thou madest for us upon the Cross', and 'His most precious Passion and Sacrifice'. One feels very much in reading and using the prayers in the *Devotions*, the centrality of the Passion in Cosin's own faith. Equally striking is the frequent affirmation of the goodness and bounty of God and the joyful potentialities of life, whereby, for example, out of his 'blessed providence', we receive 'the blessings of heaven above, and the blessings of the earth beneath'. This is on such a scale in the prayers that we cannot but be in touch with an aspect of Cosin's own faith and outlook.

Third, an unusual feature of the *Devotions* is the large amount of prefatory material that Cosin includes. In addition to the Preface itself, 'TOUCHING PRAYER, AND THE FORMES OF PRAYER', there are 'Of the Calendar', 'OF THE ANCIENT AND ACCUSTOMED TIMES OF PRAYER in generall', 'AN ADVERTISMENT CONCERNING THE DIVISION OF THE HOURES following', a separate note on 'THE ANTIQUITIE . . . ' or 'THE ANCIENT USE . . . ' of each separate Hour, a note on the Litany, and a dozen or so notes introducing and explaining the days and seasons of the church's year, accompanying the Collects, together with one prefacing the Ember Prayers. These prefatory passages are packed with scriptural and patristic allusions and quotations (there are some one hundred and twenty-six patristic references, many with quotations, most of these being, I think, in Cosin's own translation), and with references to the Councils of the Church, *The Book of Common Prayer*, Canons and Royal Injunctions, to liturgical authorities and, on several occasions, to Richard Hooker's *Of the Lawes of Ecclesiasticall Politie*. This all no doubt reflects Cosin's concern to anticipate puritan objections, but it also discloses his love of order and his care for the tradition of the church, while the individual prefaces give us a series of most attractive, learned and lucid expositions, eloquently encouraging the devout life.

Finally, the *Devotions* also provides us with a wonderfully wide-ranging demonstration of the particular character of Laudian theology and ecclesiology. In addition to the veneration for tradition, and confidence in the authority of the reformed Church of England, its doctrine and discipline being (in the words of his friend Richard Mountague) 'Ancient, Catholick, Orthodox, and Apostolicall',[8] which we have just noted, there is the claim, echoing Laud himself, and soon to be repeated by George Herbert, of a uniquely favoured reformation. With regard to the use of the canonical Hours, this was for Cosin neither merely antiquarian nor necessarily Romanizing; the Elizabethan Church had, after all, authorized them, while in Cosin's own time Laud observed them, as did the community at Little Gidding, and Lancelot Andrewes (whom Mountague called 'our Gamaliel'), and the anonymous *The Whole Duty of Man* recommended their use.[9] On this point, we need to note Cosin's emphasis on the public liturgical obligation of the Christian, these private devotions being offered as essentially a private complement to common prayer, to that obligation 'to give God a solemn and a public worship in the congregation of His saints'. A great deal more of the character of the Laudian ideal is disclosed in the *Devotions*; the encouragement of outward signs of reverence, the frequent reference to the sacraments (and to the doctrine of baptismal regeneration, the Eucharist as a re-presentation of the merits and power of Christ's sacrifice, and the value of sacramental confession 'for better preparation thereunto'), episcopal ordination as 'the ordinary custom of the Church', prayers for the dead, and so on. So comprehensive an illustration of the

Laudian ideal do the *Devotions* afford, in fact, that it is not unreasonable to describe Cosin's work as the typical Laudian text.

Those are the four main points that I would want to bring out about the distinctiveness of the *Devotions*.

We have seen that in preparing his book, Cosin seems to have tried to anticipate the criticisms of the Puritans. The onslaught to which he and the *Devotions* were subject was, nevertheless, ferocious in the extreme, making of Cosin the first victim of the Long Parliament, and indeed reverberating in continuing attacks upon him throughout the years up to his withdrawal to Paris in 1643.

Official pressure seems to have been placed upon him to revise the second edition of 1627, but his response did nothing to relieve the pressure. The full force of the puritan attack becomes evident in two pamphlets, both published in the earlier part of 1628. One of these was by William Prynne ('Marginal Prynne' as he was memorialized by Milton for his relentlessly pedantic style), and entitled *A Briefe Survay and Censure of Mr. Cozens his Couzening Devotions. Proving both the forme and matter of Mr. Cozens his booke of private devotions, or the Houres of Prayer, lately published, to be meerely Popish . . . etc*. It is a long pamphlet, over one hundred closely printed pages, full of citations of pre-Reformation and Roman Catholic texts, but it is the wide divergence of his general attitude as a religious radical from that of the conservative Cosin that is at issue as the credibility of the religious settlement crumbles. Henry Burton's pamphlet, *A Tryall of Private Devotions . . .*, also over one hundred pages, is a much more literary piece than Prynne's both in its vigorous and colourful style and its dialogue-structure. The provision of 'Houres of Prayer' suggests the return of 'Monkerie' and Burton is preoccupied with the fear of the return of papal power and influence in England. Both pamphlets are important as illustrations of the puritan position in its religious aspect as the country moves towards civil war. They were also effective, leading to Cosin's being summoned before the 1628 Parliament or one of its committees, the King's haste in proroguing Parliament to save Buckingham from impeachment serving also to let Cosin off that particular hook. The reassembled Parliament of 1629 proposed that the *Devotions* (along with some of Cosin's friend Mountague's books) be burned, and their authors 'condignly punished', the dissolution of Parliament again saving the situation for Cosin. Over the following years, Prynne continued to attack Cosin and his book in his pamphlets. Meanwhile, Peter Smart, who had referred to the *Devotions* in his sermon of 27 July 1628, and to Cosin's 'speculative and theoricall popery' therein, took up a number of Prynne's and Burton's points in a legal charge against Cosin and others, a further illustration of the success of the two pamphleteers with those who shared their views. Looking at all this, it is probably fair to state that Cosin's initial default in compiling the *Devotions* first confirmed the Puritans in that opposition to him which finally led to his flight to the Continent.

With his flight, expressions of disapproval of the *Devotions* came to an end. In contrast, evidence of a more favourable estimate of Cosin's book can be found over a far longer period. The evidence takes a variety of forms: the nineteen editions that have been published; its influence on the revision of *The Book of Common Prayer*, and on later books of devotion; and the testimony of various individuals. We can only touch upon these very briefly.

Three further editions in 1627, one at least a large one, followed the small first edition. Peter Heylyn makes the observation that:

> . . . for all . . . [the] violent opposition, & the great clamours made against it, the Book grew up into esteem, & justified itself, without any Advocate; insomuch that many of those who first

> startled at it in regard of the title, found in the body of it so much Piety, such regular Forms of Divine Worship, such necessary Consolations in special Exigencies, that they reserved it by them as a Jewel of great Price and Value . . .[10]

The 1630s, which saw the Laudian church continue to flourish under royal protection, saw also two further editions. During this period also Cosin's Hours were in use at Little Gidding. Interestingly, there was a further edition between the execution of Charles I and the Restoration, in 1655, evidence perhaps for 'the persistence of a Laudian viewpoint among the harrassed and scattered clergy, . . . [and] the re-emergence of a strong and determined High Church party'.[11]

Further editions after the Restoration, in 1664, 1672, 1676 and 1681 are perhaps corroboration of the claim that this was 'in a measure the brilliant period of Laudianism', with two further editions in 1693 and 1719 suggesting the persistence of the tradition.[12] The revival and partial re-shaping of the High Church tradition effected by the Oxford Movement, which was, in its beginnings at least, self-consciously and deliberately a recovery of Caroline or Laudian Anglicanism, saw a renewed interest in the *Devotions*, five further editions appearing in the nineteenth century. There is also a good deal of evidence of Cosin's Hours in use in that period. More recently, the only edition, that by the Clarendon Press in 1967, was a significant publisher's and printer's event. This beautiful edition won a prize at the Hamburg Book Fair and earned a handful of favourable reviews in specialist journals. However, unsold copies were soon being pulped and we are invited to make our own deductions from that.

It remains to say a brief word about the *Devotions* and later editions of *The Book of Common Prayer*. The considerable number of traces of its influence in *The Durham Book* (a very large number of which Geoffrey Cuming overlooked) support the view that in 1660 Cosin wanted to go on where he had left off twenty years previously, and that his outlook before the

Civil War and after the Restoration were not appreciably different. However, the forces of compromise that prevailed in the official stages of the revision of the Prayer Book, virtually excluding all that was distinctively Laudian in the proposals of *The Durham Book*, ensured that only comparatively undistinctive elements from the *Devotions* found their way into the edition of 1662. Let me mention just two items. First, some ninety-five small explanatory details in the Calendar are from the *Devotions*, only two of them by way of *The Durham Book*, a nice reminder of Cosin's great love for the ordered and full observance of the liturgical year as what he would have called a 'Provocation to . . . piety'. Secondly, his fine version of the *Veni Creator*, first handwritten into the copy of the service which it is believed Charles I had himself held on the occasion of his coronation (at which the young Cosin had been Master of Ceremonies), and subsequently included in his 'PRAYERS FOR THE THIRD HOURE', so strikingly an Office of the Holy Spirit, becomes a fixed and much loved element in the Ordinal, its exceptional quality even ensuring its crossing over from *The Book of Common Prayer* to *The Alternative Service Book*. These are two, among many other points from the *Devotions*, which Cosin's meticulous care forbids us to call mere details.

It is impossible not to conclude with a brief reflection on the pulping of the only twentieth-century edition of the *Devotions*, not least because of my personal involvement in its publication, as a result of which its fate has often been the subject of my meditations. May I make three points: (i) Cosin's book was produced in a context of two Englands, as Michael Ramsey reminded us, but in both of which people cared deeply about the truth of the Gospel: its pulping helps to define our very different context today.[13] (ii) The backdrop to Cosin's Hours of Prayer was a thousand-year-old monastic movement: new forms of the church today, nothing less than ecclesiogenesis say those close to them, are creating their own spirituality.[14]

(iii) I did my share of the preparation of the 1967 edition from India, where I had gone at the tail-end of the vast missionary movement from northern Europe that had not even begun in Cosin's lifetime: now as a result of that movement there is a Third Church, full of vitality and martyrdom, waiting to assist in the renewal (though not surely the restoration) of the Second Church.[15]

In spite of that, I am grateful to have had the opportunity to return to Cosin's jewel of a book, and to be recalled to 'that true devotion wherewith God is more delighted, and a good soul more inflamed and comforted, than with all the busy subtilties of the world'.

NOTES

Editor's note: Quotations have been kept in the style of the original.

1. H.B. Porter, 'Cosin's Hours of Prayer: A Liturgical Review', in *Theology* (February, 1953).
2. This paper is based on my M.A. dissertation submitted in the University of Durham in December 1964, much of the work for which found its way into the Introduction and Notes in the 1967 edition of the *Devotions* (Oxford) which I edited with P.G.Stanwood.
3. P. Heylyn, *Cyprianus Anglicus* (London, 1668), III, 174.
4. *The Correspondence of John Cosin*, edited by G. Ornsby, Surtees Society, 52 (London, 1869), I, 284, quoting an extract from Evelyn's *Diary* for 1 June 1651.
5. John Cosin, *A Collection of Private Devotions*, edited by P.G. Stanwood, with the assistance of Daniel O'Connor (Oxford, 1967), 11-15.
6. H.C. White, *Tudor Books of Private Devotion* (Madison, 1951), 8.
7. *Private Prayers put forth by Authority during the Reign of Queen Elizabeth*, edited by W.K. Clay (Cambridge, 1851).

8. R. Mountague, *Appello Caesarem* (London, 1625).

9. *The Correspondence of John Cosin*, I, 70, R. Mountague to Cosin, 23 May 1625.

10. See note 3.

11. R.S. Bosher, *The Making of the Restoration Settlement* (London, 1951), 4.

12. Y. Brilioth, *The Anglican Revival* (London, 1933), 16.

13. 'The Tercentenary of the Prayer Book' in *The English Prayer Book 1549-1662*, by A.M. Ramsey [and others] (London, 1963), 3.

14. Leonardo Boff uses the term 'ecclesiogenesis' in a book of that title to describe the *Comunidades de base.*

15. The concept of First, Second and Third Churches, the First being the (Eastern) church of the first millenium, the Second the (Western) church of the second millenium and the Third being the ('Third World'/Southern) church of the third millenium, is that of Walbert Bühlmann in *The Coming of the Third Church*, English translation edited by Ralph Woodhall S.J. and A.N. Other (Slough, 1976).

X

The Liturgical Work of John Cosin - Some Remarks on Method

Kenneth W. Stevenson

'He would be a rash man who undertook to say something completely new about John Cosin.'[1] So said my late mentor, Dr Geoffrey Cuming, a classic example of the Anglican scholar-pastor, who had the added luxury of the twofold connections with Durham as a former Vice-Principal of St John's College, and editor of *The Durham* Book,[2] which is the most important immediate background document for the 1662 *Book of Common Prayer.* As a native of what would have been for Cosin the next diocese up, that of Edinburgh, it is a special pleasure for me to round off this Conference with some disparate remarks on his liturgical work. I should perhaps add that 'method' is always a slippery term to apply to liturgical studies, whether these are delving into the past or making proposals for the present (two fields in which Cosin was equally at home). I am not going to suggest that I know Cosin's mind. Rather, I am going to look at four main areas of his output and then suggest that they add up to a fairly unified, complete picture of a man who knew his world, understood his church, and had definite ideas on how to improve its standards of worship.

Before we look into those four areas, however, it needs to be said at the outset that John Cosin's life spanned no fewer than *four* official service-books in this country: the Prayer Book of 1559 (Elizabeth I), that of 1604 (James VI and I), *The Westminster Directory* of 1645, and finally the Prayer Book of 1662. To these four one could add a fifth, that of 1637, the Scottish Prayer Book, which, although for the northern kingdom and although ill-fated, is arguably the most eloquent expression of seventeenth-century Anglicanism;[3] a book, too, on which Cosin had some influence, though the extent of that is debated. For us who live in such a different century, it is easy to merge all these together, excepting (of course) the *Directory* of 1645. But that is to do violence to the evidence we have of their differences, to say nothing of the strong debates that took place within Cosin's lifetime, which were by no means confined to the key-stages, namely the Hampton Court Conference in 1604,[4] the often fractious deliberations at Westminster between Presbyterians and Independents in 1645,[5] and the Savoy Conference in 1661.[6] Time and again when we read John Cosin's writings, we are meeting a man who not only wanted to make the best of the official service-book of his church, but also wanted to clarify its imprecisions, correct its weaknesses, and enrich its poverties. He strains repeatedly against what he sees as the minimalists, casual in their interpretation of the prescribed texts of his church, and in turn reactive - sometimes quite violently - against what they see as his retrograde traditionalism or inappropriate innovation. And although I cannot agree with those like Dugmore and Cuming[7] himself who discern in Cosin's Eucharistic theology a gradual mellowing from an initial 'high' phase to a later 'middle' one, I cannot help seeing the key to the emphatic character of his episcopate in those long, sad, financially-restrictive and personally unsettled years of exile in Paris. It was there, after all, that he met Jean Durel and Daniel Brevint, presented them for ordination by Bishop Thomas Sydserf (deposed bishop of Galloway),[8] and then took them back with him to Durham at the Restoration; and in Brevint[9] he gave the Church of England one of its finest and most original devotional theologians of the Eucharist of his time, a man, moreover, whose influence in that regard can be traced right down to the sons of Epworth Rectory, John and Charles Wesley.

Presentation of the Liturgy

Debates about liturgy often settle on points of *text,* whereas it is far more frequently questions of *context* that excite and stimulate reactions, particularly from the pew. Was it not the new fangled offertory, with the presentation of coins by the laity, instead of bread and wine by the priest, that provoked the 'Christmas game' jibe from the people of Cornwall when the First Prayer Book was imposed in 1549?[10] We have ample evidence for Cosin's tastes in how the liturgy should be done. As Archdeacon of the East Riding, he enquired in 1627 about whether each parish had 'a comely and a large surplice, with wide and long sleeves'. As Bishop of Durham, his *Visitation Articles* of 1662 were most particular about surplices, tippets and hoods being worn by the Dean, prebendaries and minor canons of the Cathedral, and he made similar demands of the parochial clergy.[11] In every job that he filled, he left his mark, either extending provisions that he inherited, such as the copes at Durham Cathedral while a prebendary there, or else innovating, such as the embellishments to Peterhouse Chapel at Cambridge; and as Vice-Chancellor of Cambridge, he built a screen in Great St Mary's. He was far from only being interested in the words of the liturgy, as his extensive notes on *The Book of Common Prayer* rubrics make clear; and we may lament that his service for consecrating churches, modelled on that of Lancelot Andrewes,[12] his old friend and mentor, was simply too late to gain entry into the 1662 edition of *The Book of Common Prayer.*

In many ways, Cosin was a creature of his time, espousing the eastward position at the consecration in the Eucharist, using the mixed chalice, and having two lighted candles on the altar, whether that was in Durham Cathedral as prebendary, rector of Brancepeth, Master of Peterhouse, a chaplain in exile in Paris, or as the Restoration Bishop of Durham in his private chapels at Auckland, Durham Castle, or elsewhere. He used his influence to add some beauty and dignity to the churches of his archdeaconry, and, later, his diocese, at a time when church architecture was hotly debated, in the sense that interior fittings to churches reflected different stances within that nervous alliance of character-traits that we have come to call seventeenth-century Anglicanism.

The symbolic character of liturgical presentation clearly held great fascination for him. He warmed to the northern conservatism of the kingdom over such matters as the survival of the medieval 'tokens of spousage' (as they are called in the 1549 Prayer Book) to be given alongside the ring at marriage, as well as the white garment (the 'chrysom') at baptism.[13] These were among the customs supposedly repressed by their non-direction in the 1552 Prayer Book. Cosin was intrigued by the innate conservatism of liturgical practice.

It is in the celebration of Candlemas in Durham Cathedral in 1628 that we can unearth some of his wider motivations. Accounts of the service vary. In the introduction to his famous sermon against Cosin, Peter Smart has this to say:

> On Candlemas Day last past: Mr COSENS invenuing [renewing] the Popish Ceremonie of burning candles to the honour of our Lady, busied himselfe from two of the clocke in the afternoone till foure, in climbing long ladders to sticke up wax candles in the said Cathedrall Church: The number of all the Candles burnt that evening, was 220 besides 16 Torches: 60, of those burning tapers standing upon, and neare the high Altar.[14]

And another contemporary account, given in Percy Osmond's *Life of John Cosin*, has this version:

> Mr. Cosin was so blind at evensong on Candlemas Day that he could not see to read prayers in the minster with less than 340 candles, whereof 60 he caused to be placed round about the high altar.[15]

One may allow for a certain measure of exaggeration, but it is worth looking more closely at such an observance.

First, although Candlemas is the term still popularly used of 2 February, a survival Smart himself employs in his account, the first Prayer Books actually use the term, 'Purification of St Mary the Virgin', which is an approximation to the '*in purificatione beate marie*' of the Sarum Missal, and later medieval Western practice.[16]

Second, it is clear that Cosin lit a greater than usual number of candles in connection with Evensong. Although there is some evidence for the survival or reintroduction of lit candles in many churches, and, indeed, of the grading of such usages in greater churches on certain festivals, this does not appear to be Cosin's intention here.

Moreover, there is no immediate liturgical tradition anterior to the English Reformation in connection with Candlemas,[17] where, as the medieval nickname implies, the 'candle' ceremonies precede the 'mass'. Cosin appears to be inventing his own observance, adapting tradition to suit his own ends. He is known to have been interested in the festival, as we shall see in another context, and he will have been aware of its eastern associations, which are not specifically about the Virgin Mary at all.

Thirdly, in practical terms, it must be noted that Durham Cathedral, in the late afternoon of early February, was probably a dark place. When I first came to Guildford in 1986, I encountered a similar custom at St Mary's, the smaller of my two churches, where the Prayer Book is used for nearly all services; at Sunday Evensong near 2 February, every single candle that could be found was lit, a practice that continues with some further development by the no longer new incumbent! To Candlemas we shall later return. We simply note here Cosin's apparent desire to adapt tradition to suit the evolving Anglican ethos, a motivation too subtle for the polemics of some of his contemporaries.

Daily Prayer

In terms of liturgical history, Cosin's *Devotions*[18] is the real instance of gunpowder wrapped up in cotton wool. In part, it stands in a line going back to the late medieval Books of Hours, which is not surprising in view of the Books of Hours in use by the Catholic members of the Court. More immediately, however, its parentage lies in the *Primer* of 1559, the *Orarium* of 1560, the *Preces Privatae* of 1564, and the *Book of Christian Prayers* of 1578.[19] There is, too, something of Lancelot Andrewes' *Preces Privatae*, not least in the multifarious sources employed in the construction of much of the material.[20]

Another reason for pinpointing the *Devotions* as of special significance is its legality. It is true that the 1559 and 1604 Prayer Books often had 'Godly Prayers' bound with them, just as later editions of the Prayer Book had supplementary material for domestic use included at the end. But there is something inherently audacious in labelling such fresh and radical material under the guise of 'Private' Devotions, even if the original invitation to compile such a book came from Charles I, already impressed with this young cleric's handling of the ceremonial at his coronation the previous year. In view of the speed of operation, one wonders if Cosin's *Devotions* are in fact made up of prayers that he had in mind for some time; but that is an imponderable question.

By the time of Charles I's death, it had run into no fewer than five editions; the twelfth appeared in 1719, and the sixteenth is that which we encounter in the nineteenth-century *Library of Anglo-Catholic Theology*.[21] Cosin clearly had copies with him in exile, for he sent one to Sir Ralph Verney on hearing of his wife's death. The influence of the book is manifestly far greater than its initial detractors ever feared.

But what of the method and motivations behind the book? We have already noted its different antecedents, which is another way of saying that it is really in a class of its own. There is nothing quite like it either in the previous centuries or in the following ones. In terms of its apparently *ad hoc* but actually scholarly background, it could be compared with the recent *Celebrating Common* Prayer, published last autumn [1992], and already into its fourth impression;[22] a version of the Daily Office of the Anglican Franciscans, but in fact an attempt to enrich the daily prayer of those accustomed to *The Alternative Service Book* of 1980 but who want something a little less anaemic in its planned successsor in the year 2000. Some of the features of the *Devotions* betray areas Cosin may well have perceived to be significant gaps in the Prayer Book.

The first is 'A TABLE OF MOVEABLE FEASTS . . . '[23] which forms the basis for that which appears in the 1662 Prayer Book. It is typical of Cosin's mind in its grasp of hypothetical possibilities and details of precedence. Anyone reading it can see at once that it was necessary, and not merely the result of people who like that kind of thing. It is a fact of liturgical history that when a great era of change takes place, a different kind of mind often comes in to do what might be called the tidying up.

Secondly, there are aspects of the *Devotions* that take this story a little further, into the text of the liturgy. Two tiny examples suffice to illustrate its possible influence on the next main liturgical project, the 1637 Scottish Prayer Book. In Morning and Evening Prayer, the response 'The Lord's name be praised' is added to 'Praise ye the Lord' after the opening *Gloria*, no doubt inserted for purely aesthetic reasons, in order to maintain the responsive character of the opening of the services. An even smaller alteration, again for linguistic reasons, is made to the *Te Deum*, where the 1549-1552 'we knowledge thee to be the Lord' is changed to 'we *ac*knowledge thee to be the Lord'. Both these adjustments appear in 1637. They may well have been debated at the time, but they show the *Devotions* as part of mainstream Anglicanism of the time.[24]

Thirdly, Cosin includes a form of private confession.[25] There was already a form for this in the first Prayer Books, though in 'The Order for the Visitation of the Sick'.[26] Cosin takes the further step of making such a provision as a normal part of one's prayer life, with versions of the confession in Prayer Book language, one of them from Morning and Evening Prayer, but all of them in the first person singular. Interestingly, there is no text given for the absolution, though one may hazard a guess that the absolution provided in the Prayer Book 'Visitation', with its 'I absolve thee' formula, would have been to his taste. Classical Anglican writers of the seventeenth century urge the practice of private confession as part of spiritual direction, and these include such divines as Jeremy Taylor and Simon [Symon] Patrick.[27] One need hardly add that private confession would have formed part of the practice of the Catholic part of the Royal Court of the time.

Fourthly, Cosin also provides for prayers with a dying person. Of all the services in the Edwardine Prayer Books, the Offices for the Sick were regarded as the least satisfactory, and, indeed, the 1604 Canons permit learned clergy to adapt them to suit local circumstances.[28] It could be that their hortatory character may have deprived the populace of that sense of continuity with the medieval past for which they may have yearned. At any rate, Cosin provides a real gem in the following commendation:

> Into thy mercifull hands, O Lord, wee commend the soule of this thy servant now departing from the body: acknowledge, we meekely beseech thee, a work of thine own hands, a Sheepe of thine owne fold, a Lambe of thine owne Flocke, a Sinner of thine own redeeming. Receive *him* into the blessed armes of thy unspeakeable mercy, into the sacred rest of everlasting peace, and into the glorious estate of thy chosen Saints in heaven.[29]

Prayer and the departed is a theological minefield, and would have been even more so at the time of writing. But one cannot help feeling the depth of piety, the sensitivity to basic theological issues, and the vividness of the imagery, that cohere in this remarkable little prayer. It breathes the air of real beauty, and it is therefore no surprise that it should make its next Anglican appearance in the American Prayer Book of 1928, and also in its most recent revision, that of 1979.[30]

Cosin's imagination and pastoral powers lie behind much of the *Devotions*, which emerge as an important supplement to the Prayer Book.

Observations on the Prayer Book

As is well known, Cosin was a great maker of notes, and there are three series of these on the Prayer Book that have come down to us, together with his *Particulars* which are now generally regarded as having been compiled in 1660 with a view to the revision of the Prayer Book.[31] The first series may stem from some of the work of John Overall, whom Cosin served as chaplain, and who died in 1619. In all three series, one can see a common mind,[32] delving into the origins of the various parts of the services of the Prayer Book, and, in the case of the *Particulars,* looking more directly at the possibilities of revision.

The First Series gives us a view into the mind of a scholar who looks selectively at the tradition and interprets Anglican use accordingly.[33] Among the lesser feasts, the Transfiguration is discussed; it had no legal provision in England until *The Alternative Service Book* of 1980, though it began to be observed with special propers in the later nineteenth century under Tractarian influence. He discusses the importance of vestments, the term 'altar' as appropriately referring to the Holy Table, and he quotes John Chrysostom[34] in relation to the union of heaven and earth in the *Preface* and *Sanctus* of the Eucharist. He waxes doctrinal in bold fashion; of the Eucharistic sacrifice he speaks of 'the unbloody offering up of this same sacrifice'. The 'unbloody sacrifice'[35] is a piece of terminology frequent in the Eastern liturgies, much less frequent in the Latin West, but which makes its appearance in the Anglican divines from time to time. It owes its origin to the cereal offerings of Judaism, hence the appropriateness of using 'unbloody' at a time when it was felt necessary in some circles to hold on to sacrificial language in relation to the Eucharist, while at the same time avoiding any sense of a repetition of Calvary.

The Second[36] and Third[37] Series continue in the same vein, sometimes in Latin, sometimes in Greek. The patristic and medieval learning displayed in countless sources is amazing, but the quotations are not piled on for their own sake. As with Andrewes in his preaching, so here in Cosin's liturgical scholarship, sources are never allowed to dominate the discussion of any issue. The writer is on top of his material.

It is in the *Particulars*[38] that we come nearest to the practical man, before we move on to look at *The Durham Book* itself.

Printer's errors are noted over lections, but he also points out the lack of provision for the Sixth Sunday after Epiphany, when it is necessary. There is no Epistle for Candlemas either, nor are there responses to the announcement and conclusion of the liturgical reading of the Gospel; he makes suggestions here, and also suggests that everyone should stand for the Gospel: he had been an enthusiast for this before. In line with Overall and Andrewes, Cosin's practice was to recite the Prayer of Oblation immediately after the Consecration at the Eucharist, which is clearly a doctrinal point, from what he had written about the meaning of that prayer, not least 'all thy whole Church' as not referring just to the particular Eucharistic gathering of the occasion concerned, but also to those absent, those departed, and those who have yet to live.[39] Recently I took my father's funeral in St Anne's, Dunbar, and used the 1970 Scottish Liturgy, the version he most preferred; in the course of the Eucharistic prayer, I made the interpolation 'with this our brother departed' after 'we and all thy whole Church' and before 'may obtain remission of our sins and all other benefits of his passion'. It was a supremely seventeenth-century insight, as much as it was patristic. Finally, Cosin wants to tighten up the directions over where Confirmation is to be held, aware of the fact that it often took place in the open air, a less salubrious survival (it must be admitted) from the Middle Ages, where bishops were not unknown to confirm from horseback. Cosin, wisely, does not mention this.

The Durham Book

When we come to *The Durham Book*[40] we encounter a new dimension to Cosin's work. So far, we have looked at his liturgical presentation, his ideas for private, lay daily prayer, and his notes and observations on the Prayer Book. The nearer we get to 1662, the closer we come to the practical politics of changing the Prayer Book's text, whether in clarification, improvement, or addition. It would, of course, be anachronistic to look on all this with the benefit of hindsight, knowing, for example, that only about two-fifths of *The Durham Book's* proposals were actually incorporated into the Charles II Prayer Book, or even to see this latter in some kind of isolation, such as some of the controversy about liturgical revision in our own day has, in some quarters, only served to exaggerate. Way back in the reign of Charles I, Cosin and others were led to believe that a revision of the Prayer Book was a possibility, which may explain the somewhat extensive and often discursive character of his three Series of notes. Nonetheless, such a revision never took place, only the ill-fated Scottish Prayer Book of 1637, though as several commentators have pointed out, its influence on *The Durham Book* was considerable.

Geoffrey Cuming's edition of *The Durham Book* is a loving and intricate result of his time both at St John's College, and as a scholar-priest later on under his former Principal, Ronald Williams, who subsequently became Bishop of Leicester. Cuming demonstrates both the complexity of the text, and the crucial contribution Cosin made to it. It is a folio copy of the Prayer Book of James VI and I, printed in 1619, and covered with annotations, corrections and elaborations in the margin and between the lines. These notes are the work of John Cosin himself, and (to a limited extent) of his chaplain, William Sancroft, and were intended to be a first draft for the revision of 1662. They appear to have been begun as far back as 1626-27, the time when Cosin had been working on the production of the *Devotions*, but for the most part they belong to the summer of 1661, and in that sense bear comparison with the *Particulars* which we have just looked at. It needs hardly to be added that whatever did *not* see the light of day in 1662 was nonetheless taken with the utmost seriousness by revisers both in England and elsewhere in the Anglican Communion in the centuries to come.[41]

It would be inappropriate and repetitious to attempt to discuss here all these suggestions of Cosin's. But it is instructive to look at a few of them, both the successful and the unsuccessful, in our quest for methodology and motivation in the liturgical mind of John Cosin.

Firstly, the 1662 Calendar owes a great deal both to the *Devotions* and also to the 1564 *Preces Privatae*, which includes traditional observances that were discarded under Edward VI. Cosin's concern for this has already been noted, including his discussion of the Feast of the Transfiguration. Although no Proper for this feast is included in *The Durham Book*, he strikes out on his own in suggesting Transfiguration lections (II Peter 1. 15-20 and Matthew 17. 1-6) for the Fourth Sunday after Epiphany. Although it is not absolutely certain that this was actually Cosin's move, it is in line with his view, annotated at the Epiphany, that

> the offices of ye Sundays wch follow ye Epiphanie untill Septuagesima Sunday, are of ye same argument wth ye Epiphanie itself, all belonging to the Manifestation of Christ.[42]

Another example of Cosin's integrated thought concerns Candlemas. The same man who lit candles in Durham Cathedral in 1628, and who had noted in the 1660 *Particulars* that the feast lacked an Epistle, not only suggests one now (Malachi 3. 1-5) but goes further and *adds* to the prescribed Gospel, which from 1549 onwards introduced Simeon to the scene, but stopped short of the *Nunc Dimittis* (Luke 2. 22-27a). There is both precedent and innovation here. The medieval Latin lections for this day were Malachi 3. 1-4 and Luke 2. 22-29. What Cosin adds is significant. Malachi comes back in, but with the extra final verse, with its theme of judgement on those who give in to sorcery (false religion) or who ignore the widow and orphan (the life of service); both these insights could be said to apply to the Candlemas scene, with the Lord in the Temple (right worship) being acclaimed by two elderly people (who themselves are messengers of truth). The Gospel passage, on the other hand, is even bolder. The almost universal practice in the Latin West was to read Luke 2. 22-29, stopping at the end of the *Nunc Dimittis*, or else to continue until the end of Simeon's second oracle (verse 35); what Cosin here directs is to read the *whole* of the Candlemas scene, with Anna's appearance as well, thus taking it up to verse 40. It is no coincidence that Anna appears in all the Byzantine rite Gospel passages for this occasion, hence her appearance, too, in iconography for this day, for the feast of the 'Hypapante', the festival of 'meeting'.[43]

Secondly, when it comes to the Eucharist, Cosin exercises himself in predictable directions, tightening up the rubrics, suggesting the isolation of a final offertory sentence (the well-known I Chronicles 29. 10-13, 17); this did not gain entrance into *The Book of Common Prayer* of 1662, with its clear sense of offering alms to the Lord. It is in the Eucharistic prayer that Cosin expresses the views of his school at the time, namely the reintegration of those parts which had been scattered since 1552, a project that had been enshrined in the

1637 Scottish Prayer Book. It meant, among other things, the restoration of the epiclesis before the institution narrative. [The epiclesis is part of the prayer of consecration in which the Holy Spirit is invoked. *Editor's note.*] Also, the recitation of the Prayer of Oblation before, rather than after, receiving Holy Communion, thus making it more obviously part of what would be called 'the Eucharistic action' by a later generation. Furthermore, Cosin wanted to commemorate the departed properly. On all these points, he was walking on explosive terrain, much as the 1549-1637 tradition was admired by many; all that resulted in 1662 was the introduction of the term 'consecration' at the appropriate point. This was no doubt how many perceived the meaning of the prayer, but its absence in the previous books may have led some to think that nothing much happened with the bread and the wine at the Eucharist. Cranmer's mild Zwinglian sacramental theology may have been an influence here! But with the prayer for the departed, Cosin showed a medial line, following the 1637 Scottish Prayer Book. The Prayer Book of 1549 had given thanks for the Blessed Virgin Mary, the prophets, apostles and martyrs, and had then commended all the departed to God's care, looking forward to the end of the world, and the cry, 'Come ye, blessed of my Father, inherit the Kingdom prepared for you from the foundation of the world' (Matthew 25. 34). In the 1552 Prayer Book, all this disappeared and the main prayer of intercession in the Eucharist ended with the suffering. The Scottish Prayer Book of 1637 left out the Virgin Mary, and the prophets, apostles and martyrs, rearranged the order so that the saints precede the faithful departed, but left the glorious eschatological conclusion. This is what Cosin proposes here. But less adventurous minds prevailed, and the 1662 Prayer Book gained instead a somewhat muted thanksgiving for the departed, with its limp reference to 'thy heavenly kingdom', limp by comparison with the proposals derived from the 1637 Scottish Prayer Book which greatly influenced the text of *The Durham Book*.[44]

Thirdly, Cosin offers a number of significant changes to the services of Baptism and Confirmation. Just as the Eucharist now has a prayer of *consecration*, so the baptismal rite now has a *blessing of the water*, a fact for which many have been grateful in the period since, not least those of us involved in revising the Baptism service of *The Alternative Service Book* of 1980. But it is in the Confirmation service that once more we can perceive Cosin's integral thought. The *Particulars* betrayed anxiety about the service in the open air. Not only is this put right, but the service has for the first time the renewal of baptismal vows. Such a practice has long been thought historic to the service, so that the fact that this was an innovation in 1662 becomes easily forgotten. To make public baptismal vows betrays a Reformation piety, and in a sense Cosin is probably doing no more than giving liturgical expression to an already-existing piety. For that we owe him a great deal. But he wanted to go further in order to make the Confirmation service more full-bodied: in the Middle Ages this rite had seemed no more than a final part of the original patristic baptism-cum-confirmation in one, taken out of its context and made into a separate service. Cosin suggested that a proper Epistle (Acts 8. 12-18) and Gospel (Luke 2. 40-52) should be included between the baptismal vows and the actual confirmation itself. This proposal did not win acceptance, but one can see, in the choice of those lections, yet another example of liturgical adaptation within tradition: the Acts reading stresses the gift of the Spirit, the Luke reading tells the story of growing up in the faith. Both are crucial and complementary interpretations of Confirmation within Anglicanism.[45]

Conclusion

From these brief observations, it will, I hope, have become yet clearer how crucial John Cosin was in the Anglicanism of the seventeenth century. He was not a theologian of the stature of Andrewes, nor a guru of souls of the style of Taylor, nor an incisive systematician of the depth of Thorndike, nor yet an engaging populariser of someone like Patrick. However, he had something of all these within him, though his lasting contribution was restricted to liturgical practice, daily prayer, the history and scope of liturgical revision, as well as the revision itself when it finally came at the Restoration.

He loves tradition, but he adapts it, whether in burning lots of candles on 2 February or attempting to celebrate the Transfiguration towards the end of the Epiphany season.

Then he wants to correct the Cranmerian tradition with a more Caroline sacramental focus, whether in restoring the Eucharistic prayer, consecrating the bread and wine facing eastwards, or in commemorating the departed.

Finally, he sees, perhaps more clearly than others, that to have one single book is neither practicable nor possible; hence the *Devotions*, which has more pastoral direction towards lay piety, and is a veritable backdoor through which to reintroduce some of those good things of tradition that were in danger of being lost.

In all these ways, and in much else, Cosin - the pupil of Overall, the controversialist with Smart, the victim of the Parliamentarians, the energetic returned exile and the dedicated man of pastoral, doctrinal and historical liturgical studies - stands out as an essential part of our Anglican story. It is, indeed, a consistent picture, with many strands converging at different points. But it is also a prophetic picture when one looks at what has happened in the period since. Not all twentieth-century liturgical revision deserves our unqualified admiration. However, the historian cannot help but draw parallels between Cosin's aspirations and some of the provisions in our time. A shortlist of these will suffice for now; this includes an enriched pattern of daily prayer,[46] taking Candlemas seriously,[47] celebrating the Transfiguration in the season after Epiphany,[48] clothing the Confirmation service with proper Bible readings,[49] and, of course, centring the Lord's Supper round a great thanksgiving prayer which is built on secure foundations and prays for the life of the Spirit in the worship and service of the church.[50] John Cosin is a universal figure for those who love the liturgy.

NOTES

1. See 'The Anglicanism of John Cosin', in Geoffrey Cuming, *The Godly Order: Texts and Studies relating to the Book of Common Prayer*, Alcuin Club Collections, 65 (London, 1983), 123-41, notes 193-94.

2. *The Durham Book, being the First Draft of the Revision of The Book of Common Prayer in 1661*, edited by G.J. Cuming (London, 1961).

3. Gordon Donaldson, *The Making of the Scottish Prayer Book of 1637* (Edinburgh, 1954).

4. G.J. Cuming, *A History of Anglican Liturgy*, second edition (London,1982), 102ff.

5. Horton Davies, *Worship and Theology in England from Andrewes to Baxter and Fox, 1603-1690*, 5 vols (Princeton, 1975), II, 405ff.

6. See note 4, 116ff.

7. See, for example, C.W. Dugmore, *Eucharistic Theology in England from Hooker to Waterland* (London, 1942), 1, 2ff.; and note 1 above, passim. The contrary view is held by, among others, P.G. Stanwood and D. O'Connor, editors of John Cosin, *A Collection of Private Devotions* (Oxford, 1967), xxiff.

8. Robert Bosher, *The Making of the Restoration Settlement: The Influence of the Laudians, 1649-1662* (Westminster, 1951), 54ff. See also Percy Osmond, A *Life of John Cosin* (London, 1913), 111-50.

9. Daniel Brevint's major work is, *The Christian Sacrament and Sacrifice: by way of Discourse, Meditation, and Prayer upon the Nature, Parts, and Blessings of the Holy Communion* (Oxford, 1847). On the influence of this important study on the

Wesley brothers, see J. Ernest Rattenbury, *The Eucharistic Hymns of John and Charles Wesley, to which is appended Wesley's Preface extracted from Brevint's Christian Sacrament and Sacrifice together with Hymns on the Lord's Supper* (London, 1948). See also H.R. McAdoo, 'A Theology of the Eucharist: Brevint and the Wesleys', *Theology*, 97 (July-August 1994), 245-56.

10. Colin Buchanan, *What did Cranmer think he was doing?* Grove Liturgical Study, 7 (Bramcote, 1978), 13ff. See also Aidan Kavanagh, 'Textuality and Deritualization: The Case of Western Liturgical Usage', *Studia Liturgica*, 23 (1993), 70-77 (especially 71).

11. *Hierurgia Anglicana: Documents and Extracts Illustrative of the Ceremonial of the Anglican Church after the Reformation*, edited by Vernon Staley, 3 vols (London, 1902-4), I (1902), 187 (Archdeacon's Visitation Articles); II (1903), 235ff. (Bishop's Visitation Articles).

12. See note 4, 128-29.

13. 'For tokens of spousage', see note 2, 237; for the white robe, see note 11, II, 248.

14. Peter Smart, *A Briefe but True Historicall Narration of some Notorious Acts and Speeches of Mr. John Cosin (1641)*; see also D.R. Dendy, *The Use of Lights in Christian Worship*, Alcuin Club Collections, 41 (London, 1959), 158.

15. P.H. Osmond, *A Life of John Cosin* (1913), 70 n. 1.

16. F.E. Brightman, *The English Rite* (London, 1915), II, 564.

17. Kenneth W. Stevenson, 'The Origins and Development of Candlemas: A Struggle for Identity and Coherence?', in *Time and Community: In Honor of Thomas Julian Talley*, edited by J. Neil Alexander (Washington, 1990), 43-76.

18. See note 7; compare also references to the pre-Reformation tradition of lighting candles which is spiritualized by Mark Frank (1613-1664) in two sermons on this day. See *Fifty-One Sermons by Mark Frank*, edited by W.H. Mill, Library of

Anglo-Catholic Theology, 43, 44 (Oxford, 1849), I, 348f., 358f. (sermon xxii), 376 (sermon xxiii).

19. Private Prayers of the Reign of Queen Elizabeth, Parker Society (Cambridge, 1851).

20. Lancelot Andrewes, *The Preces Privatae* edited by F.E. Brightman (London, 1903).

21. *John Cosin, A Collection of Private Devotions*, edited by P. G. Stanwood and D. O'Connor (Oxford, 1967), xl.ff.

22. *Celebrating Common Prayer*: A Version of the Daily Office, Society of Saint Francis (London, 1992); see also Kenneth Stevenson, 'Celebrating Common Prayer: a Postscript', in *Something Understood: A Companion to Celebrating Common Prayer*, edited by Paul Roberts, David Stancliffe and Kenneth Stevenson (London, 1993), 97-102.

23. John Cosin, *A Collection of Private Devotions*.

24. See note 23, 85. Compare G. Donaldson, *The Making of the Scottish Prayer Book of 1637* (Edinburgh,1954), 271, n. 1 and 273, n. 1.

25. See note 24, Donaldson, 235ff.

26. See note 16, 826ff.

27. Harry Boone Porter, *Jeremy Taylor - Liturgist*, Alcuin Club Collections, 61 (London, 1979), 53, 95, 99, 109; and Kenneth Stevenson, 'The Eucharistic Theology of Simon Patrick', in Carsten Bach-Nielsen, Susanne Gregersen, Per Ingesman, Nina Jørgensen, *Ordet, Kirken og Kulturen: Afhandlinger om kristendomshistorie tilegnet Jakob Balling* (Aarhus, 1993), 363-378 (374f.).

28. Kenneth Stevenson, 'Cranmer's Pastoral Offices: Origin and Development', in *Thomas Cranmer: Essays in Commemoration of the 500th Anniversary of his Birth*, edited by Margot Johnson (Durham, 1990), 82-93.

29. See note 23, 279. No source is offered, nor have the further researches of the author of this essay yielded any. The prayer

must be regarded as original to Cosin, at least for the time being.

30. *The Book of Common Prayer*, according to the use of the Protestant Episcopal Church in the United States of America (Greenwich, 1928), 319f.; and *The Book of Common Prayer according to the use of the Episcopal Church* (New York, 1979), 465. (See also the two Burial Rites, 483, 499.) It had been proposed for the 1882 *Book Annexed*; see Marion Hatchett, *Commentary on the American Prayer Book* (New York, 1980), 475. It appears also in an adapted form in the Eucharist for Commemoration of the Faithful Departed in *The Promise of His Glory: Services and Prayers for the Season from All Saints to Candlemas*, Church of England Liturgical Commission (London, 1991), 71f.

31. G.J. Cuming, *A History of Anglican Liturgy*, 113ff. See also G.J. Cuming, 'The Making of the Durham Book', *Journal of Ecclesiastical History*, 6 (1955), 60-72.

32. R.F. Buxton, *Eucharist and Institution Narrative*, Alcuin Club Collections, 58 (Mayhew-McCrimmon, 1976), 118ff. This is an indispensable study of seventeenth-century Anglican Prayer Book commentaries and Eucharistic theology.

33. *The Works of John Cosin*, Volume V, *Notes and Collections on the Book of Common Prayer*, edited by J. Barrow, Library of Anglo-Catholic Theology (Oxford, 1855), 6ff.

34. See note 33, 104 quoting John Chrysostom, *De Sacerdotio*, 4.

35. For a discussion of this term, see Kenneth Stevenson, 'The Unbloody Sacrifice', The Origins and Development of a Description of the Eucharist', in *Fountain of Life: In Memory of Niels K. Rasmussen, O.P.*, edited by Gerard Austin (Washington, 1991), 103-130.

36. See note 33, 179ff.

37. See note 33, 400ff.

38. See note 33, 502ff.

39. See note 33, the Second Series, 351-52, especially the following statement: 'the virtue of this sacrifice (which is here in this

prayer of oblation commemorated and represented) doth not only extend itself to the living, and those that are present, but likewise to them that are absent, and them that be already departed, or shall in time to come live and die in the faith of Christ'.

40. See note 1, and Cuming, 'The Making of the Durham Book' in note 31.

41. See note 4, 106ff. and passim, especially on the Scottish liturgies.

42. See note 2, 107, 109.

43. See note 42, 124f. also note 16, 564-69; and note 17, Stevenson, 'The Origins and Development of Candlemas' in note 17.

44. See note 2, 146-51 (Prayer for the Church) and 160-71 (the rest of the Eucharistic prayer); also note 3, 189-90 (Prayer for the Church) and 196-200 (the rest of the Eucharistic prayer). On Cranmer's Zwinglianism, see Gregory Dix, *The Shape of the Liturgy* (London, 1945). But it was James Wedderburn, Bishop of Dunblane, and associated with the 1637 Book, who drew attention to Cranmer's alleged doctrinal deficiency in this regard, see Donaldson, 52. On the question of how to include the saints and departed in the Prayer for the Church, it is interesting to note Simon Patrick actually quoting the 1549-1637 'Come, ye blessed of my Father', ending in his *Mensa Mystica* in 1660; see *The Works of Simon Patrick*, edited by Alexander Taylor (Oxford, 1858), I, 220. See also my essay 'The Mensa Mystica of Simon Patrick (1626-1707): a Case-Study in Restoration Eucharistic Piety', forthcoming in the Aidan Kavanagh *Festschrift*.

45. See note 2, 222-27.

46. See note 22.

47. See *The Promise of His Glory*, 259-86 for the very full provision of services in the Church of England for this day, which reintroduce simple candle-ceremonies. The focus is centred on this festival as The Presentation of Christ in the Temple, the very title Cosin himself wanted to prefix to the

Purification, as happened in 1662. See Cuming, *The Durham Book*, 125.

48. See *The Book of Common Prayer according to the use of the Episcopal Church* (New York, 1979), 165, where the Transfiguration is celebrated not only on 6 August, but also on the Sunday immediately before Lent, thus providing a watershed between Epiphany and Lent. This is followed also in the *Lutheran Book of Worship* (Minneapolis, 1978), 17.

49. The Alternative Service Book (1980), 225ff.

50. See Kenneth Stevenson, *Eucharist and Offering*, with foreword by Mark Santer (New York, 1986), passim for a discussion of issues related to the Eucharistic prayer. Since writing this paper, the author has produced *Covenant of Grace Renewed: A Vision of the Eucharist in the Seventeenth Century* (London, 1994), 86-98, in which Cosin's life and thought are discussed.

XI

Bishop Cosin's Survey of his Episcopal Estates

Peter A.G. Clack

Like all jewels, MS Sharpe 167 in the Dean and Chapter Library appears to be a nondescript, pretty battered book.[1] The title page tells you that this is no ordinary book:

> A booke conteyning the whole estate and yerely revenues of the Bishoprick of Duresme in the severall wards, manors, townships and other places therunto belonging . . . collected Anno Domini 1662 by me John Durham.

A letter of 29 January 1662 from Cosin to his auditor, Miles Stapleton, qualifies Cosin's claim to have collected the information himself:

> . . . make me up a perfect book of all . . . rents belonging to the Bishoprick of Durham . . . I pray set yourselves to it so that it may be done exactly and that I may understand the state of my revenues yeerely both in certainties and uncertainties . . .[2]

Cosin was especially concerned about money because he not only had to restore the Bishopric following the depredations of the late rebellious times, but he also had to repair the episcopal manor house at Darlington as well as the castles at Auckland and Durham. He has this to say of Auckland Castle and his 'favourite' person, Sir Arthur Haselrig:

> Here the Bishop of Durham hath his . . . castle . . . of late ruined and almost utterley destroyed by the ravinous sacrilege of Sir Arthur Hasilrig.[3]

The survey, completed within the year, was still being copied by Cosin in his own hand during 1663. At the fore of the survey is a list of who held what lands, for how many years or 'lives' and at what rent. It records not only the rent, but also the true or commercial rent of the farms at which some tenants were sub-letting them. The net annual income from leasehold rents was £1,500, considerably less than the commercial value.[4] It appears from a letter Cosin wrote to Miles Stapleton in February 1668/9 that he had a private book of leases into which he entered renewals and other necessary information.[5] One wonders whether he made two copies, one for himself and the other for Stapleton and that the latter is the one which has survived. The Lease Registers were certainly duplicated, one of which, for the years 1669-71, bears Cosin's autograph at the end of most leases.[6]

It is quite clear that the Survey Book was used by episcopal administrators from 1662 to 1718, for they recorded renewals of leases in the margins. The full text of each lease is recorded both in the Bishops' Lease Registers and in the counterpart leases signed by the tenants.

The counterpart leases are kept in bundles, each of which is supposed to relate to a single tenement. When using them, care needs to be taken as this is not always the case.[7] Because so many of the counterpart bundles have leases that predate the 1662 survey, it is possible to carry the tenurial history of individual tenements back, in some cases, to as early as 1583 or 1584.

When Bishop Cosin's survey was being prepared in 1662, frequent reference was made to the Parliamentary Survey of 1647 and occasional reference to Queen Elizabeth's Survey of 1588.[8] It is often possible to identify the counterparts of leases used when the Parliamentary Survey of the Episcopal Estate was compiled.

There are intermittent references to a 'new book' or the 'other book' in marginal notes recording lease renewals between 1688 and 1705. So far that book has not been found. There are, however, other manuscripts which are useful in checking and expanding Cosin's survey. The first is a day book in which abstracts of leases renewed and the fine paid are recorded from 1677 to 1680. From then until 1700 the record consists of a full copy of each lease renewed, as well as the fine paid.[9] [A fine is a money payment made to the lord of the manor, here the bishop, by an incoming tenant. *Editor's note*.]

By the early 1700s the pages of Cosin's survey were so cluttered with marginalia that a new book was urgently needed. A copy of Cosin's survey was made in about 1702-3.[10] This, however, only covers Darlington and Chester Wards and has no marginal entries, which suggests that it was an abandoned project. It records current leases and omits earlier ones. It is however, quite extraordinary to read Cosin's peppery remarks about individuals, which were copied verbatim long after the offenders were dead.

While we may not have the New Book noted in Cosin's survey, we do have a Lease Register which may have used it.[11] It contains much of Cosin's preliminary material copied verbatim, including the Customs of Auckland Manor, which are the only customs recorded in 1662. The earlier book had up to four entries on each page and was written on both sides of each leaf. The later text was originally written on one side of each leaf and various hands have made additional entries both on the page containing the fair copy as well as on the blank facing page. Renewals are noted as well as the fines paid for them. This Lease Register was made in about 1716-17, which coincides with the final marginal entries in Cosin's survey, and remained in use until the 1740s. The first of the Notitia Books, which follows the same format, came into being in 1718.[12]

It seems that Cosin's instruction to Miles Stapleton in 1662 resulted in a document which helped the Bishop manage his temporal estate. It also led, indirectly, to the creation of the Notitia Books some fifty years after his death, and so laid the foundations for management of the episcopal estate into this century.

Cosin's annotation of the survey provides an insight of aspects of his estate management. Tenants who had a long history of non-payment were dealt with fairly severely. In the 1640s, William Barnes had leased the Tolls of Darlington for £16 a year, but had not paid the rent for years on end. The lease was forfeited and the tolls let to Richard Neile to make sure that the rent came in on time. Barnes, however, had to pay the arrears.

> For which purpose there is an entry made and the Tolls are forbidden, by proclamation in the market, to be paid to William Barnes.[13]

The Tolls of Darlington had been in the hands of the Barnes family since before 1605. In that year William Barnes, Senior, died. He was a nephew of Bishop Barnes and had been a Bailiff of Darlington.[14] His widow and two of his sons took over the lease and finally it was taken over by William Barnes, junior.[15] A letter of 22 November 1665 from Robert Colthirst to Miles Stapleton throws considerable light on William Barnes, Junior.[16] Over the previous two days, he had first of all smashed all the windows in a house where his wife was visiting a friend, and the next day, with an accomplice, had attacked her and friends in an alehouse. Colthirst concludes his letter:

> Some course must be taken with Mr Barnes who is too subject to drinke and quarrell, and save that I presume you know him I should say more . . . If my lord should thinke of doing ought herein by some adjacent justice of the peace, Sir Francis Bowes is the onely person Mr Barnes hath any interest in.

It is also clear from the letter that the people of Darlington were frightened of him.

At Wolsingham, William Crook of Sunderland by the Sea, gentleman, had a lease for three 'lives'. When two of them were dead, he lived up to his name and pulled the wool over

Mr Farrar's eyes. He pretended that the true value of his farm was only £8 a year and so paid £25 a year and he should have paid £116 fines. 'Let my succesors be heedfull, that they also be not denied', is Cosin's comment.[17]

He wasn't only concerned with those who cheated him - and they might do so by pretending that leasehold lands were freeholds or copyholds and so subject to different rules - or those who failed to pay rent, but also with those who might try to plead poverty when it came to renewing their leases. He notes about Lancelot Trotter of Longlee in Weardale:

> He is a very troublesome tenant & hath pawned his lease to Newcastle merchants who are to receive £30 per annum out of the profits and improved rents of it for 13 yeers next to come.
>
> The true value of the farm was about £55 a year, so the merchants were to get 60 per cent of its value.[18]

Earlier seventeenth-century bishops, especially Howson and Morton, had converted leases for twenty-one years into leases for three 'lives'. A lease for twenty-one years would normally be renewed at about seven year intervals for a modest fine, which varied from about 25 per cent of the commercial rent for a small farm, up to 100 per cent for a large one. Leases for three 'lives' were renewed at irregular and unpredictable intervals. When one of the 'lives' died, a new 'life' could be put in for a fine of about 200 per cent of the commercial rent of the farm.

In contrast to Howson and Morton, Cosin was more concerned with establishing a regular flow of money through the episcopal coffers and took every opportunity to turn leases for 'lives' back to leases for twenty-one years. In a note concerning the income from fines for renewing leases, Cosin has this to say of his predecessors:

> Most of the most profitable & best Leases were lett out for 3 lives by my predecessors (& by Bishop Morton more than by any before him) . . . which still continue in being. They that have one

or two lives dead, refuse to renew their Leases, unlesse they might have them for the 4th part of the value. I desire my successors to take speciall notice herof, and to waite till all the lives of these tenants leases become voyd; which wilbe a great advantage to him, & a just, if he maketh use of his right to let their leases unto any others whom he shalbe pleased to choose.[19]

Bishop Morton had converted leases for twenty-one years to leases for three 'lives' wholesale. One example is the township of Heighington in 1634, when 65 per cent of the leases were so converted.[20] His concern over lost revenue is illustrated by the fact that the lease for Ryton Colliery had been converted to 'lives', and by this means cost Cosin £2,500 a year by his reckoning.[21]

Some people tried to persuade Cosin to change leases for many years to leases for 'lives'. William Bellasis at Murton was one such person:

He maketh great instance (having deserved well for his service done to the King and his country in the late rebellious times) that . . . his lease for years may be changed into a lease for 3 lives . . . because it was let for 70 years before. But I am not willing to do it. If his importunity chance hereafter to prevail with me or my successors, let the rent at least be advanced to £10 from £6.[22]

In contrast to Bishops Howson and Morton, Cosin was more concerned with stabilising a regular flow of money through the episcopal coffers. He took every opportunity to turn leases for 'lives' back to leases for twenty-one years.

Cosin's notes in the survey provide a flavour of the man as an estate manager and his attention to detail. A few of his letters to Miles Stapleton have been published which add a little to our understanding. A hint lies in a letter dated 17 December 1668:

When I was first made Bishop of Durham, I remember Mr Barnes came to me and askt me if I would let the demesne at Stockton for £280 a year, and my answer was that if he could get no more he

> might let them so for me. And presently after he let them to the tenants there for £320 per annum, allowing me no more than £280 for 3 yeares together, which hath made me wary ever since howe I answer any questions of that kind . . . untill I know all the true circumstances that belong to it.[23]

Problems arising from this lease rumbled on for the rest of Cosin's episcopate.

As an estate manager Cosin had two main concerns: to repair his own residences out of the clear revenues of the estate and to ensure that the rents and fines due were paid. He spent £18,000 repairing the manor house at Darlington and the castles at Auckland and Durham in the first seven years of his episcopate. A further £36,000 went on a whole range of projects, including his beloved library. All of this work had to be paid for from the revenues of the Bishopric, in particular from fines paid on the renewal of leases, which were his sole substantial source of income. During the interregnum, people had paid extortionate sums of money for their lands. Cosin had to find ways of raising money from fines without bankrupting his lessees. According to a statement prepared in 1668, Cosin could have expected £31,800 in fines over the first seven years of his episcopate. He only achieved £19,800.

> In his fines for leases he abated and pardoned his tenants of the proportion which the leases were justly worth, the summe of £12,000.[24]

What is extraordinary is that, while there are detailed records of rents paid, there is no central record of fines paid for the whole of the seventeenth century.

There still remain some two hundred letters from Cosin to Miles Stapleton[25] which were selected for entertaining detail by the editor of Cosin's Correspondence. Until these have been properly edited, we shall not fully understand Cosin as an estate manager. We know he had an eye for detail, but we do not know how he used it to avoid bankrupting the Bishopric.

NOTES

CC = Church Commission (Bishopric).

DCL = Durham Dean and Chapter Library.

DUL = Durham University Library, Archives and Special Collections.

HC = Halmote Court Records.

'p.' and 'pp.' have been omitted for printed books but used in the case of manuscripts.

1. The text of MS Sharpe 167 is being prepared for publication by the Surtees Society in two volumes. It includes cross-references to the Parliamentary Surveys (Surtees Society, 183 and 185), lease registers and counterpart leases (calendared when they precede 1662).
2. *The Correspondence of John Cosin*, edited by G. Ornsby, Surtees Society, 55 (1872), II, 88-89, letter xxxiv.
3. DCL, MS Sharpe 167, p. 1.
4. DCL, MS Sharpe 167, pp. iii-v.
5. *Northumbrian Documents of the Seventeenth and Eighteenth Centuries*, edited by J. C. Hodgson, Surtees Society, 131 (1918), 196.
6. DUL, Lease Register CC 184963a, in use from 1669 to 1671, is duplicated in Lease Registers CC 184963 and CC 184964. The last lease signed by Bishop Cosin is dated 21 February 1670/1.
7. The worst example of jumbled counterpart leases which has been found concerns Ryton and Ryhope Mills (DUL, CC 447: 186765).
8. *Parliamentary Surveys of the Bishopric of Durham*, edited by. D. A. Kirby, Surtees Society, 183, 185 (1971,1972). Queen Elizabeth's Survey is contained in DUL, Halmote Court Records, Misc. M64.
9. DCL, MS Sharpe 111.
10. DCL, MS Sharpe 113.

11. DUL, CC 216814.
12. DUL, HC 54001.
13. DCL, MS Sharpe 167, p.44
14. *Darlington Wills and Inventories 1600-1625*, edited by J.A. Atkinson, B. Flynn, V. Portass, K. Singlehurst and H. J. Smith, Surtees Society, 210 (1993), I, 64-73.
15. DUL, CC 395:185369/1.
16. See note 15, n. 5, p. 139.
17. DCL, MS Sharpe 167, p. 58.
18. See note 17, p. 62.
19. See note 17, p. v.
20. See note 17, p. 12.
21. See note 17, p. v.
22. See note 17, p. 138.
23. See note 15, n. 5, p. 190.
24. See note 15, n. 2, letter xc; DCL, MS Sharpe 167, pp. i-vi.
25. DUL, Cosin's Letter-Books.

1. Portrait of an unknown young man *'Aetatis Suae 20 anno 1615'*. Is this John Cosin? *Reproduced by kind permission of the Master and Fellows of St Peter's College, Cambridge*

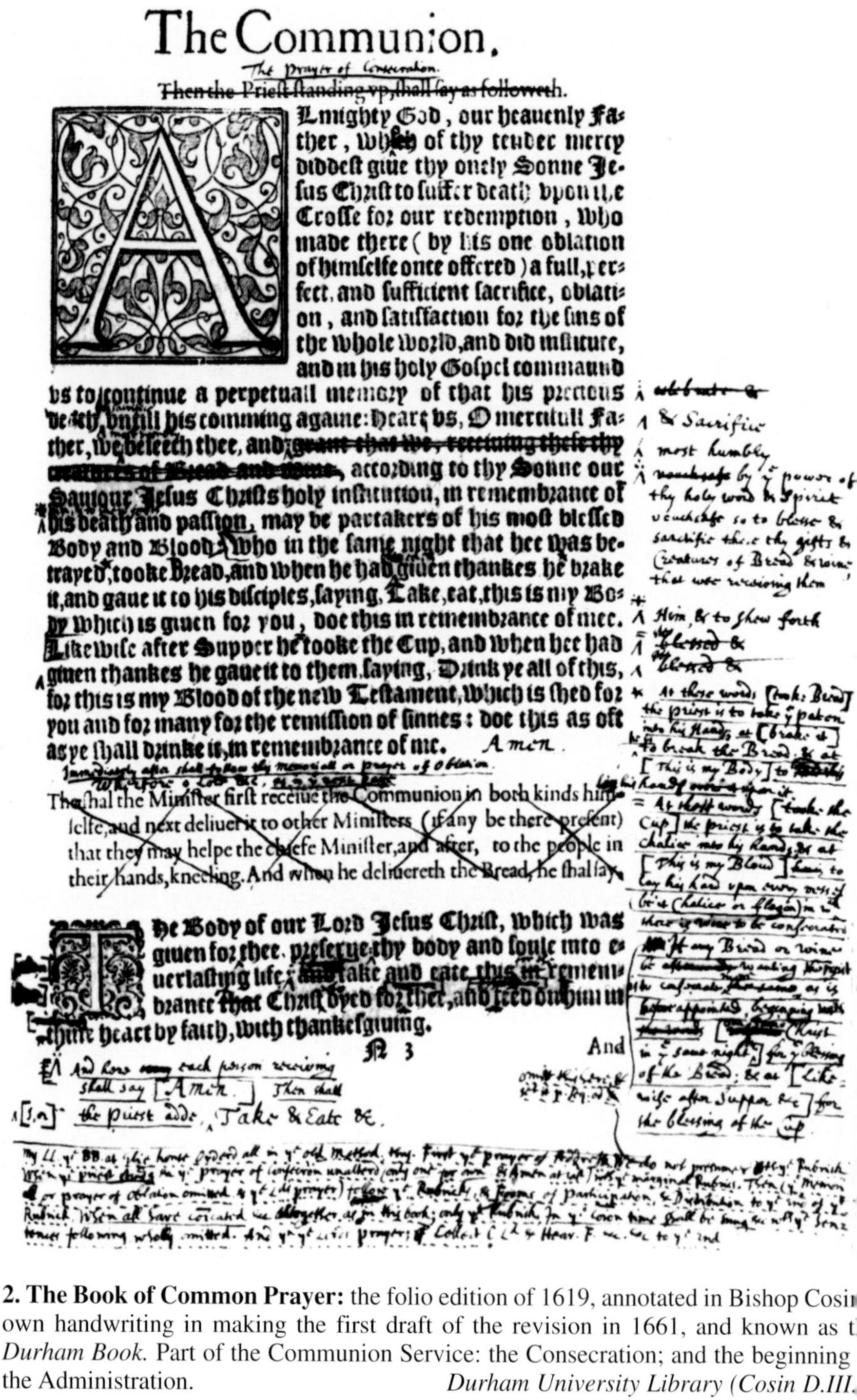

The Communion.

The Prayer of Consecration.

~~Then the Priest standing vp, shall say as followeth.~~

Almighty God, our heauenly Father, which of thy tender mercy diddest giue thy onely Sonne Jesus Christ to suffer death vpon the Crosse for our redemption, who made there (by his one oblation of himselfe once offered) a full, perfect, and sufficient sacrifice, oblation, and satisfaction for the sins of the whole world, and did institute, and in his holy Gospel commaund vs to continue a perpetuall memory of that his precious death, vntill his comming againe: Heare vs, O mercifull Father, we beseech thee, and ~~grant that we, receiuing these thy creatures of Bread and Wine,~~ according to thy Sonne our Sauiour Jesus Christs holy institution, in remembrance of his death and passion, may be partakers of his most blessed Body and Blood: who in the same night that hee was betrayed, tooke Bread, and when he had giuen thankes he brake it, and gaue it to his disciples, saying, Take, eat, this is my Body which is giuen for you, doe this in remembrance of mee. Likewise after Supper he tooke the Cup, and when hee had giuen thankes he gaue it to them, saying, Drinke ye all of this, for this is my Blood of the new Testament, which is shed for you and for many for the remission of sinnes: doe this as oft as ye shall drinke it, in remembrance of me. Amen

~~Then shal the Minister first receiue the Communion in both kinds himselfe, and next deliuer it to other Ministers (if any be there present) that they may helpe the chiefe Minister, and after, to the people in their hands, kneeling. And when he deliuereth the Bread, he shal say,~~

The Body of our Lord Jesus Christ, which was giuen for thee, preserue thy body and soule into euerlasting life: ~~and take and eate this in remembrance that Christ dyed for thee, and feed on him in thine heart by faith, with thankesgiuing.~~

N 3 And

& Sacrifice

most humbly

Him, & to shew forth

Take & Eate &c.

2. The Book of Common Prayer: the folio edition of 1619, annotated in Bishop Cosin's own handwriting in making the first draft of the revision in 1661, and known as the *Durham Book.* Part of the Communion Service: the Consecration; and the beginning of the Administration. *Durham University Library (Cosin D.III.*

3. Brancepeth, St Brandon: the reading pew, from the south side against the a nave pillar, was moved to the north of the chancel arch in the 19th century to serve as a pulpit; the original pulpit disappeared. *P. Mussett*

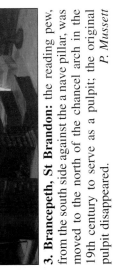

4. Brancepeth, St Brandon: chancel screen pinnacles. *P. Mussett*

5. Brancepeth, St Brandon: north side, with Cosin's porch, 1843. *Drawn by R.W. Billings and engraved by George Winter*

6. Sedgefield, St Edmund the bishop: the nave, looking east to the choir and pinnacled screen, 1841.

Drawn by R.W. Billings and etched by J.H. Le Keux

7. Durham Cathedral: Dean Hunt's altar, now hidden beneath another altar except in Passion week. *Janet Thackray*

8. Durham Cathedral: Litany Desk given by Cosin and with his coat of arms. *Janet Thackray*

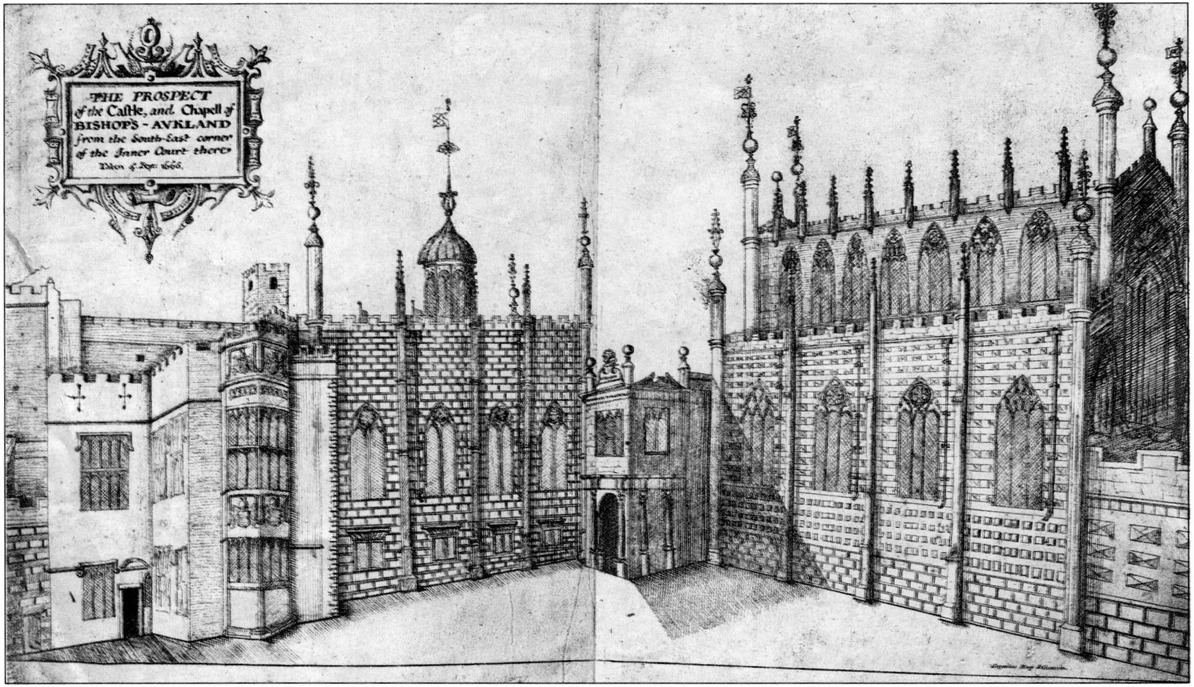

9. Auckland Castle: south-east corner of the inner court, 1666; drawn by Gregory King. *Reproduced from a copy (kindly loaned by the Bishop of Durham) from an original in the College of Arms*

10. Inner Farne, St Cuthbert's chapel: built in 1370 and restored by Archdeacon Thorpe in 1848, who re-used Cosin's 17th-century stalls formerly returned against the choir screen in Durham Cathedral. *Fleur Coppock*